THE FEDERAL CONSTITUTION OF SWITZERLAND

THE FEDERAL CONSTITUTION OF SWITZERLAND

TRANSLATION AND COMMENTARY

BY

CHRISTOPHER HUGHES

With German Text

OXFORD
AT THE CLARENDON PRESS
1954

Oxford University Press, Amen House, London E.C. 4

GLASGOW NEW YORK TORONTO MELBOURNE WELLINGTON
BOMBAY CALCUTTA MADRAS KARACHI CAPE TOWN IBADAN

Geoffrey Cumberlege, Publisher to the University

PRINTED IN GREAT BRITAIN

PREFACE

THERE are many books about Swiss government in English and German, but the English books are nearly all elementary, and the German books either very long or exclusively concerned with details. My intention here has been to provide an introduction to Swiss government which shall go farther than my English predecessors, and yet not so far as the great German works upon the subject—to bridge in fact the gap between English and German studies of Swiss institutions.

There is, however, no better introduction to Swiss law and politics than the Federal Constitution itself, and therefore I have presented a new translation of this, together with a running commentary upon the matters with which it deals—for neither its implications nor its bare legal meaning can be understood without a commentary, nor is it easy even to read attentively a foreign legal document.

My tone in this commentary is perhaps more critical than is usual in English examinations of Swiss institutions, and it is therefore necessary to explain that this springs from a pessimism towards government in general, and not from a prejudice or adverse judgement concerning the Swiss form of it. I do in fact rate Swiss government, particularly local government (with which, however, this book is not concerned), very highly, and consider that their ways of thought are inferior only to our own vocabulary of Crown, common law, and Parliament. It is my special hope that no words I have used will give offence in Switzerland: if I have reintroduced certain matters into controversy it is to increase interest in Swiss institutions. It has been my aim to provide the materials for a balanced judgement, by presenting Swiss constitutional documents in a form in which they can be studied, for the benefit of those already interested either in Switzerland, or in comparative government, or foreign affairs in general.

C. J. H.

MORETONHAMPSTEAD, DEVON
Sept. 1953

ACKNOWLEDGEMENTS

I MUST in the first place acknowledge my gratitude to the Carnegie Trust for the Universities of Scotland, whose trustees elected me as Research Fellow to undertake a year's investigation into Swiss public law. I am most grateful for their generosity. I should like also to acknowledge that the University of Glasgow has at various times afforded me certain courtesies, including a year's leave of absence. To those kind Swiss scholars who helped me at Berne and Zurich I must repeat my thanks —and especially to Dr. Hans Lang who read the proofs—but to enumerate my debts to them would be inappropriate in a work designed for an English-speaking audience. To Professor K. C. Wheare of All Souls College, who encouraged my first interest and who read through my manuscript, I owe special thanks.

C. J. H.

CONTENTS

I CONSTITUTION OF THE SWISS
CONFEDERATION 1
    ALPHABETICAL ANALYSIS 143

II PARLIAMENTARY PROCEDURE 149
    LAW OF 1902 ON THE RELATIONS
    BETWEEN THE COUNCILS 153
    ALPHABETICAL ANALYSIS 166

III EMERGENCY FULL POWERS 169
    FEDERAL ARRÊTÉ OF 30 AUGUST 1939 170

GERMAN TEXT OF THE FEDERAL
CONSTITUTION 172

SELECT BIBLIOGRAPHY 213

GENERAL INDEX 219

I
FEDERAL CONSTITUTION*

OF THE

SWISS CONFEDERATION

(of 29 May 1874)

IN THE NAME OF ALMIGHTY GOD!

The Swiss Confederation

Desiring to confirm the Union of the Confederates, and to maintain and promote the unity, strength, and honour of the Swiss nation, has adopted the following Federal Constitution:

The best opinion is that this preamble has no juristic meaning, but that is no guarantee that it will not be referred to in order to support an extension of the competences of the central government in an emergency. The

---

* The Constitution is given as revised to 1 Jan. 1953. The German text of the Constitution on page 173 seq. contains all the revisions down to 1 Aug. 1953, and also includes the Additional Provisions in force on that date.

The translation printed here of the Constitution, and of the other legal texts included in this book, is by the author of the commentary. It is based on a comparison between the French and German texts. Where the texts conflict the German text has usually been relied upon, unless there is any special reason for regarding the French text as more authoritative or clearer: important conflicts are noted in the commentary. It has often been possible to steer, as it were, between the French text and the German, but frequently the little consistency between the original texts, or the structure of the English language, has compelled me to be arbitrary in small matters. The reader who would like to exercise his talent of translation is invited to try to render the two texts of Article 102 into consistent English.

It should be added that the original text even in a single language is by English standards carelessly drafted. The same expression (e.g. 'Federal supervision') is occasionally used to describe different things, while the same thing (e.g. 'within the Federal competence alone') is rendered by a number of different expressions (steht dem Bund zu, ist Sache des Bundes, ist Bundessache) without plan, and without consistency between the French and the German text. Swiss jurists, however, in general refrain from making distinctions where the authors of the Constitution intended none, unless for good cause.

It has been convenient to use some expressions which are not normally pardonable in English, such as 'votation' for a vote upon a project by the public (while retaining 'election' for a vote for a person), 'competence' (for a power legally

claim that Switzerland is a 'nation'—the word has a stronger racial connotation in French and German than in English—is a bold one, deliberately made.

The German text uses the words 'Bund' and 'Eidgenossenschaft' indifferently, and these are both usually translated by *Confédération* in French, with the adjective *fédéral*. 'Eidgenossenschaft' means literally 'oath-fellowship', that is to say, a society formed by oath rather than, for example, contract. The invocation of the Almighty is a common form in the older Federal treaties and in charters, and is appropriate in a document founding an 'oath-fellowship'.

exercisable, e.g. 'the Federal competence', 'the Cantonal competence'), and 'universally binding' (since 'public general' draws a false analogy) as a transliteration of 'allgemeinverbindlich'.

The commentary was actually written during the first part of the year 1952, but has been revised so as to refer to the same date as the English version of the Constitution.

FIRST SECTION

GENERAL PROVISIONS

ARTICLE 1. The peoples of the twenty-two sovereign Cantons united by the present alliance, that is to say: Zurich, Berne, Lucerne, Uri, Schwyz, Unterwalden (Obwald and Nidwald), Glarus, Zug, Fribourg, Solothurn, Basle (Town and Country), Schaffhausen, Appenzell (the two Rhodes), St. Gall, Grisons, Aargau, Thurgau, Ticino, Vaud, Valais, Neufchatel, and Geneva, comprise the Swiss Confederation.

Nature of the Constitution. Is it a Law or a Contract? The best Swiss opinion holds that the Constitution is not in any of its parts a contract, but that it is a law of a particular kind—not a Treaty but a Constitution. All parts of it can therefore be changed by the procedure described in the Constitution (Articles 118–23). This view is supported by consideration of the nature of the society that is described in the Constitution, but is against the actual phrasing of the first part of the document, which rather supports a contractual theory.

The claim that the Cantons are sovereign stands or falls with the claim that the Constitution is a contract.

The Enumeration of the Cantons.[1] The implication of the list of Cantons is that a constitutional amendment would be needed for the secession of a complete Canton, or for the accession of an additional Canton to the Confederation (e.g. the Vorarlberg, whose request for admission was repulsed by the Executive in 1919–20). The extension or diminution of the area of an existing Canton is apparently not covered by this Article, but is perhaps covered by Article 5, or in the case of cession to another Canton, by Article 7. In any case, the matter is in the competence of the Confederation rather than of the Canton concerned (see also Article 8). The problem is what can be effected by legislation and what needs a constitutional amendment.

The text of the constitutional document would, of course, have no relevance to *de facto* secession.

The Half-Cantons. The position of the half-Cantons is perfectly clear, but is difficult to describe; it would be simpler if the number of Cantons were given here as 25 rather than as 22. In respect of autonomy, a half-Canton

---

[1] The territory of the Principality of Lichtenstein is for many purposes, but not for the purposes of defence, Swiss territory. The relationship of the principality to the Confederation is *sui generis*: it is not the same as that of the 'sovereign' Cantons, but it is closer than mere treaty-alliance. See *Le Liechtenstein: ses institutions*, by Pierre Raton, Paris, 1949, 254 pp.

differs not at all from a whole Canton: it has, for example, its own Constitution and its own citizenship. There is no institution of government corresponding to the theoretical whole Canton of Unterwalden, Appenzell, or Basle. Both halves vote independently in the Council of States and in referendums (Article 123, para. 2 of the present Constitution removes the last doubts). A half-Canton is in fact a Canton which has unequal representation in Federal affairs, with *half* representation. The originality of this device, which preserves the theoretical equality of all Cantons while giving only half representation to six small ones, has not been adequately recognized.

To what extent Unterwalden was ever united is hard to say. Appenzell finally split in 1597 into a Protestant and a Catholic area—the Outer Rhodes (i.e. districts) being Protestant, and the Inner Rhodes remaining Catholic.[1] Basle split in 1832–5 on a political issue.

The question of the reunion of the two Basles has often been raised and has given rise to interesting discussions—the matter is complicated by a provision made at the time of separation for reunion by agreement. During the last century and a half the division of Schwyz, Fribourg, Ticino, and Berne has at various times been proposed: the proposed division of Berne into French (Catholic) and German (Protestant) is once more highly topical today. The threat to form a separate half-Canton is a potent one in the hands of a large, grouped, minority, and it is one of the permanent facts of political life in Switzerland. According to the practice of the Federal authorities, the effect of the enumeration of the half-Cantons in this Article is that a constitutional amendment is needed for separation and for reunion.

The matters in which half-Cantons have half votes are Articles 80 (Council of States) and 123 (Votations). Articles 82, 86, and 89 are ambiguous; 13, 72, and 73 explicit. The best opinion is that, where there is ambiguity, 'Canton' everywhere means 'Canton or half-Canton'.

ARTICLE 2. The purpose for which the Confederation is formed is to secure the independence of the fatherland against foreign nations, to maintain peace and good order within, to protect the liberty and the rights of the Confederates, and to foster their common welfare.

When the Confederation was a treaty-society, proclamation of the purpose of the treaty had a sense, for the obligations of the parties were limited to the purposes of the alliance—common defence, &c. The declaration of intention was carried over from the Federal Treaty to the Constitution as a harmless piece of high-sounding rhetoric: time, however, has conferred a

---

[1] Rhodes (Rhoden) are, according to one etymology, 'clearings' or 'uprootings' (cf. Ruetli or Gruetli = a little clearing) and the word was used to describe the communities of which the little rebel state of Appenzell was composed. The two half-Cantons have different, but equally characteristic, perversities, and rarely agree in a Federal referendum. The vote of one half thereby can be said to cancel the vote of the other.

more sinister meaning upon this Article. For if it is interpreted as conferring a competence upon the central government ('the Confederation') as against the Cantons, then it is virtually an alternative centralistic Constitution in itself. A central government which has all the powers necessary to secure independence, maintain peace and good order, and foster the common welfare of its subjects, hardly has need of any more. Moreover, if a competence is conferred by this Article, it appears to be conferred upon the Executive (compare Article 102, ss. 9 and 10, with Article 85, s. 6). Most jurists agree, however, that the use of this Article as a competence is illegal; the question of emergency powers is discussed on page 169.

No constitutional right of the citizen (in the sense of Article 113) is conferred by this Article.

ARTICLE 3. The Cantons are sovereign in so far as their sovereignty is not limited by the Federal Constitution, and, as such, they exercise all rights which are not transferred to the Federal power.

This Article is one of the most difficult to interpret, and one should be cautious about drawing any conclusions from it; its juristic meaning is highly disputable, and it may have none. It is tempting to regard the Article as a product of the habit of mind represented by declarations of the Rights of Man ('The freedom of XYZ is guaranteed, within the limits of the rules which restrict it') and to dismiss it. But it might well be a mistake to yield to this temptation, for there remains in spite of all a very attractive savour of sovereignty about the Cantons, which places them in another class to English counties. Item by item this sovereignty may come to very little, and may seem to elude the eye when examined at any point as if it were an illusion, but nevertheless it is there, and does not allow itself to be explained entirely away. It is a fact, of a sort.

CANTONAL SOVEREIGNTY. SOME CONSIDERATIONS

1. There is no field at all in which the Cantons are in a narrow sense 'sovereign', since some principles of the Federal Constitution (e.g. Equality before the Law, Article 4) cover all fields.

2. The limitation 'as far as their sovereignty is not limited by the Federal Constitution' understates the case, for the rule of daily application (and the rule which should be quoted) is 'Federal law breaks Cantonal law'—see Article 2 of the Transitory Provisions. One may notice that, whereas during the first thirty years of the Constitution of 1874 the rule that 'the Cantons are sovereign . . .' was an important one in the jurisprudence of the Federal Tribunal, it is now seldom or never cited in litigation before that court; Article 2 of the Transitory Provisions has taken its place.

3. The most important of the powers specifically 'of sovereignty' are in the hands of the Confederation. The powers held by the Cantonal authorities are mainly those usually delegated to local authorities, not indeed by virtue of delegation (as a rule) but generally as a result of original powers. But some rights traditionally 'of sovereignty' are in the hands of the Cantons,

and the delegated powers they possess are becoming as important as the 'original' ones.

4. The Constitution is an unreliable guide to what is in the competence of the Cantons, for a Federal competence does not supersede a Cantonal competence *until it is actually made use of* by the Confederation (e.g. Article 47, Settlement and Temporary Residence).

5. The Cantons enjoy, or at least play, sovereignty as against other Cantons. This Article, however, is not concerned with this relationship, but with sovereignty in itself and with sovereignty as against the Federation. See Article 5.

6. If the Cantonal Constitution and the concordats and treaties by which the Canton is bound are regarded as a part of Federal law, then we can say that the individual can only attack Cantonal law on the grounds of repugnancy to Federal law (including the Federal Constitution as Federal law). In other words, the Canton is sovereign as against the individual except in so far as its sovereignty is infringed by Federal law. But whether that is a consequence of this Article can be doubted.

7. It is probable, but not quite certain, that the Cantons have no personality in international law; see Article 9 below.

8. There is no justification for thinking this Article provides a presumption in favour of the Cantons. A case under Article 113, Conflict of Competence, is decided strictly on its merits. And the Constitution provides ample remedies for the central government if the Cantons infringe Federal law, but none for the Cantons if the Confederation infringes Cantonal competences.

ARTICLE 4. All Swiss are equal before the Law. In Switzerland there is neither subjection nor privilege of locality, birth, family, or person.

The Old Confederation was composed of the thirteen sovereign Cantons (Orte) and the territories subject to them jointly or severally, and the recognized permanent allies of all or any of them. It was a structure whose cohesive forces were its antiquity, its legitimacy, and the complexity of its relationships—including the common possession of subject 'bailiwicks' (Vogteien) and the various alliances with France. And the Cantons themselves were seldom more homogeneous than the Confederation, for within the district which we should now call the Canton a particular city or district was in general alone sovereign, and within that district membership of the citizenship which alone was sovereign was everywhere strictly hereditary, and in general within that citizenship certain families had hereditary claims to pre-eminence which tended to harden into legal rights.

This Article commemorates the destruction of old relationships of subjection in 1798, and the destruction of the restored Cantonal patriciates between 1830 and 1848.

But although originally erected as an historical monument, this Article is now a rule of law, and incontestably the most active rule of law of the whole Constitution.

Equality before the Law

Of the pack of constitutional rights, Equality before the Law is the Joker. The Federal Tribunal has interpreted Article 4 as conferring nothing less than a jurisdiction in equity over all Cantonal decisions, legislative or executive.

Case Law. One-half of the Appeals in Public Law to the Federal Tribunal against violation of constitutional rights[1] arise out of Article 4. The best idea of the extent of 'Equality before the Law' can be obtained by looking at the cases over a period of years and the way in which they are classified.

In the period chosen the cases under this Article are classified as follows (1925–35, *Répertoire général, Arrêts du Tribunal fédéral*):

1. *'Généralités.'* (Half-a-dozen reported cases.) Can a foreigner domiciled abroad bring a case under this Article? Can someone not personally affected bring a case? Need Cantonal procedure first be exhausted? &c.

2. *'Inequality of Treatment.'* Need Cantonal legislation provide for free judicial assistance? May communes subsidize cremation to the extent they are saved burial costs? Should Federal employees be excluded from jury service? Can a commune decide that privately employed gardeners must not tend graves for others, but may do so for their own family? What happens if the lower courts refuse to apply the Federal Tribunal's decisions? Can proof of need be required for new inns and not for established inns? Is it lawful to refuse to permit posters decrying a shooting-match on a publicly owned notice-board? What limitations on the choice of advocates are lawful?, &c.

3. *'Formal Denial of Justice.'* (Only two cases.) The right to be heard in defence. The withholding in certain cases of some papers in a dossier.

4. *'Material Denial of Justice (Arbitrariness).'* (Very numerous indeed.) Violation of principle *ne bis in idem*, of *nulla pœna sine lege*; permissibility of certain Cantonal judicial procedures; an ill-formulated Cantonal referendum; the claim of a particular political party to a vacant Cantonal judgeship; Cantonal taxation; permission to inhabitants of one Canton to perform acts not permissible to others; exclusion of children from certain juvenile films; refusal to license hawking of Nazi anti-Semitic literature; refusal to allow a non-doctor to be a chiropodist; &c.

Many of these cases had a slender chance of success, and a criticism of the Article 4 jurisdiction is that there are so many eccentric and hopeless cases brought 'on the chance'. The control of Cantonal taxation is particularly important, since in principle all direct taxation is Cantonal.

Connexion between the wording of the Constitution and the Case Law. There are several lines of approach to this problem. One may say that all injustice leads to inequality, for injustice is either favouritism or unfair discrimination. A rule against inequality is therefore a rule against injustice or 'inequity'. Alternatively one may start from the Kantian position that the justice of a rule is the same as its universality (or universability), and therefore a just rule applies to all alike. In either case a Swiss jurist would consider the question one to be argued philosophically rather than historically or empirically. As a matter of *history*, 'denial of justice' was at first considered to be a rule on its own merits; it was only later that it came to be considered as falling under Article 4.[2]

---

[1] See Article 113.
[2] The student should in general note the changes in the interpretation of the

Equality before the Law as a Political Programme

Aristocracy. Before the French Revolution the Swiss aristocracy did not cut much dash among the European aristocracies. From the standpoint of the years after the Revolution, however, the old régime in Switzerland appeared very much a part of the old régime in Europe. Democracy, which makes ancient aristocracy exclusive by refusing to create new titles, and the recent stability of Swiss currency which has made aristocrats of other countries applicants for Swiss charity, have together altered the picture, and the aristocracies of Switzerland bid fair to outlive all others. They remain for the most part local aristocracies, with names illustrious in the history of a town or village or 'democratic' Canton, but outside that area only distinguishable by the connoisseur from their fellow doctors, architects, and lawyers who are not in the 'Geschlechterbuch'. A few great names like Burckhardt, Escher, and Salis have called ancient virtues out of abeyance and commanded respect in their own right, but today even these are producing less copious talent. The local aristocracies constitute rather than exert an influence. They play nearly no part in public political life.

Women. The principle of equality is complied with when like things are treated alike, and is violated when unlike things are treated alike. There is nothing more certain than that men and women are in all their qualities and works unlike (though it cannot be said that one is undeniably superior to the other). There is therefore no case at all (in the Swiss view) from the argument of equality against the exclusion of women from all political, all judicial, and most administrative offices, and for depriving them of all political rights. While it is admitted that the arguments for admitting women to these rights and offices are weak, it must nevertheless be conceded that the arguments against it are unconvincing. Swiss people in conversation often trade the referendum, &c., against votes for women.

It is sometimes said that the position of women in civil law in Switzerland is particularly favourable. Examination of the Civil Code suggests that this claim is exaggerated.

ARTICLE 5. The Confederation guarantees to the Cantons their territory, their sovereignty within the limits of Article 3, their Constitutions, the freedom and the rights of the people and the constitutional rights of citizens, as well as the rights and powers which the people has conferred upon the authorities.

Before 1848 the Cantons guaranteed *each other's* governments and sovereignty, and the present Article is a not completely logical attempt to substitute the central government's guarantee for that of the collectivity of the Cantonal governments. The first phrase of the Article completes Article 1 of the Constitution by inscribing the territories of the Cantons as in 1874 into the Constitution. This guarantee of territory can only be a guarantee

Constitution which have followed upon the adoption of neo-Kantianism as the source of revealed truth for lawyers.

as against other Cantons, since violation of the territory of Switzerland by a foreign country is primarily a violation of Federal, not of Cantonal, territory.

The guarantee of Cantonal sovereignty (that is to say, the guarantee of the autonomy of one Canton as against another Canton, not against the Confederation itself) and the guarantee of the constitutional structure of the Canton—and the Federal competence to maintain this autonomy and structure—should not be confused with Article 6, which speaks of the 'formal' guarantee, a Resolution approving a document. The sanction behind the present material guarantee of sovereignty is armed 'Intervention' of Federal troops under Federal command (Articles 16 and 17). The guarantee is given to the citizen as against the Cantonal government, however, as well as to the Cantonal government itself, and the sanction behind this guarantee to the individual is of a different sort—it is the decision of the Federal Tribunal or Council in individual cases, backed up if necessary by Federal 'Execution' (see note to Article 85, s. 8).

ARTICLE 6. The Cantons are obliged to ask of the Confederation the Federal Guarantee of their Constitutions.

The Confederation grants this guarantee, providing:

(a) that the Constitutions contain nothing contrary to the provisions of the Federal Constitution;
(b) that they assure the exercise of political rights according to Republican (representative or democratic) forms;
(c) that the Constitutions have been accepted by the people and can be amended whenever the absolute majority of citizens demand it.

The Cantons must have their new Constitutions and alterations to their existing Constitutions sanctioned ('guaranteed') by the Confederation. That is to say, the Federal Assembly has to pass an *arrêté* granting, or refusing, the 'guarantee'. This procedure follows from reading the present Article with Articles 85, ss. 7 and 8, and 102, s. 3. If the guarantee is refused the Canton must withdraw the offending passage. Because there is doubt concerning the validity of a constitutional provision not yet granted or denied the Federal guarantee, the Cantons in practice generally make alterations in such a way that they only go into force if the guarantee is accorded. Acts under the guaranteed Constitution can still be challenged for repugnancy to Federal law, for although the guarantee must be sought its grant does not make valid what is otherwise unlawful. It is probable that the Cantonal Constitution itself may also be challenged for repugnancy to Federal law in the Courts, even though guaranteed by the political authorities, but the question is uncertain.

Paragraph 2, section (a). If the Federal authorities find part of the Cantonal Constitution to be contrary to Federal law, then that part is void *ab initio*.[1] It frequently happens that parts of the Cantonal Constitution duplicate parts of the Federal Constitution, guaranteeing for example the same freedom-rights. It is generally agreed that such Cantonal provisions have no effect, and that even if the Federal provisions were repealed, the Cantonal provisions would not revive. An interesting case which turned on this point is that of Hauri *versus* Aargau (1889; Curti, No. 1374).

Section (*b*). Neufchatel used to be a constitutional monarchy. This section is directed against a royalist revival there, but in view of Article 4 it appears to be superfluous.

Section (*c*). This section contains more than might appear at first sight:
(i) Cantonal Compulsory Referendum. The Cantonal Constitution and all amendments to it must be submitted to the people.
(ii) Cantonal Constitutional Initiative. There must be a procedure whereby the majority of citizens can at any time alter the Constitution, viz. a right of popular initiative for total revision, and probably also a right of initiative for partial revision.
(iii) Arising from this that no particular sanctity (a delay of two years, for example, or a requirement of a two-thirds majority) may be attached to any part of a Cantonal Constitution.

These provisions in practice are no hardship. In Switzerland, as far as political rights are concerned, the Cantons set the pace. All Cantons go farther and have the legislative referendum also and an assortment of other devices (varying from Canton to Canton) such as a budget referendum, or a compulsory legislative referendum for laws incurring expenditure beyond a certain limit. The effect of all these political rights is that the citizens are called to the polls from four to eight (or more) times a year, and each time will have to vote on several issues.[2]

The Cantons would be entitled to require a majority of all qualified voters, but in practice only require a majority of those voting.

ARTICLE 7. All separate alliances and all treaties of a political character between Cantons are forbidden.

On the other hand, Cantons have the right to conclude conventions among themselves upon matters of legislation, administration, and justice. In all such cases they are to bring the conventions to the cognizance of the Federal authorities, who shall prevent their being executed if they contain anything repugnant to the Confederation or to the rights of other Cantons. If there is no repugnancy, the Cantons are entitled to

---

[1] Article 2 of the Transitory Provisions.
[2] For example, the approval of a communal budget, the election of half a dozen school teachers, the approval of a Cantonal law and constitutional amendment, and a Federal referendum—all at the same time. For this reason alone figures of participation in Federal referendums should be used with caution: moreover, in certain Cantons voting is in various degrees compulsory.

claim from the Federal authorities co-operation in the execution of such conventions.

'Treaties' between Cantons, like all Cantonal acts, must be in accordance with Federal law: the sanction of the Federal authority[1] is analogous to the Federal sanction of Cantonal Constitutions under Article 6. Without sanction, the validity of the treaty is in doubt, but if a sanctioned treaty is, or becomes, contrary to Federal law, the treaty is *pro tanto* void: the treaty is Cantonal law for the purposes of the rule 'Federal law breaks Cantonal law'. As to the subject-matter of the treaty, it may deal with anything that is within the legislative competence of the Canton. Now that the Confederation has made use of its competences in the sphere of civil and criminal law (Articles 64 and 64 *bis*) the subject-matter of intercantonal treaties is limited.

Nevertheless, such treaties are still fairly frequent. They are of two sorts: the 'agreement' between two or more Cantons on a matter within the Cantonal competence (e.g. a hydro-electric scheme for a river flowing between two Cantons); and the 'concordat', an agreement between several Cantons to which other Cantons may at any time adhere, e.g. the concordat on the maintenance of paupers on the territory of the contracting Cantons. Both these types are in general use; the procedure and the validity of both sorts are the same.

The prohibition of treaties with a political content is a reminiscence of the Old Confederation and of the Sonderbund war; the Cantons are not now in a position to think of making such treaties.

The validity of the 'treaty' within the contracting Canton is, as far as enforcement by the Federal authorities is concerned, similar to that of the Cantonal Constitution, i.e. it is a part of the Canton's law which the central government applies against the government of the Canton in the interests of an aggrieved party (cf. Article 113, s. 3).

ARTICLE 8. The Confederation has the sole right of declaring war, of making peace, and of concluding alliances and treaties with foreign Powers, and, in particular, treaties concerning customs duties and trade.

The Confederation in practice concludes treaties upon all subjects. The boundary between Federal and Cantonal treaty competences drawn by the Constitution is, presumably, that the Confederation makes treaties on all subjects within its competence, while treaties (with foreign countries) concerning subjects within the competence of the Cantons are to be made by the Cantons.

For Cantonal treaty powers (with foreign countries) see Articles 9 and 10. For competence of the Federal Council in foreign affairs see Article 102, ss. 7, 8. For approval of treaties by the Assembly see Article 85, s. 5; for the treaty-referendum (challenge) see Article 89. The constitutionality of Federal

---

[1] i.e. the Federal Council, with the possibility of discussion by the Assembly in certain cases (Articles 102, s. 7, and 85, s. 5).

treaties cannot be challenged by the Federal Tribunal (Articles 113, para. 3, and 114 *bis*). Customs treaties are again mentioned in Article 29. Article 11 forbids 'capitulations'. The special status of neutrality in Swiss constitutional practice is discussed on page 94.

ARTICLE 9. In special cases, the Cantons retain the right of concluding treaties with foreign Powers upon the subjects of public economic regulation, cross-frontier intercourse, and police relations; but such treaties shall contain nothing repugnant to the Confederation, or to the rights of other Cantons.

The Cantons now seldom make use of their constitutional powers of making treaties with foreign countries. The existing treaties—especially those dating from the days of larger sovereignty before 1874—are sometimes in the name of the Canton, but now usually in the name of the Federal authority on behalf of the Canton. It seems that the party bound by them in international law is the Confederation and not the Canton—the subject is a nice one for the theoretical ingenuity of jurists. The relation, in fact, between the Confederation and the Cantons in this matter is rather that of a parent who sometimes used to let his infant sons sign cheques needing parental counter-signature, but who is now too busy to play infant-sovereignty any more.

The Cantonal treaty competences are probably not limited by the particular mention of economic regulation, &c., in this Article, but extend to the whole field of Cantonal competences, in the same way as the Federal power is not limited by the explicit mention of customs in Article 8. The procedure for Federal sanction is the same as for treaties between Cantons, for which see Article 7. This is perfectly logical.

The usual subject-matter of Cantonal treaties is Double Taxation, direct taxation being in principle a Cantonal matter.

ARTICLE 10. Official relationships between a Canton and a foreign Government or its representatives take place through the intermediacy of the Federal Council.

Nevertheless, upon the subjects mentioned in Article 9, the Cantons may correspond directly with the inferior authorities and the officials of a foreign State.

That is to say, the diplomatic and consular services are exclusively Federal. But when a Canton wishes to make a treaty with a foreign country on a matter within its competence it may (sc. with Federal permission?) enter into negotiation with 'the inferior authorities' of a foreign State. What is meant by 'inferior authorities' is disputed; it is possible that it does not include the officials of another country's Foreign Office, but only local government officials, or perhaps only those of private enterprises, &c.—this last interpretation appears too narrow. For a recent example see Bundesblatt 1949, ii. 744 (the Basle–Mulhouse airport astride the French–Swiss frontier).

Treaties concerning local cross-frontier traffic sometimes leave certain matters to be settled by the Cantonal government and (for example) the French *préfet* concerned.

ARTICLE 11. No military capitulations may be concluded.

Military capitulations were treaties between Cantons and foreign Powers, whereby the Cantons permitted recruitment of mercenaries in their territories in exchange for money and other advantages. These treaties obtained special privileges for the mercenary forces amounting to something like extra-territoriality. This Article (dating from 1848) limits Cantonal, and indeed Federal, sovereignty in this respect. Recruitment of mercenaries by foreign Powers under conditions often popularly called capitulations continued more or less openly into the 1870's.[1] The Pope still has a Swiss Guard, but this is held not to be *military* service under a foreign Power.

The word 'capitulation' is apparently the same word as the Ottoman and other capitulations: the etymology is disputed.

ARTICLE 12. No members of the Federal authorities, Federal civil or military officials, or representatives or commissioners of the Confederation, nor members of Cantonal governments or legislative assemblies, may receive from a foreign Government pensions, salaries, titles, gifts, or decorations. An infringement of this rule effects loss of office or function.

Whoever possesses such pension, title, or decoration is only eligible as member of a Federal authority, as Federal civil or military official, as representative or commissioner of the Confederation or as member of a Cantonal government or legislative assembly, if, before entering upon the duties of the office, he expressly renounces the enjoyment of the pension or the carrying of the title, or has returned the decoration.

No order or title conferred by a foreign Government may be worn or used in the Swiss army.

No officer, non-commissioned officer, or private soldier may accept a distinction of this nature.

Transitory Provision. Anyone who had honourably received a decoration or title before the revised Article 12 came into force may be elected or appointed member of a Federal authority or Federal civil or military official, or representative or commissioner of the Confederation, or member of a Cantonal

---

[1] Swiss citizens who serve in foreign armies as mercenaries (e.g. in the French Foreign Legion) now commit an offence under Swiss military law.

government or legislative assembly, provided that he renounces the use of the title or the wearing of the decoration for the term of his office or function. An infringement of this rule effects loss of office or function.

The severity of this Article was increased by a popular votation on 8 Feb. 1931. The text is an Assembly counter-project to an initiative. It is of some social-psychological interest that republican virtue was strong enough to take all this trouble.

Paragraph 4 contains the sting. All men capable of it belong to the army from 20 to 48 years old, or longer, and they can be victimized by military punishments when they do their annual service if they accept, for example, the Medal of Honour of a foreign branch of the Red Cross during those years.

Honorary and other doctorates are not included in this prohibition, since they are not conferred by a foreign sovereign or State.

The position in the Constitution of this Article immediately after the prohibition of capitulations reveals its historical origin. The receipt of pensions and bribes from foreign sovereigns was one of the important industries of the Cantons in the Old Confederation, especially of the primitive alpine democracies.

ARTICLE 13. The Confederation is not authorized to maintain a standing army.

No Canton or half-Canton may, without the sanction of the Federal government, maintain a standing force of more than 300 men. The *gendarmerie* are not included in this number.

The wording of this Article is misleading. By 'standing army' is meant a mercenary army independent of the Federal army described in Articles 18–22; the expression is not understood as prohibiting the Confederation from maintaining a cadre of instructing-officers and N.C.O.s for the Federal army nor as prohibiting it from retaining volunteer soldiers permanently to man and maintain fortifications. What the Article does do is to provide that the Federal Army, instructors, maintenance troops, and conscripts, shall be the only army.

In this sense the Cantons maintain no troops. That the army is composed on a territorial basis follows from Article 21, not from this Article.

ARTICLE 14. When a dispute arises between two Cantons they shall not take any independent action nor resort to arms, but are to submit duly to the decision of the Federation.

This Article gives a misleading picture of what is likely to happen when two Cantons quarrel, but a good picture of the Federal Treaty of 1815–48 and of the Old Confederation. Until 1874 the Article was an important one.

Under the present Constitution, Articles 110, s. 3, and 113, s. 2 provide for conflicts between Cantons which can be brought before the Courts, and Article 102, s. 5 for other cases; logically, however, both depend upon this Article, which creates the Federal competence.

ARTICLE 15. If a Canton is threatened by a sudden danger from a foreign country, the government of the Canton threatened is obliged to seek the aid of other confederate Cantons, and at the same time to inform the Federal authorities, without prejudice to any dispositions the latter may make on its own account. The Cantons whose aid is sought are bound to afford it. The expenses thereof are borne by the Confederation.

This describes the procedure of the Old Confederation and of the Federal Treaty period. The picture it evokes—a messenger on a steaming horse, the patriotic Landamman in his nightshirt hoisting the Cantonal and the Federal flags, messengers with bandoliers galloping amid barking dogs and bugle-calls to the next Canton—is agreeable but untrue to life. Wireless, codewords, and an efficient military machine entirely under Federal control determine the present procedure.

ARTICLE 16. In cases of internal disturbance, or if danger is threatened from another Canton, the government of the Canton threatened shall give immediate notice to the Federal Council, so that the latter may, within the limits of its competences (Article 102, ss. 3, 10, 11), take the necessary measures or summon the Federal Assembly. In urgent cases the [Cantonal] government in question is authorized to seek the help of other Cantons, which are bound to afford it. The Federal Council must be at once informed.

If the government of the Canton is not in a position to call for aid, the Federal authority *can*, and if the security of Switzerland is endangered, the Federal authority *must*, intervene of its own motion.

In cases of Federal Intervention, the Federal authorities shall see that the provisions of Article 5 are observed.

The expenses are to be borne by the Canton asking or occasioning Federal Intervention, unless special circumstances cause the Federal Assembly to resolve otherwise.

Federal Intervention (Eidgenössische Intervention). 'Intervention' under this Article to restore public order is to be distinguished from Federal Execution (see Article 85, s. 8), which is the last sanction the central government can exert against a Canton reluctant to obey Federal law.

Under Article 19, para. 4, the Cantons may use their own defence forces on their own territory to maintain public order. It sometimes happens, however, that their own forces are insufficient or disaffected, and in this case they must ask help of the Confederation. In practice the government of the Canton concerned sends a telegram to the Federal Military Department, who obtain the consent of the Federal Council and dispatch troops by train. These troops are under Federal command (Article 17). In all this there is nothing much different from the conduct of local governments in other countries. The problem then comes up whether the dispatch of troops is to be called 'Federal Intervention' in the legal sense, because if it is an 'Intervention' the Canton must pay the expenses unless the Assembly passes a resolution excusing it. That is the crux of the matter.

It was formerly the practice for the Confederation to send a 'Commissioner'. This was a temporary plenipotentiary of the central power, in practice appointed by the Federal Council, who took charge of civil and military operations (in the capacity of a civilian) and assumed all powers necessary for the fulfilment of his task according to his instructions. During the last 'Intervention', in Geneva in November 1932, no Commissioner was appointed; it is therefore uncertain what would be the practice if serious riots occurred again. The office of Federal Commissioner is nowhere mentioned in the Constitution (unless the reference in Article 12, Prohibited Decorations, means Commissioner in this sense, which is doubtful); it is somewhat similar to that of 'General', discussed under Article 18.

In war-time the Cantons have no troops under their control and so must always use Federal troops: the strict meaning of Intervention thereby is blurred, and it is hard to say what is Intervention and what is not.

It is not the practice of the central government to wait to be invited to intervene. In the language of the Constitution, it always considers that the troubles 'endanger the security of Switzerland'. In 1890 the government of Ticino (a Canton which at that time was frequently 'in a state of *coup d'état*') actually did seek the help of two neighbouring Catholic Cantons—who were too slow—but that is the only time it has been done. The Assembly has always remitted the costs, except once (Zurich in 1871). 'Danger from another Canton' is an anachronism.

For other mentions of 'Intervention' see Articles 112, s. 3, and 85, s. 7. Cf. Article 5, from which the necessity for Intervention logically springs.

ARTICLE 17. In the cases mentioned in Articles 15 and 16 every Canton is obliged to allow free passage to troops. These are to be placed at once under Federal command.

This refers to an incident of 1845. The Cantons must allow the passage of troops while they are still under the command of another Canton as well as troops under Federal command. The rule about Federal command is an important one in the event of internal disturbances; see Article 16 above.

ARTICLE 18. Every Swiss is liable to military service.

Servicemen who as a result of Federal military service lose their lives or suffer permanent injury to their health are entitled to support from the Confederation for their families or themselves, if in need.

Servicemen shall receive their first equipment, clothing, and arms without payment. The weapon shall remain in the hands of the soldier, subject to conditions to be determined by Federal legislation.

The Confederation shall lay down unified provisions on service-exemption tax.

The Swiss Army. The Swiss army consists of conscripts, a very small cadre of regular officers, and some maintenance troops. All Swiss young men of an adequate physical standard must do military service: the only exemptions are for certain officials while in office, and for the clergy of recognized denominations. The initial stage of military service lasts several months, but in later years is only for a week or two—the claims of service diminishing with age. A university student can do it in his vacations. After the end of the first period the conscript keeps his rifle and equipment at home until his liability for service is past. The experiment is now being started of also permitting him to retain a small quantity of sealed ammunition at home. This practice is perhaps the culminating sign of political liberty: it is also of military value in facilitating a rapid mobilization.

The military value of the Swiss army is disputed; it is not known. A feature of Swiss military training seems to be the emphasis placed on carrying heavy packs long distances, and the concentration upon accuracy of rifle fire. One has the impression of a good infantry of an old-fashioned sort, tempered by the faults and virtues of a territorial service where military relationships are continuous with those of civilian life. The relationships with the civil power appear good, perhaps because of the great weight the army, and the executive power generally, has in Swiss estimation.

Those unable to perform military service for any reason (incapacity, residence abroad, &c.) pay a tax for exemption. Half this tax goes to the Cantons: see p. 48.

The General. Article 85, s. 4 (cf. Article 92), mentions incidentally the office of General-in-Chief of the Federal army, who is to be elected by the two Chambers in joint session. It is only on the rare occasions when there is a mobilization in consequence of imminent threat of war that a General is elected, and he retires when the threat is past. Only four Generals have been elected since 1848 (Dufour, in 1849 and again in 1856; Herzog, 1870; Wille, 1914; Guisan, 1939). It is a typical institution of the period before 1848, like the 'Federal Commissioner'.

The General holds a remarkable position. Chosen by the Assembly on the advice of the Federal Council, he is in effect an independent estate of the realm while the war lasts, and is revered by the whole population. Every other power is held by the civilian executive, to whom a grant of Full Powers is given during war, except the one power which it is essential that it should have—the power of commanding and dismissing the General. This power is reserved to the Assembly (which by Article 204 of the Law on Military Organization of 1907 can only exercise it on the proposition of the Federal Council). The Federal Councillor in charge of the Military Department and the General stand to each other in the relationship of two hostile legislative chambers—the Councillor irremovable during his term of office and the General responsible to, and removable by, two separate multi-party legislative councils; the General with a soldier's liability to alternate between panic and routine, and the Councillor with the cares and responsibility of State on his shoulders.

The problem as to who makes the decisions of policy is not easy to answer, and is perhaps not to be couched in those terms. There are traditionally two schools of military policy, one advocating a flexible defence of the frontier, the other retirement to the 'alpine redoute' astride the Gotthard. Neither policy is a purely military one, and it is unlikely that an officer who at the time of mobilization favoured the unfashionable view would be elected. One wonders what the relationships of the General and the Federal Council would be in the alpine redoute! On the other hand, the General does form a sort of *raison d'être* for the Assembly in war-time: if the Assembly gave up its power to dismiss the general there would not be much likelihood of its meeting in war-time at all, for the Federal Council holds all authority and power. The solution has been put forward of distinguishing between armed neutrality, which a peace-time General can after all run, and real war, which should be left in the hands of responsible civilians. The matter is still occasionally under discussion.

ARTICLE 19. The Federal army is composed:
(*a*) of the Cantonal military contingents;
(*b*) of all citizens who, not belonging to such contingents, are nevertheless liable to military service.

The right of disposing the Confederate army, including the military equipment by law pertaining to it, belongs to the Confederation.

In time of danger, the Confederation has also the exclusive and direct control of men not included in the Federal army and of all other military resources of the Cantons.

The Cantons dispose the defence forces of their territory, so far as this authority is not limited by the laws or the Constitution of the Confederation.

Under the Federal Treaty of 1815–48 each Canton had to provide a stipulated number of men reckoned according to the population of the Canton, and the Federal army was composed of these Cantonal 'contingents'.[1] Under the Constitution of 1848 the Confederation raised its troops directly, leaving training and equipment to the Cantons, with Federal inspection. The system was more picturesque than efficient. The Cantons managed to make an adequate showing at inspections by masking shortages of equipment by time-honoured ruses, but the real discrepancies between equipment and the number of men was revealed in the mobilizations of 1858, 1866, and 1870. The language of this Article is a sentimental reminiscence of the days of the Federal Treaty. One of the chief purposes of the Constitution of 1848 was precisely to abolish the Cantonal contingent system.

The true position is described in Articles 20 and 21. The army is Federal, but a sphere of administration remains to the Cantons, and the infantry and horsed cavalry are organized on the territorial system.

Section (*b*) of para. 1, and para. 3, give the central government the competence to enrol those not otherwise liable to military service (through youth, old age, disability, &c.) into some sort of military formation if the worst comes to the worst.

ARTICLE 20. Legislation upon the organization of the army is a Federal matter. Execution of these laws in the Cantons is entrusted to the Cantonal authorities, within limits which shall be fixed by Federal legislation, and under Federal supervision.

All military instruction, and likewise the arming of the troops, belongs to the Confederation.

The provision and maintenance of clothing and equipment is a Cantonal matter, but the Cantons shall be reimbursed therefor by the Confederation, according to a scale to be laid down by Federal legislation.

The compromise described here for the division of authority between Confederation and Cantons seems a happy and stable one—Federal legislation, command, and supervision, Cantonal management of details, and the emblem of the Canton on announcements which affect the individual infantry soldier. The Cantonal provision of equipment has become somewhat fictitious.

ARTICLE 21. Corps of troops shall, unless military considerations stand in the way, be formed from men of the same Canton.

The composition of these corps, the maintenance of their effective strength, the appointment and promotion of officers

[1] For the Cantonal (money) contingents see Article 42. The same expression is used of both institutions.

is a Cantonal matter, subject to general regulations to be laid down for them by the Confederation.

Only the infantry and horsed cavalry are as a rule constituted on a strictly territorial basis. One of the 'military considerations' for transfer to the troops of another Canton would be inability to understand the main language of the Canton of residence. But for the most part a territorial basis is rather found desirable on military grounds. It is the Canton of permanent residence which counts.

Cantonal patronage in the matter of commissioning and promoting officers only applies to those bodies of troops in fact composed on a Cantonal basis. Cantons can only commission men who have the qualifications the Confederation lays down, i.e. who are trained and passed out as potential officers, and if the Canton is unable to provide enough of these from its own corps the Confederation allots to it officers resident in another Canton. The situation is really that as far as possible the men of a Cantonal body of troops are commanded by officers living in that Canton. The patronage is unimportant.

ARTICLE 22. The Confederation has the right to take over, permanently or temporarily, parade-grounds and military buildings and their appurtenances on the territory of a Canton, upon payment of fair compensation.

The conditions governing this compensation shall be laid down by Federal legislation.

The Confederation has never needed to invoke this Article, as it has always purchased or rented barracks and parade-grounds, &c., in the ordinary way by agreement.

Exemption of Federal Property from Cantonal Taxation. Article 10 of the Federal Law concerning Political and other Guarantees in favour of the Confederation of 26 March 1934 (Garantiegesetz), reproducing a provision of the Law of 1851 of the same name, provides that 'Federal funds, or funds administered by the Confederation, and land, buildings, and materials devoted directly to Federal purposes, are not liable to the direct taxation of the Cantons'. Among property included in this exemption are barracks and parade-grounds, the Federal railways, customs houses and post offices, and the Swiss National Bank.

ARTICLE 23. The Confederation has the right to construct at its own expense or to subsidize public works which are to the advantage of the whole Federation or a large part thereof.

For this purpose it may expropriate property, against payment of just compensation. Further provisions shall be laid down by Federal legislation.

The Federal Assembly may forbid public works which run counter to the military interests of the Confederation.

This Article confers four competences upon the Confederation: (1) to erect, and (2) to subsidize, public works; (3) to expropriate on payment of a fair indemnity; and (4) to prevent Cantonal, &c., constructions which are against military interests.

1. Article 26 (Railways) is the most important particular case of this competence. The Confederation prefers not to undertake direct construction.
2. The competence of subsidizing public works is much used. The wording of the Constitution does not make it clear how 'considerable' a part of the Confederation the works must interest. Must it interest several Cantons, or is a large project within one Canton sufficient? Is a water-supply for one country town sufficient? The central authority has not permitted itself to be unduly restricted in its interpretation, and a certain amount of control has followed subsidy. Article 24 (Torrents) is an important particular case of public work.
3. The Federal Law on Expropriation of 1850 was replaced in 1930 by a new law designed to be in harmony with the Civil Code. The purposes for which expropriation may be used are not confined to 'works which are to the advantage of the whole Federation or a large part thereof' but include 'any purpose of public interest recognized by Federal law'. Moreover, the Confederation has long exercised the power to expropriate ground on which to build its own buildings (e.g. post offices) when necessary. The power may be exercised directly or it may be delegated. The indemnity must be 'full and entire' (Article 16 of the Law) and there is an eventual appeal to the Federal Tribunal on compensation. The Cantons also possess the right to expropriate by virtue of their 'sovereignty' and may empower their communes to do so also.

Article 22 (Barracks) is a particular case of this competence.

The law of expropriation is a good point at which to test the quality of a nation's justice and freedom.

4. The *arrêté* of both Councils which this clause necessitates, and the confinement of the wording to public works, make this competence valueless. The Federal Council (i.e. the Executive) can use other methods against Cantons in the unlikely event of their being uncooperative in this matter, and would in any case not permit private works which, for example, spoilt a fortified area from a military point of view (cf. 'Burckhardt', No. 2256): the only question is that of compensation.

ARTICLE 23 *bis*. The Confederation shall maintain such reserves of cereals as will ensure the country's food-supply. It may compel millers to store corn, and to take over its own supplies of corn in order to facilitate turnover of its reserve.

The Confederation shall encourage the growing of cereals within the country, facilitate selection and acquisition of high quality home-grown seed, and give assistance to those growing corn for their own use—taking especial account of the needs of the upland areas. It shall buy home-grown corn of good quality suitable for milling at a price which makes production possible. Millers may be compelled to repurchase this corn on the basis of its market value.

The Confederation shall take steps to maintain the national milling industry and, at the same time, safeguard the interests of the consumer of flour and bread. Within the limits of the powers transferred to it, it shall supervise trade in cereals and bread-flour, and the prices thereof. The Confederation shall take the necessary measures to regulate the import of bread-flour and may reserve to itself the exclusive right of such importation. The Confederation shall grant cheap transport facilities to millers where need exists, so as to lessen their costs of transporting (corn) to the interior of the country. It shall take measures designed to equalize the cost of flour to the advantage of the upland areas.

The cross-frontier duty (*droit de statistique*) levied on all merchandise crossing the Swiss customs frontier shall be increased. The yield of this duty shall go towards covering the expenses of provisioning the country in cereals.

This was the Assembly counter-project accepted in the votation of 3 March 1929. The legislative history of the project is instructive. In 1915 a Federal monopoly of corn, &c., was introduced by an *arrêté* of the Federal Council under war-time Full Powers, which was modified two years later and in 1922 was replaced by a Federal Arrêté guaranteeing government purchase at a fixed price; the *arrêté* was declared 'urgent' to withdraw it from challenge to a referendum. At various times in the years following the *arrêté* was revised and extended, all instruments being withdrawn from the referendum by being declared 'urgent'. At length in 1926 the Assembly submitted to the people and Cantons a constitutional amendment making a cereal monopoly, and the previous practice, legal. The amendment was rejected at the votation. Notwithstanding this the Assembly continued its protection and subsidy of corn-growing, by *arrêtés* withdrawn from the referendum, until at last the voters accepted the present revised Article, granting the Confederation the competence to do what it had been doing since 1915, in 1929.

The Article prescribes control and subsidy, but not monopoly. In 1939 a monopoly was reintroduced, 'provisionally', and it still continues (in 1952).

ARTICLE 24. The Confederation has the right of high supervision over the control of water-regulation and forests.

It shall give assistance to the work of correcting the courses and the embanking of mountain streams, and to the afforestation of their collection areas. It shall lay down rules to ensure the upkeep of these works and of the forests already in existence.

Federal Supervision. This is a rather vague conception; the expression is used in at least five different senses: (*a*) this Article and 24 *bis*, (*b*) Article 37, (*c*) Articles 20, 40, and 69 *bis*, (*d*) Article 34, (*e*) Article 85, s. 11.

Here and in the next Article the words are interpreted as meaning a concurrent power of the Confederation and Cantons in the same field; typically the Confederation issuing the general rules by which the Cantons are bound and which supersede Cantonal law inconsistent with them ('Federal law breaks Cantonal law'), whereas the Cantons issue subsidiary rules. This relationship must be distinguished from the situation where the Confederation is alone competent (posts, railways, &c.), and where the Cantons are alone competent (income tax, &c.), and where the Cantons are to execute Federal legislation (a frequent relationship, e.g. Article 53, Register of Births, Deaths, and Marriages, which merges into the relationship of supervision in the sense of this Article).

Until 1897 the words 'in mountain districts' stood at the end of the first paragraph, but other districts came to desire subsidies, and an amendment in that year cut the words out.

The visitor to Switzerland will have noticed the canalized torrents and the extensive areas of forest.

ARTICLE 24 *bis*. Water-power is under the supervision of the Confederation.

Federal legislation shall lay down general provisions to safeguard the public interest and to ensure the rational exploitation of water-power. This legislation shall, as far as possible, take into account the interest of inland navigation.

Subject to these reservations, the regulation of water-power belongs to the Cantons.

Nevertheless, when a stretch of water is claimed as a source of water-power and is under the sovereignty of two or more Cantons, and the Cantons are unable to agree in a joint concession, then the granting of the concession belongs to the Confederation. In the same way, the Confederation has the right to grant the concession when the stretch of water forms the national boundary, subject to the consultation of the Cantons concerned.

Payments made for the use of water-power belong to the Cantons, or to those entitled to them under Cantonal legislation.

The Confederation fixes the amounts of payment for the concessions it grants after consultation with the Cantons interested, and with reasonable regard for Cantonal legislation. Within the limits to be fixed by Federal legislation the Cantons determine the amounts of payment for other concessions.

Export to a foreign country of energy produced by water-power may only take place by consent of the Confederation.

In all concessions of water-power made after the coming into force of the present article there shall be a reservation that the terms are subject to any future Federal legislation.

The Confederation is authorized to make legislative provisions on the subjects of transmission and distribution of electric power.

In the early years of this century a new sort of 'patriotism' came to the surface in Switzerland, a Conservative, as opposed to the old Liberal, patriotism. It expressed itself in various ways, among which we may notice: (1) attacks on foreigners and foreign influences (Articles 12, Orders; 44, 69 *ter*, Foreigners; 89, para. 3, Treaties; and protectionism); (2) attacks on supposed national weaknesses (Articles 32 *bis*, *ter*, and *quater*, Alcohol; 35, Gambling); and (3) a reinterpretation of history whereby the aristocratic Old Confederation is the hero and the Helvétique is the villain. The present Article is, to some extent, an example of the anti-foreign and protectionist movement.

The potentialities of water-power, which can make Switzerland self-sufficient for fuel for most purposes (e.g. for railways), were not foreseen by those who made the Constitution of 1874. In 1891 there was a movement for public ownership of water-power, but the matter was brought to a head in 1905 when it was proposed to export electricity from Ticino to Italy. In December of that year the Federal Assembly issued an *arrêté*, and withdrew it from the referendum by declaring it 'urgent', forbidding the export of electricity without the permission of the Federal Council. This was an early example of the use of the 'urgency clause' to supersede the Constitution itself—the matter was probably not in the Federal competence (but see Article 24, and Article 64, Civil Law) and was a precedent for what is now a not uncommon practice. In 1906 an initiative was launched to confer on the Confederation the competence to legislate on such matters and to legalize Federal control for the future. This initiative was later withdrawn by the committee which launched it in favour of the Assembly's counter-project, which alone was voted upon and which was accepted by all Cantons except Inner Rhodes.

Legislation was not passed under this Article until 1916. Note that a Federal monopoly has not been created, and Federal and Cantonal powers are concurrent except on frontier rivers (e.g. the Rhine) and where several Cantons are unable to agree. The water-power is usually exploited by private firms who pay a royalty to the Cantons.

ARTICLE 24 *ter*. Legislation upon navigation is a Federal matter.

Introduced by the votation of 4 May 1919. The Article settles the doubt as to Federal competence in this field, and was perhaps unnecessary. The wording is the same as that of Article 26, and leaves it open to the Confederation to introduce a Federal monopoly or to control private enterprise by police measures.

The Declaration of Barcelona (1921) created—or admitted—the right of countries without a seaboard to fly their national flags at sea, and Switzerland now does this. Navigation on the high seas and in inland waterways alike comes under the scope of this Article.

For Posts (which potentially include all forms of transport) see Article 36; for railways, Article 26; for aerial navigation, 37 *ter*.

ARTICLE 25. The Confederation is authorized to make legislative provisions concerning shooting and fishing, particularly with a view towards preservation of alpine game, and the protection of those birds beneficial to agriculture and forestry.

The ancient hunting and fishing rights were abolished by the Helvétique in 1798, and today the 'Jagdhoheit' (supremacy or sovereignty over sporting rights) belongs to the Cantons—subject to rather extensive Federal restrictions, and Federal supervision over Cantonal legislation.

The Cantons adopt one of two systems for sporting rights: either the licence system, whereby a permit to shoot in the whole, or part, of a Canton is sold to all who pay the fee and are otherwise entitled to a permit, or the block (Revier) system, where the shooting rights in a limited area, e.g. a commune, are let to a person or limited number of people for a period of years. Sporting rights are in general independent of ground-ownership.

Fishing is also a Cantonal monopoly (*régale*). But Cantons have variously recognized titles in particular waters, e.g. of corporations, private persons, or riparian owners. Administration is often handed over to the communes.

The monopolies of hunting and fishing are understood as being Cantonal monopolies reserved from the operation of Article 31.

ARTICLE 25 *bis*. The killing of any animal whatsoever for meat by bleeding the animal to death without stunning it first is forbidden.

An initiative accepted in 1893. It was originally a project of animal-lovers, but was taken up with enthusiasm in order to annoy the Jews, whose mode of ritual slaughter it forbids. It was necessary to pass the prohibition in the form of a constitutional amendment because Cantonal legislation, which forbade the Jewish methods of killing by bleeding an animal to death while it is conscious, had been voided by the Federal political authorities on an Appeal in Public Law as a violation of Article 50, Freedom of Worship.

The Article is therefore not the classic example of legislation masquerading as a constitutional amendment which it might be supposed.

Ingenious fictions and the blind eye of authority have made it of no effect. Under the Old Confederation Jews were tolerated in two rural communes of Aargau (Oberendingen and Lengnau). The Constitution of 1848 extended them some civil liberties throughout the Confederation, and they have benefited from all the freedom-rights since 1866. They play conspicuously little part in public life in Switzerland, and are concentrated in the large towns.

ARTICLE 26. Legislation concerning the construction and running of railways is a Federal matter.

That is to say, legislation concerning railways is an *exclusively* Federal matter. The power of legislating on this matter may not be delegated to the Cantons, nor may the legislation be executed by the Cantons. The same is the case with Articles 20, 24 *ter*, 28, 36, 37 *ter*, 38, 39, and 41. The competence to build railways and expropriate private owners would belong to the central government even without this Article (under Article 23, Public Works, or perhaps Article 36, Posts). What is provided under this Article is the exclusion of the Cantons.

With the legislative competence goes the 'Konzessionshoheit' or supremacy in the matter of issuing rights of making and running railways. This power is, somewhat surprisingly, exercised by the Assembly, and not by the Federal Council, by means of *arrêtés* not subject to the legislative challenge. It is a nice point whether road-trams are to be understood as railways, for the road 'Hoheit' belongs to the Cantons.

Exercising its legislative powers under this Article and Article 23 the Confederation nationalized the principal railways (Law of 15 Oct. 1897), a very bold legislative act in those days, and of doubtful constitutionality. The Law was challenged to a referendum, but passed. At the present day about one-half of the railway mileage of Switzerland is run by the Confederation. The trains are nearly all electric.

Railway officials are Federal civil servants. Under the Law on Political and other Guarantees of 1934 all Federal property is exempt from Cantonal direct taxation, and this applies to the Federal railways.

During the second half of the nineteenth century the granting of railway concessions, in Switzerland as elsewhere, was a passionately felt issue of constitutional as well as political importance.

ARTICLE 27. The Confederation is entitled to establish a Federal university and other institutions of higher education, in addition to the already existing Polytechnic School, and to subsidize institutions of this nature.

The Cantons provide for adequate primary education, which shall be exclusively under the control of the civil authority. Such education is compulsory and, in the public schools, free.

The public schools shall be such that they may be attended by adherents of all religious sects without any offence to their freedom of conscience or belief.

The Confederation shall take the necessary measures against Cantons which fail to fulfil these obligations.

Universities. A Federal Technical University (Eidgenössische Technische Hochschule, ETH, as it is now called) was created in 1853 and is situated in Zurich. It was created by the Confederation, and the Confederation plays a large part in its management. The Federal university visualized in this Article has never been established, though the Confederation has possessed this competence since 1848. The Cantons retain their 'sovereignty' in this field and have created Cantonal universities (all under direct political control by the Cantonal governments), so that there is no longer any need for a Federal university. The Swiss universities are: Basle (founded for the first time in 1460), Zurich (1833), Berne (1834), and Geneva, Lausanne, Fribourg, and Neufchatel. Of these only Fribourg is Roman Catholic. All the universities are exclusively Cantonal in that they receive no regular direct Federal subsidies. The Confederation has subsidized various specialist (e.g. commercial) training colleges.

Primary Schools. The supremacy in this field belongs to the Cantons, but the Constitution lays upon them certain obligations which apply to 'primary' schools only, i.e. until the children are about 13 or 14, for the Cantons interpret the word 'primary' variously.

These obligations are:

1. The Cantons must provide education in public schools or lay on their communes the duty of providing it.

2. This education must be 'adequate' as respects the teaching staff, length of schooling, number of school hours, attendance, number of children in the class, books, and subjects taught.

3. It must be obligatory, at least for normal children.

4. The education in public schools must not be under Church control, i.e. a Roman Catholic Canton or commune may not run a Catholic primary school even if it runs an undenominational school as well: all public primary schools must, theoretically, be non-sectarian. This means that the *ex officio* presence of a clergyman on the school board is illegal, that there must be no religious services in school hours, that the teaching must not be pervaded by religion—though religion may be administered in labelled doses set apart from the main school teaching—and that there must be no pictures of what might be called a party-religious character exposed in the school. These restrictions are offensive to Catholics, but they bear more lightly upon the authorities of Protestant Cantons, whose teachers are apt (as a type) to be radicals more inclined to a gentle *laissez-faire* atheism than to religious proselytizing. The bark of the Constitution, however, is not followed by an effective bite.

5. It must be free in the public schools.

Enforcement. The Federal Council entertains Appeals (under Article 102, s. 2 of the Constitution) by parents who complain, for example, that a school is not cost-free, or is confessional. But those provisions of this Article which do not give rise to a tangible private grievance when infringed appear to be nearly unenforceable: there exist, no doubt, certain means of Federal moral pressure—especially upon Cantonal officials and Executive Councillors, but no study of these seems ever to have been made. Since the ultimate control is in the hands of the Federal Council, which is a political body and which now always contains Roman Catholic clericalist members, the equilibrium which has been reached allows the Catholic Church at least a certain influence upon primary education in clerically minded Cantons. And the fact that military education is exclusively Federal (Article 20) and that recruits are examined in 'general education', enables the Confederation to impose a certain standard upon an educational system which is otherwise almost exclusively Cantonal or communal.

Quality of Swiss Education. The minimum standard of education in Switzerland, and the average achievement, is very high, and the general result is satisfactory, especially as a training for political democracy. But from an academic point of view the achievement is short of exhilarating: one receives an impression of too little intellectual inquisitiveness. Some sort of intellectual life is well spread throughout the country and exists in all the principal provincial capitals, but perhaps nowhere, at least in German Switzerland, does it achieve any great intensity. As with the political system as a whole, one is uncertain whether to regard the cultural system with solid satisfaction or with a certain disquiet.

ARTICLE 27 *bis.* Subsidies shall be paid to the Cantons to help them fulfil their obligations in the field of primary education.

The details shall be settled by law.

Organization, control, and supervision of primary schools remain Cantonal matters, subject to Article 27.

The last paragraph of Article 27 appears to mean that the Confederation has some duty to see that the provisions of the Article are enforced, that public primary education is in fact available, adequate, obligatory, free, and secular. But it is not clear whether it gives the Confederation a competence to legislate, for example, upon what is to be understood by such words as 'primary' or 'adequate', or whether the Confederation may subsidize education in the poorer, or in all, Cantons.

The Federal Council understood the Article as conferring a Federal competence in the matter. In order to pave the way for legislation, an examination of what happened in the various Cantons was necessary, and this needed a staff, or at least an official. The Federal Council therefore got the Assembly to pass an *arrêté* authorizing this. The *arrêté*, however, was challenged to a referendum by the Catholics and localists, and rejected at the votation (26 Nov. 1882). The project for an 'Education-Bashaw' (Schulvogt) was rightly seen as an attempt to centralize the control of education. A few years later, however, there was a movement that the Confederation should subsidize the Cantonal schools—always a popular move—to which the Federal Council, expecting that control would follow subsidy, agreed. The contention that a subsidy was not authorized by the Constitution was made, and appeared to have something in it—though the Executive declared itself quite ready to give the subsidy nevertheless, and even succeeded in finding a distinguished jurist to agree that it was constitutional—and scrupulousness won the day. The above Article was submitted to the people and Cantons and accepted (23 Nov. 1902) by a very large majority and all Cantons except Appenzell Inner Rhodes. One suspects that Inner Rhodes was right for once.

The Federal subsidy is at a flat rate per head of population, except that the mountainous and Italian-speaking (and incidentally predominantly Catholic) Cantons get a higher flat rate. The subsidy is not large and has never been withheld to exert pressure. The Law of 25 June 1903 is the one in force, as amended.

ARTICLE 28. Customs duties are a Federal matter. The Confederation has the right to levy import and export duties.

The Constitution of 1848 made Switzerland a free-trade area internally, and allotted the control of customs duties at the frontier to the Confederation, to the exclusion of the Cantons.

In the French text the word *péages* is used instead of *douanes* as a gesture that customs duties were to be used for revenue rather than protection. The boundary was already overstepped in the 1880's. Switzerland is now becoming the classic land of protection and subsidy.

ARTICLE 29. The following principles shall govern the assessment of the rates at which Federal customs duties shall be levied.
1. Import duties.
(*a*) Materials necessary for the industry and agriculture of the country shall be taxed as low as possible.
(*b*) The same principle shall apply to the necessaries of life.
(*c*) Luxuries shall be subject to the highest duties.
These principles shall be observed whenever commercial treaties are negotiated with foreign countries, unless there be compelling reasons to the contrary.
2. Export duties shall be as low as possible.
3. Customs legislation shall include appropriate provisions for cross-frontier and market trading.

Notwithstanding the provisions above, the Confederation

retains the right to take extraordinary measures temporarily in exceptional circumstances.

The implication of this Article is that customs duties should be levied for fiscal purposes, subject to the interests of the consumer, and particularly of the poorer consumer.

The present policy of all parties appears to be that customs duties and the prohibition of imports should be extensively used to compel citizens to consume indigenous products and imitations of foreign goods rather than the products of neighbouring countries which are often better and usually cheaper. This Article must therefore be read with the new 31 *bis*, subject to a somewhat pessimistic interpretation of the phrase 'whose survival is threatened' there. While conceding the constitutional propriety, one may doubt the political and economic necessity for this policy at the present time. The adoption of the policy of mutual subsidy at the expense of the unorganized consumer may indicate a weakness in the constitutional structure of the country, hence its interest for the student of government.

ARTICLE 30. The yield of the customs duties is paid into the Federal exchequer.

The indemnities previously paid to Cantons for the redemption of customs duties, road and bridge tolls, and other charges of this nature, are abolished.

As an exceptional case, and on account of their international alpine roads, the Cantons of Uri, Grisons, Ticino, and Valais receive an annual indemnity, which is fixed at the following amounts with effect from 1 Jan. 1925:

Uri	160,000 francs	[240,000]
Grisons	400,000 ,,	[600,000]
Ticino	400,000 ,,	[600,000]
Valais	100,000 ,,	[150,000]

After 1848 the greater part of the Federal income from the customs was used to compensate the Cantons for the sources of income they had lost, mentioned in paragraph 2 of this Article. The present Article presents the decision taken in 1874 to abolish this compensation, with the exception of payments to four poor Cantons which had previously done well out of their international passes, the roads over which they had themselves constructed. This explains why these three paragraphs are brought together in one Article.

At times some of the Cantons mentioned have got more compensation than they spent on the passes: the compensation was originally for loss of an historical income, not for upkeep of the roads (but see Article 37).

The sums were increased in 1927, and a paragraph which had become superfluous since the completion of the Gotthard tunnel was dropped at the same time.

(The figures in brackets are the sums payable to the Cantons for the years

1951–4 under the Temporary Provision adopted in the votation of 3 Dec. 1950; see note to Article 42, Federal Finance.)

ARTICLE 31. Freedom of Trade and Industry is guaranteed throughout the Confederation, except in so far as it is restricted by the Constitution itself or by laws made under it.

Exception is made for Cantonal regulations of trade and industry and taxation thereof. These regulations shall only infringe the principle of the Freedom of Trade and Industry if the Federal Constitution authorizes it. The Cantonal monopolies (*régales*) are also excepted.

Freedom of Trade and Industry was not guaranteed under the Constitution of 1848, and its introduction in 1874 had the effect of immediately voiding a number of Cantonal laws and administrative provisions, especially Cantonal laws controlling the trade in alcohol (see Article 32 *bis*). The present Article dates from the 'Economic Articles' revision of 1947 (see note to Article 31 *bis*), but the first phrase is retained from the old Article.

The original interpretation included in the guarantee of the Freedom of Trade, &c., both free-trade in the English sense as opposed to protection, and free competition as understood by the classical economists. As regards protection, Articles 28 and 42 make customs duties the chief, and almost the sole, source of income for the Federal government, and the political structure of the country provides little resistance to the protectionist pressures of vested interests. As regards free competition, as a freedom-right the Freedom of Trade and Industry is a right available to the individual, and by analogy to juristic persons of a private-law character (not to communes or Cantons), against the powers of the State. It therefore provides no method whereby the individual may proceed against a trust or a trade union, nor does it by itself confer on the State a competence to prevent restrictive practices (see *Verwaltungsentscheide der Bundesbehörden*, 1927, No. 7. The competence is probably given under 31 *bis*, not as part of the Freedom of Trade, &c., but as an exception to it).

Now that the Confederation has resigned itself to subsidizing and protecting all those who can exert an effective political pressure, it is rather with wistfulness that the Swiss consumer recollects that the words 'Freedom of Trade and Industry is guaranteed' are still in the Federal Constitution. And, indeed, the first reaction to the statement as now qualified with 'except in so far as Federal legislation restricts it' is that it is a statement of the type 'Buns can be bought in the shops which sell them'.

This, however, would be a mistake. In the first place the proclamation of freedom is still there. And a Constitution does more than provide a set of rules enforceable in a Court, it sets forth a programme which the people in a moment of sovereignty has ordained for its successors. The programme is rather more than a rule of discarded morality, it influences the whole vocabulary of political thought—there is a difference between saying 'We must follow the policy which made Britain rich' and saying 'We must observe Article 31'. Secondly, the rule provides a presumption that in the sphere of commerce all is lawful which is not either criminal or against public order. No doubt this presumption would have been made even had the freedom not expressly been guaranteed, but having once been guaranteed, it would be hard to repeal the rule: the consequences would be unpredictable and perhaps far-reaching, as with an alteration to a rule of common law. Thirdly, as against the Cantons it remains an enforceable rule, for 'Federal law breaks Cantonal law'. It is true that Federal legislation can now extend the Cantonal competence to infringe the subsidiary rules which have been derived from the rule of Freedom of Commerce, but until this legislation is passed the Cantons remain bound: the Cantons cannot go faster than the Confederation in this field. Fourthly, one may observe that many Cantonal Constitutions also proclaim Freedom of Commerce, Trade, Industry, &c., and may be restricted from carrying out competences (not duties) given them by Federal legislation thereby—the matter is not quite certain. And lastly, Article 32 provides special restrictions (referendum, &c.) on certain rules infringing this freedom-right.

ARTICLE 31 *bis*. Within the limits of its constitutional powers, the Confederation shall take measures to increase the general welfare and to ensure the economic security of the citizens.

While safeguarding the general interests of the national economy, the Confederation may regulate the exercise of trades and industry and take measures in favour of particular economic classes or professions. In the exercise of this power the Confederation shall respect the principle of Freedom of Trade and Industry, except as provided in paragraph 3.

When the public interest justifies it the Confederation has the power to make provisions infringing, if necessary, the Freedom of Trade and Industry:
- (*a*) to preserve important economic classes, or professions, whose survival is threatened, and to encourage independent producers in such economic classes or professions;
- (*b*) to preserve a strong peasantry, to encourage agriculture, and to strengthen the position of rural property-owners;
- (*c*) to protect districts whose economic life is threatened;
- (*d*) to prevent harmful social or economic effects of cartels or similar organizations;
- (*e*) to take precautions against the event of war.

Professions and economic classes shall only be protected under the headings (*a*) and (*b*) if they have themselves taken such measures of mutual assistance as can be fairly expected of them.

Federal legislation under (*a*) and (*b*) shall safeguard the development of groups based upon mutual assistance.

The '*Economic Articles*' (Articles 31, 31 *bis*, *ter*, *quater*, and *quinquies*, 32, 34 *ter*, a verbal amendment of 34 *quater*, and the repeal of Article 6 of the Transitory Provisions) are a large extension of Federal legislative competence. They choose the type of liberty which is to be obtained by being able to control— or rather, to legislate upon—the country's economic circumstances, and discard the type of liberty involved in local freedom and constitutional rights.

The project for the new Articles was introduced by a message of the Federal Council in 1937, but the discussions were held up by the war. A further message (Bundesblatt, 1945, i. 905; it contains the names of the interests consulted) reintroduced the project. The Articles were accepted in the votation of 6 July 1947 by a majority not over great.

The constitutional amendments of 1947 were many years overdue. There is a tendency in Switzerland for the Constitution to follow in the wake of unconstitutional practice, declaring the stable door open long after the horse has escaped. The tendency is not without harmful effects, for the Constitution makes it easier for the Federal Council to effect an illegal act than for the Assembly, and easier for the central government (which is not subject to judicial control) than the Cantons. Unconstitutionality in fact favours the Executive against the Legislature, and the Confederation against the Cantons.

ARTICLE 31 *ter*. The Cantons may by legislation make the trade of keeping restaurants and cafés dependent upon proof of professional knowledge and personal suitability, and make the number of such establishments dependent upon the need for them, to the extent that the existence of the trade is threatened through excessive competition. Such provisions are to take adequately into account the importance of each class of establishment to the public welfare.

The Confederation may also, within the limits of its legislative competence, empower the Cantons to make regulations in those matters which do not need a uniform Federal control, and to regulate which the Cantons are not already competent.

See note to Article 31 *bis*.

ARTICLE 31 *quater*. The Confederation may legislate concerning banking institutions.

Such legislation shall take into account the special position and functions of Cantonal banks.

Each of the twenty-five Cantons has its own Cantonal bank. The right to have a State Bank is for various reasons one of the most valued perquisites of sovereignty. These banks generally enjoy privileges in the matter of Cantonal taxation as against private-enterprise banks, and this is not considered a breach of Article 4.

For the Swiss National Bank see Article 39.

ARTICLE 31 *quinquies*. The Confederation shall take measures in conjunction with the Cantons and private enterprise to prevent economic crises and, if necessary, to combat unemployment. It shall issue regulations upon the means of obtaining employment.

This Article increases the powers of the Confederation, but not at the expense of the Cantons. The original Article 31 restricted the powers of the Cantons without (except perhaps implicitly) increasing those of the central government. The present Article is an example of how a new economic theory may affect the balance of a Federal Constitution.

ARTICLE 32. The regulations foreseen in Articles 31 *bis*, 31 *ter*, para. 2, 31 *quater*, and 31 *quinquies* may only be couched in the form of a Law or of an *arrêté* subject to the popular vote. In circumstances of urgency during times of economic disturbance the provisions of Article 89, para. 3 apply.

The Cantons shall be consulted during the drafting of the laws carrying out these Articles. As a general rule they shall be entrusted with the execution of the Federal provisions.

The economic groups concerned shall be consulted during the drafting of the laws carrying out these Articles, and may be called upon to help apply the regulations.

This is one of the Economic Articles of 1947. The old Article 32 was a temporary regulation of the Cantonal wine duties which were abolished in 1890 and had had no meaning since that date. The Article in its present form alludes to the practice of the Assembly of withdrawing its *arrêtés* from the legislative challenge by declaring them 'urgent' or 'not universally binding'.

The mention of the practice of preliminary consultation is of particular interest. The rule laid down in paragraph 2 represents the normal practice—consultation of the Cantons, and Cantonal execution of Federal legislation.

'Article 89, para. 3' should now read 'Article 89 *bis*', which has replaced the old third paragraph of that Article.

ARTICLE 32 *bis*. The Confederation is authorized to legislate upon the manufacture, import, rectifying, sale, and taxation of distilled drinks.

This legislation shall be directed towards reducing the consumption, and the import and manufacture, of spirits. It shall encourage the production of dessert fruits and the use of home-grown materials as food or fodder rather than for spirit. The Confederation shall reduce the number of stills by agreed purchase.

Concessions to produce spirits industrially shall be granted to co-operative societies and other private enterprises. Concessions shall enable the waste products of fruit, wine, and sugar-beet, and the surplus fruit and potato harvest, to be used; provided that these materials cannot reasonably be employed elsewhere.

Non-industrial production of brandies from fruit and fruit-waste, from cider, wine, grape-skins, lees of wine, gentian-roots, and similar materials, is permitted in domestic stills already in existence or in movable stills; provided that the materials are exclusively home-grown or gathered wild inside the country. These brandies are untaxed, in so far as their production is necessary to the domestic or agricultural economy of the producer. Those domestic stills working at the end of a period of fifteen years after the adoption of this article shall, if they wish to continue, apply for a concession, which shall be granted free under conditions to be fixed by law.

Specialities produced from distilled stone-fruit, wine, grape-skins, lees of wine, gentian-roots and similar products, shall be taxed. Nevertheless, the producer shall receive a fair price for his home-grown raw materials.

Brandies produced within the country, other than the quantities retained by the producer and exempt from tax, and specialities, are to be surrendered to the Confederation, which shall take delivery at a fair price.

Brandies exported or in transit, and methylated spirit, are exempt.

Receipts from retail licences and from retail trade within the Canton belong to the Canton. Licences for intercantonal and international retail trade are issued by the Confederation; the money received from them shall be divided among the Cantons in proportion to their normal resident populations.

One half of the Confederation's net receipts from the taxation of spirits is divided among the Cantons in proportion to their normal resident populations, and each Canton is obliged to spend at least 10 per cent. of its share in combating the causes and results of alcoholism. The other half belongs to the Confederation and is to be allotted to old age and widows' insurance: until such insurance is introduced it is to be paid into a fund for that purpose.

The Schnapps Articles (32 *bis*, *ter*, and *quater*). With the proclamation of Freedom of Trade and Industry in 1874, under Article 31 in its original wording, the old Cantonal restrictions on inns and the alcohol trade were voided as unconstitutional—with the exception of certain Cantonal taxes leviable until 1890 under the (former) Articles 32 and Transitory Provisions 6. Consequently there was a great and uncontrolled increase of inns and consumption of alcohol. In 1885 the Assembly submitted to the people and Cantons a proposed amendment of Article 31 and a new 32 *bis* providing for a partial restoration of the old Cantonal competences and for a tax discriminating against spirits in favour of wine and beer. The amendment was accepted; the evil, however, continued. A further amendment was submitted in 1903, but was voted upon on the same day as an unpopular law and an unpopular initiative, and shared their fate. An initiative forbidding absinthe (32 *ter*) in 1908, had, however, the good fortune to be voted upon on the same day as an amendment so popular that only Inner Rhodes voted against it—and was successful. Article 32 *bis* was again amended in 1930, and Article 32 *quater* introduced. Minor amendments to the latter were made in 1947 (Economic Articles).

Article 31 *bis*, para. 3, gives the Confederation power, *inter alia*, to subsidize the wine-growing industry. Swiss wines are pleasant, but cannot compete on equal terms with the wines of France and Italy, and Swiss dessert grapes are smaller, dearer, and often sour; export is therefore impossible. The policies of discouraging the consumption of wine and encouraging the production of it are both pursued energetically, with curious results.

The wording of Article 32 *bis* gives the Confederation the option of making spirits a Federal monopoly. The Confederation has done so (Law of 21 June 1932), and grants concessions for manufacture to co-operatives and private enterprise.

ARTICLE 32 *ter*. Manufacture, import, transport, sale or holding for sale of the liqueur called absinthe is forbidden throughout the Confederation. This prohibition applies to all drinks under whatever name which resemble absinthe. From this prohibition carriage in transit and use in medicine are excepted.

This prohibition shall come into force two years after its

adoption. Provision shall be made by Federal legislation for all that is necessary as a consequence of this prohibition.

The Confederation is authorized to introduce by legislation the same prohibition with respect to other drinks, containing absinthe, dangerous to the public.

See note to Article 32 *bis*.

ARTICLE 32 *quater*. The Cantons may by legislation control in the public interest the trade of innkeeper and the retail sale of spirituous liquors. Sale in quantities less than 2 litres is reckoned as retail sale in the case of non-distilled spirituous liquors.

For trade in non-distilled spirituous liquors in quantities from 2 to 10 litres the Cantons may by legislation, within the limits of Article 31, para. 2, require a licence and a small payment, and impose liability to inspection by the authorities.

The Cantons may not make the sale of non-distilled spirituous liquors liable to special taxes other than registration fees.

Corporate persons may not be treated less favourably than individuals. Producers of wine, cider, and fruit-juice may sell their own home-grown products in quantities of 2 litres or more without licence or fee.

The Confederation may provide by legislation for the trade in non-distilled spirituous liquors in quantities of 2 or more litres. Such provisions may contain nothing contrary to the principle of Freedom of Trade and Industry.

Hawking from door to door and the travelling sale of spirituous liquors are forbidden.

See note to Article 32 *bis*.

ARTICLE 33. The power is reserved to the Cantons of making the exercise of a liberal profession dependent upon a certificate proving competency.

Provision shall be made by Federal legislation that certificates valid throughout the Confederation can be obtained.

This Article empowers the Cantons to infringe the Freedom of Trade and Industry in respect of the liberal (or in the German text 'scientific') professions. It also grants the Confederation a competence to legislate in this field.

The present position is that the Confederation has legislated for certain professions—doctors, dentists, and veterinary surgeons—and has established for these a Federal standard and a Federal-controlled examination. If the Cantons require a certificate of competence from doctors, &c., then they must recognize the Federal certificate, but they are free to require no certificate and to let everyone practise who cares to put up a brass plate, and some rural Cantons do so: the Confederation thus obtains the advantages of control and of liberty. In the case of other professions, notably the Bar, the Confederation has not made use of its legislative competence, and therefore Article 5 of the Transitory Provisions prevails. That is to say, the Cantons which require certificates of capacity grant them and recognize each other's certificates, so a lawyer qualified in one Canton can in principle practise in another Canton once he has mastered the Canton's court-procedure. The certificates of those Cantons which grant them too freely are correspondingly despised.

Cantons are not permitted to require proofs of erudition from those exercising professions not liberal or learned in the sense of this Article. The definition leads to a certain amount of litigation. It is possible to get round this restriction, however. If the Court shows an old-fashioned reluctance to recognize the calling of cemetery-path weeder as a learned one, then the Canton makes it a public office, appointing whom it pleases.

For innkeepers see Article 32 *quater*. For trade-unionism, considered as a different problem, see 34 *ter*. Clergy are a special case: if the Church is established, then they are a category of officials from whom qualifications may be required; if unestablished, then they enjoy the protection of Freedom of Religion, Article 49, paras. 2 and 4.

ARTICLE 34. The Confederation is authorized to make uniform provisions concerning the employment of children in factories and the hours of work of adults therein. Furthermore, it may issue regulations to protect workers in unhealthy and dangerous industries.

The transactions of emigration agencies and of private enterprise undertakings in the sphere of insurance are subject to Federal supervision and legislation.

The Factory Law at present in force is that of 1914, modified by the Law of 1922 (Young People) and by numerous *ordonnances* made under these laws. The whole legislation is to be found in volume viii of the *Recueil systématique des lois et ordonnances*, pp. 3–248. The Federal Law of 1877 is repealed under the Law of 1914 mentioned above.

The first paragraph of this Article is now rendered superfluous by the new Article 34 *ter*, and is retained only to show that protection of workers was not introduced in 1947 but is moderately ancient. It will be noticed, however, that Article 34 *ter* is qualified by certain safeguards, which are lacking in this Article: it is not yet apparent whether the difference is ever likely to be important.

Private insurance and emigration are still 'supervised' by Federal officials. Cantonal and communal insurance agencies remain under Cantonal legislation.

ARTICLE 34 *bis*. The Confederation shall introduce by legislation insurance against accident and illness: it shall have regard to the benefit funds already existing.

It may make such insurance compulsory, either for everyone or for particular classes of persons.

Accepted in the votation of 26 Oct. 1890. The Law on Insurance against Sickness and Accidents of 13 June 1911 gave effect to the first paragraph. Most paragraphs of this Law only came into force in 1918, but some were declared in force earlier—and some have not yet come into effect. The Law declares accident-insurance obligatory for certain classes of workers, and delegates to the Cantons the competence to make sickness-insurance compulsory.

Article 122 of the Law provided for the setting up of a Federal Insurance Court (Eidg. Versicherungsgericht; *Tribunal fédéral des Assurances*) in Lucerne. The Court hears appeals from decisions of Cantonal Insurance Tribunals set up under the Law, and also deals with 'military insurance' (Article 18, para. 2), with Federal contributory pension funds, and, since 1918, with old age and widows' insurance (Article 34 *quater*).

The Law of 1911 is of constitutional interest in that it delegated to the Assembly the power to set up an Insurance Court: in other words, the Assembly delegated to itself the power to pass subordinate legislation—an early and successful attempt to evade the legislative challenge. That this procedure is not more extensively used is not due to scrupulousness on the part of the Assembly, but to the modern practice of withdrawing *arrêtés* from the referendum illegally, which is simpler.

ARTICLE 34 *ter*. The Confederation may legislate upon the following subjects:
- (*a*) The protection of employees.
- (*b*) The relationships between employers and employees, especially as concerns the joint regulation of professional and trade matters.
- (*c*) The legally binding effect of collective contracts on terms of work, and other agreements between associations of employers and employees calculated to improve industrial relations.
- (*d*) Compensation for loss of earning power due to military service, at rates related to the earning power lost.
- (*e*) Labour exchanges.

(*f*) Unemployment insurance and assistance.
(*g*) Technical education in industry, crafts, trades, agriculture, and domestic service.

Legally binding effect under section (*c*) may only be declared in the case of contracts affecting the industrial relations of employers and employees, and where the terms thereof take sufficient account of local differences and the legitimate interests of minorities, and respect the principles of Equality before the Law and Freedom of Association.

Unemployment insurance may be undertaken by public or private insurances and be contributable to by one or by both parties. The right of introducing public unemployment insurance or of making insurance compulsory for all is reserved to the Cantons.

The provisions of Article 32 apply where appropriate.

'Collective contracts declared legally binding' (allgemeinverbindlicherklärte Gesamtarbeitsverträge) are a new type of Federal legislative instrument, declaring generally applicable the rates of wages, &c., agreed by employers' and employees' organizations and sanctioned by the Federal Executive. It is too soon to judge the success of this experiment on the Federal level. The contracts are approved by the Federal Council at its discretion, but can only be initiated by the interests concerned. The Arrêtés of the Federal Council approving them are published in the *Feuille fédérale*: they are not subject to referendum.

ARTICLE 34 *quater*. The Confederation shall by legislation introduce insurance against old age and widowhood: it may thereafter introduce insurance against sickness.

It can declare these insurances compulsory for all, or for particular categories of, citizens.

The insurances shall be effected in collaboration with the Cantons; both public and private insurance funds may be called upon to lend assistance.

The two first-mentioned types of insurance shall be introduced simultaneously.

The financial contributions of the Confederation and the Cantons shall not together exceed one-half of the total sum required for the insurance.

From 1 Jan. 1926 the Confederation shall devote the whole yield of the tobacco duties to insurance against old age and widowhood.

The Confederation's share of the net yield of a tax on brandies shall be devoted to insurance against old age and widowhood.

This Article, and 41 *ter*, were accepted by a substantial majority of people and Cantons on 6 Dec. 1925. The project had been introduced by a message of the Federal Council in 1919. The Federal Law introducing the old age and widows' insurance which this Article foresees, however, was challenged to a referendum and rejected by a correspondingly substantial majority of voters—the Catholic, the French- and Italian-speaking, and the rural votes being cast against it—on 17 June 1931. After the War another project was introduced, challenged to a referendum, and accepted, the voting being held on the same day that the Economic Articles (31, &c.) were accepted (6 July 1947). The time-lag since 1919 is noticeable. The financial provisions came into effect twenty years before the insurance, and the fund was raided by the Confederation—cf. Articles 41 *ter* and 32 *bis*, para. 9, and see note to Article 42. For the Federal Insurance Court see Article 34 *bis*.

ARTICLE 34 *quinquies*. The Confederation shall, while carrying out its existing competences and within the limits of the Constitution, take account of the needs of the family.

The Confederation is empowered to legislate on the matter of family insurance funds. It can declare membership compulsory for all, or for certain classes of the population. It shall take account of the funds already existing, shall support projects of the Cantons and of trade groups to establish new funds, and is empowered to set up a central insurance-fund. The Confederation may make its own contributions conditional on a fair Cantonal contribution.

The Confederation is authorized in the matter of housing and workers' settlements to support measures designed to assist the family. A Federal Law shall determine the conditions under which the Confederation will give financial aid; the Law shall not disregard the Cantonal housing regulations.

The Confederation shall by legislation introduce maternity insurance. It can declare membership compulsory for all, or for particular classes of the population, and may require those to contribute who will not be able to benefit from the insurance. The Confederation may make its own contributions conditional upon a fair Cantonal contribution.

The Laws passed under the present Article shall be put into effect in collaboration with the Cantons; public- or private-law associations may be called upon to assist.

The Catholic-Conservative party, while not supporting progressiveness blindly, is in favour of 'something vague about the family'. The family is the emotional apanage of the Catholics, as the working class is of the Socialists. This Article is the counter-project of the Assembly to an initiative launched by a committee calling itself 'For the Family', sponsored by the Catholic-Conservatives. The initiative was withdrawn in favour of the counter-project, which was accepted by all Cantons except the Protestant half-Canton of Appenzell Outer Rhodes on 25 Nov. 1945. The Confederation has not yet passed any legislation under this Article: the matter therefore remains in the competence of the Cantons.

ARTICLE 35. The opening and keeping of gaming-houses is forbidden.

Cantonal governments may, subject to the requirements of the public interest, authorize until the spring of 1925 the types of game usual in kursaals, in so far as the appropriate authority considers it necessary to the maintenance or extension of the tourist industry and the organization of play is vouched for by a body engaged in running a kursaal for this purpose. Alternatively, the Cantons may forbid such play.

An *ordonnance* of the Federal Council shall determine what restrictions the public interest requires. The stake shall not exceed two francs.

Every Cantonal authorization is subject to the Federal Council's approval.

One-quarter of the gross receipts from running the betting shall be paid to the Confederation, which shall, without deducting expenses, apply it to the relief of damage caused by natural phenomena and to works of public utility.

The Confederation may also take appropriate measures in respect of lotteries.

This Article has been twice amended (21 Mar. 1920 and 2 Dec. 1928). It was originally intended to impose a distinctively Protestant morality on the Canton of Valais, and to some extent on Uri, Schwyz, and Zug. At the present day publicly run lotteries are a feature of Switzerland which immediately strikes a foreigner: there seems to be one well-publicized lottery or another in progress the whole time.

This Article and Article 41 contain the only mentions in the Constitution of the Federal *Council*'s legislative powers. The acts of the Federal Council are known by various names—Arrêté of the Federal Council (as opposed to 'Federal Arrêté', of the Federal Assembly), *ordonnance*, and *règlement*—but in legal documents they are usually all included under the term *ordonnance*. In bulk and number the acts of the Federal Council much exceed those of the Assembly. A distinction must be made between those subordinate legislative powers exercised by delegation of the Assembly and those powers exercised directly under the Constitution, and out of reach of the Assembly.

It is a characteristic of the Swiss Constitution that some of the most interesting and distinctive aspects of Swiss constitutional practice are only mentioned there, as it were, by the tail. Other examples are: neutrality, 'Federal law breaks Cantonal law', 'denial of justice' as remedied under Article 4, emergency Full Powers, the rule against Double Taxation, the exclusion of women from political rights, and the Cantonal execution of Federal laws. These institutions receive at most an oblique notice in the constitutional document, which goes into details concerning institutions like the Federal Assizes (Article 112) that have little more than a theoretical existence.

ARTICLE 36. Posts and Telegraphs throughout the Confederation are a Federal matter.

The yield of the Post and Telegraph administration is paid into the Federal exchequer.

The rates shall be fixed throughout the territory of the Confederation according to the same principles and as reasonably as possible.

The inviolability of the secrecy of letters and telegrams is guaranteed.

The words 'a Federal matter' in themselves only mean that the matter is Federal to the exclusion of the Cantons, but they have here been interpreted as entitling the Confederation to deprive the individual of the Freedom of Trade and Industry within this sphere: the Posts have been a Federal *monopoly* ever since the Constitution of 1848. The extent of the monopoly is greater than appears at first sight. The word 'Posts' includes all the services run by the Post Office, including an excellent system of 'postal cheques' and a Post Office Savings Bank (from which payments may be made by cheque), and the word 'Telegraphs' includes telephone and wireless, which is also a Federal monopoly under a corporation supervised by the postal administration.[1] In addition to all this the transport of passengers according to a timetable has always been understood as falling within the postal monopoly, and in fact most bus services other than buses in towns are run directly by the Postal Department all over the country (though some routes are run by private persons under Federal 'concessions'): the yellow 'Post-autos' will be familiar to the visitor to Switzerland. Any investigation of the historical origins of the Federal railway monopoly, or of the control of inland

---

[1] The relationships between the Confederation and the *Societé suisse de radiodiffusion* are now (1953) undergoing revision. A description of the present relationships and their history, and the draft project of the new Law, can be found in the report of the Federal Council, *Feuille fédérale*, 1953, vol. i, p. 17.

navigation or of the supervision of roads and bridges, would have to take the implications of the Federal postal monopoly into account.

Paragraph 2 of the Article is in contrast to the system before 1874, when a part of the receipts from the Posts went to compensate the Cantons for the loss of their former postal monopolies, and to remove any doubts whether the Confederation receives all the income from the Posts, or only a part (cf. Article 30; see Article 1 of the Transitory Provisions). At the present day the Confederation incurs a loss on the purely postal services.

Paragraph 4. *Guarantee of the Inviolability of Postal Secrets.* This appears at first sight to be an individual freedom-right, but it is in fact doubtful whether it deserves this status. It is not a penal provision, for although it is a crime for a postal official to divulge the contents of a letter or telegram passing through his hands to a person not entitled to the information, the crime is merely a special type of breach of confidence or official duty, it is not a crime 'under this Article'. The guarantee seems rather to be of the same nature as a separation of powers; it is a command to the Confederation that the Postal Department is to be separated for this purpose from the other departments. The extent of this separation is not large—public policy can override it (e.g. to prevent a crime or to detect one). It is not a constitutional right in the sense of Article 113, for there is no Appeal in Public Law for the individual against violation of it (cf. Article 116, Freedom of Languages, which is in the same case). At times it seems rather to be a right of the Posts and Railways Department enabling it to resist having to undertake such troublesome tasks as opening letters containing lottery advertisements, &c.

ARTICLE 37. The Confederation exercises high supervision over the roads and bridges in the maintenance of which it is interested.

The money due to the Cantons named in Article 30 on account of their international alpine roads shall be kept back by the Confederation if the roads are not properly maintained.

Article 23 allows the Confederation to subsidize public works, and a measure of control follows these subsidies, which include subsidies to Cantons for road building and maintenance. The measure of control that follows subsidy at present exhausts the 'high supervision' of the Confederation over the Cantonal roads (which in principle are within the Cantonal *Hoheit*) and is found sufficient by the Confederation and not excessive by the Cantons. There is thus no need to invoke this Article.

A proportion of the customs duty on petrol by law is given to the Cantons for road building and maintenance.

ARTICLE 37 *bis*. The Confederation is entitled to make provisions concerning cars and cycles.

The Cantons preserve the right to limit or forbid car and cycle traffic. Notwithstanding this, the Confederation may declare particular roads essential for long-distance traffic either unrestrictedly or conditionally open. The use of roads on the Confederation's service is unaffected.

This Article and 37 *ter* were accepted in the votation of 22 May 1921. If the Confederation possessed a competence to legislate before that, it was under its postal monopoly. There is a rich crop of Federal legislation on this subject, to be found in volume vii of the *Recueil systématique*. The principal Law is now that of 15 Mar. 1932, which repeals the concordats of 1904, 1914, and 1921.

ARTICLE 37 *ter*. Legislation upon aerial navigation is a Federal matter.

Accepted 22 May 1921, with Article 37 *bis*.
The principal Law on the subject is now that of 1948. For the meaning of the words 'is a Federal matter' see note to Article 26 (Railways).

ARTICLE 38. The Confederation exercises all rights included in the State monopoly of coinage.

It alone strikes coin.

It determines the coinage system and may as need arises fix tariffs of the exchange value of foreign coins.

Before 1848 the coinage was Cantonal. In practice there had always been a shortage of locally minted coins, and foreign coins were used and were often even legal tender. It was therefore necessary to fix a tariff for those foreign coins (sovereigns, napoleons, &c.) which were in circulation. Now, of course, all money is Swiss and Federal.

Banknotes are dealt with separately in the following Article.

ARTICLE 39. The right to issue banknotes and other fiduciary money belongs exclusively to the Confederation.

The Confederation can exercise its monopoly of banknotes through a State Bank under a separate administration, or it can grant the power to a central joint stock bank (with a reservation as to the right to repurchase) which shall be administered with the help and under the control of the Confederation.

The principal tasks of the bank entrusted with the monopoly of banknotes shall be to regulate the money market in Switzerland, to facilitate the making of payments, and to follow, within the framework of Federal legislation, a credit policy and a money policy in the general interest of the country.

At least two-thirds of the net profit of the bank, after deduction of a reasonable interest or dividend for the founding or share capital and of payments to a reserve-fund, shall be returned to the Cantons.

The bank and its branches shall not be liable to taxation in the Cantons.

The Confederation cannot suspend the obligation to repay banknotes and other fiduciary money, nor can it declare the acceptance of such money obligatory, except in time of war or monetary crisis.

Banknotes issued must be covered by gold or short-term securities.

Federal legislation shall make provision for the execution of this Article.

The Constitution of 1874 gave the Federation general power to legislate in the matter of banknotes provided it neither created a monopoly nor made notes legal tender. The Law to give effect to this power was, however, rejected on 18 Sept. 1875. A further Law in 1881 got through unchallenged. In 1879–80 an attempt to present a popular constitutional initiative for a Federal monopoly of notes caused the Assembly to submit to the people a project for a total revision of the Constitution (see note to Article 118, below) which was the prelude to the introduction of the popular initiative in its present form. The proposed total revision (aimed only at this Article as it then was) was rejected at the votation.

In 1891 the Assembly submitted with success a cunningly worded amendment to the people and Cantons, drafted so as to leave the question open where the seat of the bank was to be and whether it was to be a private or a State bank, but establishing clearly a Federal monopoly: the present paragraph 1 dates from that year. A further amendment accepted on 15 Apr. 1951 gave the Article its present wording.

Swiss banknotes are issued by the 'Swiss National Bank', and bear that designation (in three languages, Article 116).

ARTICLE 40. The determination of the system of weights and measures is a Federal matter.

The Cantons shall execute the laws on this subject, under the supervision of the Confederation.

In 1835 certain Cantons agreed, by concordat, to introduce some decimal features into their weights and measure systems. The Federal Constitution of 1848 empowered the Confederation to universalize the concordat, which in 1861 it did. In 1866 the Confederation sought competences to introduce a full-blooded decimal metric system, but the Cantons' votes refused permission in the disastrous referendum of that year. The Confederation thereupon introduced the metric system nevertheless in 1868. The present provision legalizes this, and the Law of 1875 gave effect to this Article. The scope of the Article is held to include not only length, weight, &c., but also measurements of heat and electricity, and even the universalization of Central European time.

ARTICLE 41. Manufacture and sale of gunpowder belong exclusively to the Confederation.

Manufacture, purchase, sale and distribution of arms, munitions, explosives, and other materials of war and their components are subject to the authorization of the Confederation. This authorization shall only be granted to individuals and undertakings able to provide the guarantees the national interest demands. The Federal state-monopolies are reserved.

Import and export of materials of war within the meaning of this Article shall take place only with the authorization of the Confederation. The Confederation may also make transit of such materials subject to authorization.

Subject to Federal legislation, the Federal Council shall by *ordonnance* lay down the regulations which are needed in order to give effect to paragraphs 2 and 3. In particular, it shall provide in detail for the grant, duration and withdrawal of authorizations and the control of the licensees. It shall further determine what arms, munitions, and component parts are included in the present Article.

This Article in its present form dates from the votation of 20 Feb. 1938. The Federal monopoly of gunpowder dates from 1848: it is an exception to the Freedom of Trade and Industry. The profit to the Confederation from this monopoly is unimportant, the motive being not gain but public security and the control of an industry potentially anti-social.

ARTICLE 41 *bis*. The Confederation is authorized to levy stamp duties on negotiable instruments, receipts for insurance premiums, bills of exchange and similar documents, on bills of lading and other commercial documents: documents concerning the transfer of real property and mortgages are not covered by this authorization. Documents upon which the Confederation has levied a stamp duty, or which it has exempted from such duty, cannot be subjected to stamp or registration duty by the Cantons.

One-fifth of the net revenue from the stamp duties is allotted to the Cantons.

The execution of this Article shall be provided for by Federal legislation.

Accepted in the votation of 13 May 1917. See note to Article 42. Section (*g*) of that Article is a consequential amendment accepted in the same votation.

ARTICLE 41 *ter*. The Confederation is authorized to tax raw and prepared tobacco.

Accepted in the votation of 6 Dec. 1925, as a part of the scheme for old age and widowhood insurances (Article 34 *quater*). See note to Article 42, Federal Finances. The taxation of tobacco is an issue on which public opinion is rather sensitive.

ARTICLE 42. Federal expenditure is covered by:
  (*a*) The income from Federal property.
  (*b*) The income from Federal customs duties levied at the Swiss frontier.
  (*c*) The income from Posts and Telegraphs.
  (*d*) The income from the monopoly of gunpowder.
  (*e*) The income from half the gross yield of the service-exemption tax levied by the Cantons.
  (*f*) The contributions of the Cantons, on a scale to be laid down by Federal legislation, which shall take into account their taxable capacity.
  (*g*) The income from stamp duties.

This Article mentions some of the main sources of income of the Confederation, but it does not include all the constitutional sources (e.g. tobacco, alcohol, banks, gambling), and the list as a list has no juristic meaning. Nor does the Federation rely upon this Article for its constitutional right to moneys, but upon the separate sources granted to it in other Articles. The services the Confederation runs, for example the railways, may also provide an income.

Section (*e*) contains a rule of law, that the Confederation only gets one-half of the service-exemption tax (Article 18). And section (*f*) is of considerable constitutional interest as implying clearly that the Confederation should be dependent on the Cantons for its income, that is to say, that the Cantons possess the 'fiscal supremacy' (Steuerhoheit). The scale of contributions still exists, on paper, but since 1849 no such Cantonal contributions have ever been made. Section (*g*) was introduced in 1917.

Federal Finances. The Constitution of 1874 placed the Confederation in a favourable financial position by allotting to it the whole yield of the customs duties. The Cantons also had no grievance, for they retained the 'Steuerhoheit' and they alone could levy direct taxation, e.g. an income tax. About three-quarters of the Federal income was derived from customs duties, and around half of the expenditure was on the Federal army. The system continued without raising many difficulties until 1914, when war on Switzerland's borders exposed the weakness of the financial arrangements: as military expenditure rose, income from customs duties sank.

For this situation, however, the Constitution provides; the Cantons are to make contributions—the 'Cantonal contingents'—according to a scale laid down by Federal legislation. The refusal to take this course, whether from unpreparedness, or short-sighted localism, or from a feeling that the scheme was impracticable, is the turning-point in modern Swiss financial history.

The subsequent history of Federal finance is as follows:

1. In 1915 the Confederation for the first time levied a direct tax. It did this in a perfectly constitutional manner, submitting to a compulsory referendum a temporary constitutional amendment providing for a once-for-all 'war-tax' (Kriegssteuer), which was accepted by the people and by all Cantons on 6 June 1915 (*Amtliche Sammlung*, 1915, p. 336).

2. The next year the financial need was as great as ever, and this time a direct tax on war profits (Kriegsgewinnsteuer) was imposed by an Arrêté of the Federal Council (not challengeable to referendum), relying on the grant of Full Powers made in 1914. The *arrêté* was amended from time to time, and repealed in 1933 (ACF of 13 Feb.).

3. In 1917 a new constitutional Article, 41 *bis*, gave the Confederation a new source of income permanently. But in June of the next year a proposed constitutional amendment to grant the Confederation a permanent tax on property was rejected by the people and Cantons.

4. Faced with a burden of debt, the Federal authorities asked for the war-tax (no. 1, above) to be repeated until the costs of mobilization were paid off. At a votation on 4 May 1919 the people and Cantons granted this tax, which came to an end in 1932 when the costs of mobilization had been met.

5. In 1925 the Confederation got two new taxes (see Articles 34 *quater* and 41 *ter*). Both were supposed to be applied to old age insurance, but the proposal for this insurance not being accepted by the people, the fund formed by the yield of these taxes lay ready to be pirated by the Federal authorities. By 1925 the Confederation had turned the corner financially, and by 1928 was even showing a surplus on the annual balance of accounts. All seemed set for a return to the historic principle of the Constitution 'No direct taxes for the central government', when the storm of economic depression broke.

6. In 1933 the Federal Assembly passed an *arrêté* levying a Federal direct tax, the 'crisis offering' (Krisenabgabe), and granting the Federal Council certain taxing powers (A.F. of 13 Oct. 1933, *A.S.* 49, p. 839, and the ACF in *A.S.* 50, p. 49). The *arrêté* of the Assembly was declared 'urgent', that is to say, it was withdrawn from challenge to the referendum (under the old Article 89). The double breach of the Constitution in peace-time—

amendment of a basic constitutional rule by the Assembly alone, and the declaration of 'urgency'—was unprecedented. The *arrêté* was renewed as it lapsed, and the renewals were also declared 'urgent'.

7. A movement was set on foot for 'return to the Constitution', that is, for adapting the Constitution to the *fait accompli*. On 27 Nov. 1938 the people and Cantons accepted in a votation the Temporary Provision granting the Confederation, among other sources of income, the 'Krisenabgabe', that is to say, direct taxation. This temporary Article is still, in a sense, in force: it is known as the Federal Arrêté of 22 Dec. 1938. Originally for three years, it was prolonged until Dec. 1945 by the Federal Council Arrêté of 30 Apr. 1940 (under the grant of Full Powers made on 30 Aug. 1939) and prolonged again by the Federal Assembly, by *arrêté* of 21 Dec. 1945, until 31 Dec. 1949. Both these prolongations were, in different ways, unconstitutional.

8. A limited purchase-tax (Warenumsatzsteuer, *impôt sur le chiffre d'affaires*) was granted to the Confederation by the people and Cantons on 4 June 1939.

9. By virtue of its war-time Full Powers the Federal Council granted itself direct taxes (Kriegsgewinnsteuer, Jan. 1940; Wehropfer, and Warenumsatzsteuer, Apr. 1940; other taxes, Oct. and Nov. 1942 and Sept. 1943).

10. (i.e. nos. 7, 8, and 9 prolonged). On 3 Dec. 1950 the people and Cantons accepted a Temporary Provision prolonging the *arrêté* of 22 Dec. 1938 and the Federal extra-constitutional direct taxation still in force—notably the purchase- and income-taxes—until 31 Dec. 1954. What happens then is a matter of speculation. Federal direct taxation is thereby reluctantly and 'temporarily' legalized.

Causes of Instability. Unconstitutionality and living from hand to mouth in the matter of Federal finances having now become an institution of Swiss public life, in the same way as cabinet instability is a feature of French public life, speculation is justified on what are its underlying causes. Among these may be found the following:

1. The policy of the Federal administration. Either the ship of state is adrift, or it is being steered by the Federal Council and the senior civil servants. One may suspect that, behind the elaborate parade of helplessness, the administration is steering the state firmly into a position where Federal direct taxation is inevitable.
2. The unpreparedness and indecisiveness of the Federal Assembly, capable neither of obtaining power nor of exercising it, nor of responsibility.
3. The resentment of the people, faced with a choice between two policies it dislikes, for it must either force the Federal Council to resort to illegal means of raising taxes or it must sanction in a referendum a tax it dislikes on constitutional grounds, and thus rivet chains round its own neck—but is unable to resist a subsidy or the offer of further artificial 'protection'.
4. A central power whose ambitions outrun its legal powers, and whose legal powers outrun its income, in an age when bureaucratic centralization has all the charms of progressiveness.

It may be added, though it is paining to the legal purist, that a temporary régime, alternating with periods when the Executive acts illegally (and thereby takes the full responsibility), is by no means a bad solution of the problem of how to get certain things done by the central government while keeping a firm check on its powers.

Federal Income in 1950–1.

	(in millions of francs)	
	1950	1951
(a) Constitutional sources		
Customs	477·85	492·72
*Stamp Duties	100·20	101·59
Tobacco	69·07	72·6
*Service Exemption	16·04	15·62
Other Sources	13·93	19·59
(b) Extra-constitutional sources		
*Defence Tax	427·85	219·45
*Defence 'Offering'	5·93	3·34
*War Profits Tax	22·98	11·57
Tax at source, credited	77·64	74·46
Purchase Tax	414·50	426·57
Luxury Tax	17·71	20·38
Compensatory Tax	12·94	14·04
Beer Tax	12·02	13·04
TOTAL	1668·49	1484·64

(Figures from *Feuille fédérale*. Headings and arrangement by the author.)

* Gross amount, before deduction of the Cantonal quota.

ARTICLE 43. Every citizen of a Canton is a Swiss citizen.

By virtue of this citizenship he may take part in all Federal elections and votations at his place of residence so soon as he has established in due form his claim to vote.

No one may exercise political rights in more than one Canton.

A Swiss citizen who has obtained settlement enjoys at his place of residence all the rights of a citizen of that Canton and, with these rights, all the rights of a citizen of that commune. Participation in the property of the citizenship-commune or of a Corporation, and the right to vote in matters exclusively concerning the citizenship-commune, are not included in the above, unless Cantonal legislation decides otherwise.

In Cantonal and communal matters he enjoys voting rights after three months' settlement.

Cantonal laws on settlement and the electoral rights in

communal affairs of those who have obtained settlement are to be submitted to the sanction of the Federal Council.

Citizenship. The word 'citizenship' is used in Switzerland in three slightly different, but connected, senses:

1. 'Swiss citizenship' denotes the status of a Swiss subject, which secures him the protection of his diplomatic representatives abroad, and of his constitutional rights at home.

2. 'Cantonal citizenship' is a purely internal matter. For the foreigner who wants to become a Swiss subject it represents an extra stage in the protracted process. For the Swiss citizen who does not live in his home Canton it represents an inherited sentimental link with a name, and an area to which he may some day be confined, but out of which he can never be driven. To the citizen who does live in his home Canton it may mean certain minor differences of a procedural character in certain cases. This hereditary Cantonal citizenship is of undeniable spiritual and emotional value, but its abolition would leave the constitutional structure of the country unaffected and would simplify certain matters—it survives by force of habit and on its historical merits. The *vocabulary* of Cantonal citizenship is still carefully retained.

3. Communal 'citizenship' (*bourgeoisie*) is a most important and original institution, and one that has profoundly affected the Swiss national character. For the foreigner seeking Swiss nationality it means that he must first 'buy himself in' to a commune, and membership of that commune will thereafter be a hereditary and nearly indelible status for him and his descendants. For the citizen who lives outside his home commune, communal citizenship designates an area that will be the ultimate refuge of his family in poverty, disgrace, or difficulty, and constitutes a strong sentimental link. It may also designate a poor-law authority (see Article 45), and in all cases it will mean a police control, through the 'Heimatschein' or document of origin, which serves as a sort of internal passport for settlement outside his home commune.

And for the citizen who lives in his home commune, communal citizenship often means more. In many Cantons there are two classes of citizen: those without a claim on the private-law property of the citizen commune, and those with such a claim. The latter are the innermost council and core of the town or village, enjoying certain perquisites (usually including free wood from the commune's forests) and subject to certain taxes. The *patriziato* (as it is called in Ticino) would not be human if it did not look down upon those without the full citizenship. The citizens without claim to a share of the private-law property of the commune remain as it were strangers in their own home commune. Article 44, para. 5, refers to this distinction, which some Cantons have abolished. Some communes only grant citizenship to those who buy themselves also into the inner group. The distinction therefore does not everywhere arise. Connected with this idea of an inner citizenship are the ancient Corporations and guilds (Zuenfte) which have here and there survived. The membership of some of the rural Corporations is very closely confined; in some cases it is restricted to families with full rights of citizenship before 1798, or to families named in the Corporation's constitution. It is not easy to determine when in fact a new member was last admitted into some Corporations of this sort, for some claim (for example) to have admitted no one since the seventeenth century. These remarkable exclusive privileges of place, birth, family, and person are locally of considerable social and economic importance, and bring hereditary distinctions of status into the daily lives of quite humble people. The urban guilds are differently constituted in different towns, and are not always strictly hereditary in their membership. In Berne, however, they form miniature citizenship-communes within the citizenship of Berne itself. They mostly have a conservative, even faintly aristocratic, flavour.

About one-third of resident Swiss live in their home communes, one-third in their home Canton outside their home commune, and one-third outside their Canton of origin (see *Annuaire statistique de la Suisse*).

PARAGRAPH 1. The people affected by survival of Cantonal citizenship are the high civil Federal officers elected by the Assembly (Article 96, Federal Councillors; and Article 9 of the Law on Political and other Guarantees), criminals (Articles 45 and 66), those living abroad (e.g. for military taxation), paupers, and those seeking Swiss nationality.

PARAGRAPH 2. The meaning of the word 'residence' is unclear. It does not always coincide with the tax-domicile or with the civil-law domicile. The Swiss citizen merely staying temporarily in a place cannot vote there, but if he intends to live in a place he can vote in Federal matters as soon as he can get his name inscribed on the register. In Cantonal and communal matters, on the other hand, under Federal law he only need receive a vote after three months' settlement. Otherwise all three franchises are normally exercised at the same place.

PARAGRAPH 3. There is no plural vote. For this reason domicile for political rights does not always coincide with settlement, for a citizen may have settlement in several Cantons.

PARAGRAPH 4. This refers to the distinction—which is not everywhere made—between the 'inhabitant commune' (sometimes called 'political commune') of all those exercising political rights in the commune, and the 'citizen commune' of those who hold that commune's citizenship. Both sorts of commune normally own property. The inhabitant commune is the important one in political affairs. The paragraph also refers to the distinction between those enjoying the common property of the citizen commune (or of a Corporation) and those excluded from it: this distinction is also not everywhere made.

PARAGRAPH 5. The Cantons are free to give Cantonal and communal voting rights before the three months are up.

ARTICLE 44. No Swiss citizen may be expelled either from Switzerland or from his home Canton.

The conditions to be fulfilled for acquisition or loss of Swiss citizenship shall be laid down by Federal legislation.

Federal legislation may enact that the child of foreign parents is Swiss from birth if the mother was Swiss by origin and its parents are resident in Switzerland when the child is born. The child acquires citizenship in the mother's home commune. Federal legislation shall determine the principles governing reception back into citizenship.

Persons acquiring citizenship under these provisions enjoy the same rights as other citizens of a commune, with the restriction that they have no claim to a share in property belonging solely to a citizen-commune or Corporation, unless Cantonal legislation determine otherwise. The Confederation takes over from the Cantons and communes at least half the expenses of assistance incurred by those acquiring citizenship from birth, until the eighteenth birthday. It takes over the same share in the case of those received back into citizenship, during the ten years following reception back.

Federal legislation shall determine when the Confederation is to share the expenditure of the Cantons and communes in assistance of naturalized *Heimatlosen*.

Except for the first paragraph and the substance of the second, this Article was introduced in the votation of 20 May 1928. An initiative designed to make naturalization of foreigners harder, and of Swiss-born 'foreigners' easier, was defeated in June 1922. This amendment is a substitute for the defeated initiative. The problem with which the legislator was faced was the presence on Swiss soil of Swiss-born people who were in some ways in the position of the 'Hintersassen' of the Old Confederation—citizens without full rights; the comparison with the old régime is not altogether to the advantage of the present practice. The first solution proposed was more liberal naturalization, but when it came to the point this was felt to be too generous. The problem arises out of the lack of a *jus soli*, and a reluctance to let other people share the good thing of citizenship.

As things turned out, the Article was not necessary. The 'Fremdenpolizei' (foreigners' police) were given a freer hand, and the problem of excessive numbers of foreigners without means voluntarily on Swiss soil gradually became a thing of the past.

The imprescriptibility of Swiss nationality is found to be a most useful device for extending the work of diplomacy through the intermediacy of Swiss citizens who have acquired citizenship in other countries while retaining their Swiss nationality. It is probably only a small country which could give so little and obtain so much as Switzerland does by the law of citizenship.

PARAGRAPH 1. Banishment as a penalty is therefore illegal. By virtue of this provision the home Canton becomes an *ultimum refugium*—very necessary in view of the possibility of withdrawing or refusing settlement in certain cases (Article 45). Within the Canton, settlement can be withdrawn or refused in certain cases by the commune; therefore, in order to leave some substance in the Cantonal refuge, the commune of origin is the ultimate refuge inside the Canton. This is a right which has always been respected, even by emergency legislation.

PARAGRAPHS 2, 3, AND 4. The Law on Naturalization of 1903 continues in force, amended, and now in part superseded by emergency legislation. It was altered in 1920 in the sense of making the procedure more wearisome for the foreigner seeking naturalization, and thereby went some way towards meeting the demands of the initiative of that year. The Law delegates the competence to the Cantons to make the reforms detailed in paragraph 3, but none of the Cantons has actually passed legislation in that sense, so its provisions have remained a dead letter.

Since 1848 Swiss nationality has been imprescriptible.[1] An exception was made during the last war by emergency legislation for those holding two nationalities 'and endangering Swiss neutrality &c.', i.e. embarrassing Switzerland's foreign policy.

PARAGRAPH 5. This paragraph is somewhat reactionary, as it only admits those incorporated under this Article (i.e. born of a Swiss mother of parents domiciled in Switzerland) to the 'lesser citizenship' of those excluded from the enjoyment of the property of the citizen-commune or Corporation. Previous practice had been more generous.

PARAGRAPH 6. For *Heimatlos* see Article 68, in the note to which citizenship is further discussed.

The Law of 1903 makes the Cantonal grant of citizenship dependent generally upon the consent of the Federal Department of Justice and Police. In practice, the two authorities consult together. In 1949, 1,236 foreigners were naturalized (with 1,200 dependants, making 2,436 in all); of these 500 were born in Switzerland. (Figures from *Annuaire statistique de la Suisse*, 1949.)

ARTICLE 45. Every Swiss citizen has the right to obtain settlement in any part of Swiss territory provided he is in possession of a Certificate of Origin or similar document.

In exceptional cases settlement may be refused, or may be withdrawn from, those who as a consequence of a criminal sentence are not in enjoyment of civil rights.

Furthermore, settlement may be withdrawn from those who have been repeatedly sentenced by the Courts for serious criminal offences, as well as from those who are a permanent charge on public charity and to whom the commune or Canton of origin, as the case may be, refuses adequate support after having been officially requested to afford it.

---

[1] The Law of 1 Jan. 1953 on Swiss Nationality provides that the children born abroad of Swiss parents themselves born abroad will lose Swiss nationality in certain circumstances unless they specially claim it before coming of age. The new Law also provides that a Swiss woman marrying a foreigner may retain her Swiss nationality if she makes a declaration before marriage that she wishes to do so. These are innovations of principle.

In Cantons where there is resident poor-relief, permission for settlement of citizens of that Canton may be made subject to the condition that they are capable of working and that they were not already a permanent charge on public charity in their former place of residence in their home Canton.

Any expulsion on grounds of poverty shall be ratified by the government of the Canton of settlement and prior warning thereof sent to the government of the Canton of origin.

The Canton in which a Swiss citizen establishes settlement cannot ask of him any deposit or levy any special charge for settlement. In the same way no commune may levy any charge on Swiss citizens resident on its territory other than what it levies on its own citizens.

A Federal law shall fix the maximum chancellery fee for a permit of settlement.

Freedom of Settlement. When a Swiss citizen wishes to change his place of residence he must obtain permission to settle from the communal authorities of the place where he goes to. In normal times this permission can only be refused on the grounds which are stated in this Article, that is to say: (1) loss of civil rights as a consequence of a criminal sentence (Swiss Penal Code, Article 52; Constitution, Article 66); (2) in Cantons with resident poor-relief, on the grounds described in paragraph 4 of this Article; (3) lack of a Certificate of Origin (Heimatschein) in proper form.

Settlement (Niederlassung, *établissement*) means 'living outside the home commune'. A person may be 'settled' in several places (since Cantons may require people merely trading or exercising a profession on their territory to take settlement there, without real residence, so as to bring them under their own Cantonal legislation), but there may only be one civil-law domicile (Swiss Civil Code, Article 23). For this reason the place of residence for settlement purposes need not always coincide with the civil-law domicile. The place of residence for purposes of Double Taxation (Article 46) is independent of all these, and the place of residence for exercise of political rights is also, on occasion, different.

PARAGRAPH 1. The form of a Certificate of Origin (Heimatschein) is given in ACF of 16 Mar. 1885, *Recueil systématique*, i, p. 105. The home commune is bound to issue the document, and the authorities to whom it is surrendered are bound to release it again without attaching unreasonable conditions. The issue or release is not automatic, however. It can be refused if the applicant is in arrears with certain forms of taxation, or to soldiers in certain circumstances, to an accused person when a criminal trial is pending, or upon non-payment of certain classes of fine. It may also be refused to a wife upon application of the husband even if the wife wants to live apart, and to minors and wards (Civil Code, Article 25).

PARAGRAPHS 2 AND 3. Distinguish between grounds of refusal and deprivation. *Deprivation* follows from the two grounds mentioned here (repeated criminal sentences, poverty when the home commune refuses support) and also for the reasons for *refusal* listed in the first paragraph of this note. The reason why the grounds of refusal are a smaller class included in the grounds of deprivation is that refusal potentially closes all except the home Canton, while deprivation only closes the expelling Canton. If it does not take action at the proper moment, the Canton's right of deprivation lapses.

The word 'repeatedly' has been illumined by much legal subtlety. The crime deemed the last straw gives the Canton the right to expel. The criminal on expulsion is thereafter limited, as it were, to one crime per Canton until he reaches his home Canton, where he has a crime per commune until he reaches his home commune, whence no enormity can expel him.

PARAGRAPHS 4 AND 5. Originally all poor were supported by the home commune, wherever they lived, although that was also normally required to be the home commune. Support by the home parish seems to have been consistently required in the Old Confederation. It was a consequence of the Reformation, which secularized poor-relief,[1] and may be said to date from about 1551. In recent days, however, many Cantons, and notably Berne, have for some time supported poor (in principle) in the commune where they happen to be settled. This is called the 'residence system', and the Cantons adopting it have by concordat agreed among themselves to support each other's citizens in this way. The 'Concordat Cantons' must still support their citizens who become paupers on the territory of non-Concordat Cantons. In order that one Concordat Canton does not become victimized by the others —who might otherwise have exported their poor—the Concordat Cantons are given this right of refusal. The wording of the Constitution is confusing, for it only concerns itself with the problem of one commune within a Concordat Canton exporting its poor to another commune of the same Canton.

PARAGRAPH 6. This rule of non-discrimination appears to be merely a special case of Article 4 or perhaps Article 60 (and, on occasion, of Article 31, i.e. settlement for trade purposes). But Appeals in Public Law under this Article to the Federal Tribunal have the advantage of those under Articles 4 and 31 in that, by Article 86 of the Law on Judicial Organization, the Cantonal judicial instances need not be exhausted before appealing to the Federal Tribunal.

PARAGRAPH 7. Fixed at 6 francs by the Law of 10 Dec. 1849, as modified, still in force.

Emergency Legislation. From 1918 to 1923, and from 1941 to Oct. 1950, the Freedom of Settlement was suspended by the Federal Council, the *ultimum refugium* of the home commune being always respected. This legislation is now repealed.

'Freedom of Settlement' as a freedom-right. On examination, Freedom of Settlement appears to be a grandiloquent way of describing the fact that all Swiss citizens in their own country must always register their comings and goings with the local police, and that certain classes of citizens are

[1] *Proceedings of the Federal Diet—Eidg. Abschiede—*iv. 2. 113; but see also iii. 1. 386 of 30 May 1491.

narrowly restricted in where they can live. It describes a system whereby a criminal is moved on, often at the discretion of the Cantonal executive, to fresh fields in another Canton, not regularly but haphazardly and perhaps to an area where he does not speak the local language, a system whereby the wife is tied to the husband's home, where children and wards are tied to their parents and guardians, where the pauper is carted back to his home parish, and much else. All these restrictions are tied together by the antique idea of 'settlement', and called 'Freedom'.

ARTICLE 46. In matters of civil law persons settled in Switzerland are as a general rule subject to the jurisdiction and to the legislation of the place where they reside.

Federal legislation shall lay down the provisions necessary in order to give effect to this principle, and to prevent Double Taxation.

PARAGRAPH 1. Since the Civil Code came into operation in 1912 the question of which Canton's Courts are competent has lost its interest for the student of the Constitution, while retaining it for the practical lawyer. The Civil Code now determines in most cases which Court is competent, and has superseded the greater part of the Law of 1891 on the Relationships in Civil Law of those in *Séjour* and Settlement (Article 61 of the Final Provisions of the Swiss Civil Code).

PARAGRAPH 2. *The Rule against Double Taxation.* In principle, the Confederation levies only the taxes allowed by the Constitution, and no direct taxation (for emergency taxation, see note to Article 42). The 'Steuerhoheit', fiscal supremacy or primacy, belongs to each of the twenty-five Cantons. There are numerous cases where a citizen gets pinched between two Cantonal tax supremacies and has to pay the same tax twice. This is called Double Taxation. Double Taxation also arises between nations, but this is held not to be Double Taxation in the sense of this Article; and Double Taxation arises between communes of the same Canton, but the Federal Tribunal leaves this to the Cantonal authorities, and only intervenes when Double Taxation crosses a Cantonal boundary.

Before 1848 there was neither a serious problem of Double Taxation nor the possibility of remedying it if there had been one: Cantons were sovereign, and derived their income from customs duties and other indirect taxes. The Constitution of 1848 deprived the Cantons of their customs duties and set up an effective central authority, thus changing the situation in both respects.

From 1848 to 1855 it seems that Cantons taxed double and people paid. With greater freedom of movement the matter became more serious, and especial difficulties arose from the conflict of poor-laws. In 1855, however, a case arose of a citizen of Thurgau, settled in St. Gall. In Thurgau taxation for poor-relief was based on commune-citizenship, in St. Gall on residence. Consequently the citizen concerned paid poor-taxes twice, and he appealed to the Federal Council (under the procedure then in force). The Federal Council decided against him, and the appeal went to the legislative

Councils (Articles 90, s. 2, and 74, s. 15 of the Constitution of 1848). The Councils decided in the citizen's, and St. Gall's, favour, namely that St. Gall being sovereign need only apply its own legislation in its own Courts—where the case was to be brought under an interpretation of Article 59 (present Constitution) now discarded. The Federal Council thereafter accepted this decision as a binding precedent (see 'Ullmer', No. 128, or *Feuille fédérale*, 1853, ii. 594, and 1855, ii. 479). It may be noticed that whereas the original conflict arose out of a conflict of citizenship and settlement, the present difficulty arises out of divided *de facto* settlement.

The legal basis of this decision being dubious, the Federal authorities later relied upon the simple, but wish-fathered, rule that Double Taxation was somehow forbidden, though no law stated it and the matter was outside the Federal competence. An attempt to give the Confederation the power to decide by legislation whether the laws of the home or of the settlement-Canton should prevail in taxation failed—a proposed amendment to this effect being one of those rejected in the disastrous referendum of 1866.

The Constitution of 1874, containing the present provision, transferred jurisdiction in such matters from the political authorities to the reconstructed Federal Tribunal, which inherited the case-law of its predecessors. Appeals against Double Taxation soon came before the Tribunal, which was embarrassed by the delay in the appearance of the legislation which this Article visualizes. In the meantime the Appeals had to be decided, and the Tribunal felt itself unable to depart from its predecessors' case-law. At first it relied on precedent, but later, growing bolder, interpreted the Article as if there were a guaranteed constitutional 'Freedom from Double Taxation' somewhere in the Constitution. The legislation has never appeared. The case-law of the Tribunal fills the gap.

In one of its earliest decisions the Federal Tribunal produced the definition which has become classic: 'A case of Double Taxation only occurs when the *same* person, under the tax legislation of two *Cantons*, is liable to the *same* tax on the *same* property at the *same* time' (Case of the Commune of Willihof, 1875). As time went on the full stature of the task became apparent. The situation of corporate persons gives rise to exceptional difficulties. Typical problems are those of companies with subsidiary undertakings in other Cantons, or of a slot machine in one Canton whose owner was in another, or of a steamboat on the Lake of Four Cantons, or of workers in one Canton who live in another, or who have shops in another. Such difficulties are the stuff of daily life. On occasion the Tribunal has followed lines of thought later proved unsound—such as a presumption that tax should if possible not be split—and time has compelled it to abandon its precedents. In general, it is *de facto* residence, not formal residence, which counts.

The Federal Tribunal's case-law is a remarkable achievement, which is of interest to those who wish to introduce into Great Britain a local-government income-tax. Conflicts between two or more local governments give rise to difficulties which appear, but which are not, insoluble. Swiss experience affords warning and encouragement: warning as to the great difficulty, encouragement that the difficulty can be overcome by the ordinary Courts of the land acting in particular cases.

ARTICLE 47. A Federal law shall determine the difference between 'settlement' and 'temporary residence' and at the same time decide what is the position of the Swiss citizen in temporary residence as regards civil and political rights.

Three attempts have been made to frame a Law determining the difference between settlement and temporary residence (*séjour*) so as to give effect to this Article. On the first two occasions the Laws were challenged and rejected at referendums in 1875 and 1877. The third attempt in 1882 did not get so far. The Federal Law visualized therefore has never come into force, and consequently the definition of *séjour* and the determination of the political rights of those in *séjour* are left to the legislation of the Cantons. The Cantons are restricted by the practical necessity of not making *séjour* more difficult to obtain than settlement, for if they did so everyone would choose settlement.

The position 'as regards civil rights' is determined by the Law of 25 June 1891, *Recueil systématique*, vol. ii, p. 727.

ARTICLE 48. A Federal Law shall enact the necessary provisions concerning the costs of illness and burial of pauper citizens of one Canton taken sick or deceased in another Canton.

Legislation has been passed under this Article (the Federal Law of 22 June 1875, which is still in force). Sick paupers are not to be sent back to their home Canton if this would injure their health. They are to be cared for, and if they die, buried, in and at the expense of the Canton where they happen to be.

For Poor-Relief, see note to Article 45; for Unemployment Insurance, Article 34 *ter*; Right to a Decent Burial, Article 53.

ARTICLE 49. Freedom of conscience and belief is inviolable.

No one may be compelled to be a member of a religious association, to receive a religious education, to take part in a religious ceremony, or to suffer punishment of any sort by reason of religious opinion.

The father or guardian has the right of determining the religious education a child shall receive, in conformity with the principles stipulated above, until the child's sixteenth birthday.

Exercise of civil or political rights may not be restricted by any religious or ecclesiastical conditions or prescriptions whatever.

No one is released from performance of his civil duties by reason of his religious beliefs.

No one is obliged to pay taxes devoted especially to the special expenses of the ritual of a religious community to which he does not belong. Further execution of this principle is reserved to Federal legislation.

Historical Background. The religious settlement of the Old Confederation followed the principle *cujus regio, ejus religio* of the Peace of Augsburg (1555). The religious boundaries therefore coincided with the political boundaries, and the religious map of the present day is a patchwork which reproduces the sovereignty-structure of the Old Confederation.

The most important of the towns, Berne, Zurich, Basle, and others, became Protestant. Consequently the territories subject to these towns became Protestant also, and for this reason the present Canton of Vaud is Protestant, for it was anciently subject to Berne, and for this reason the present Bernese Jura is Catholic, for it was anciently subject to the prince-bishops of Basle. A difficulty, however, arose with respect to some common bailiwicks—territories subject to several, or all, sovereign Cantons, and ruled by representatives of each sovereign in rotation—where a Catholic sovereign alternated with a Protestant. The solution adopted was 'parity' of the two confessions, both of the official denominations being protected and the *status quo* guaranteed (though there was usually a slight bias in favour of the Catholics, who were in the majority in the Federal Diet). Parity was also adopted in Glarus, where the communes enjoyed a wide autonomy—traces of the old system can be seen there at the present day—and for a time in Appenzell. In the Grisons, where the communes enjoyed something approaching sovereignty, the religious patchwork of the Swiss Confederacy proper was (and is) reproduced in miniature.

The French Revolution introduced a new factor, for the progressive, and centralist, party espoused a type of deism—a sort of protestantism within Protestantism—hardly distinguishable in its practical implications from atheism. The Liberal party, victorious in battle over the Catholics in 1848, were at once hostile to Roman Catholicism and to Cantonal autonomy: the Catholics, on the other hand, being in a minority in the whole Confederation, but commanding the votes of a disproportionately large number of diminutive Cantons, had a vested interest both in Cantonal autonomy and in the influence of Cantonal votes in Federal affairs. The issues of religious freedom and decentralized government have therefore become inextricable from one another. And the Constitution of 1874, no less than that of 1848, had its roots in religious conflict, and was carried against the votes of the Catholic-Conservative Sonderbund Cantons.

The position of the central government in religious matters, neutral or almost atheist, must be distinguished from that of the individual Cantons, in almost all of which Church and State are most intimately connected.

PARAGRAPH 1. The expression 'conscience and belief' is to be taken together with the qualified protection of religious ceremonies in Article 50, that is to say as covering religious belief, belief whose object is the worship of a deity by a ceremony, but not a political or other belief. The form of words 'inviolable liberty of conscience' should not be taken too seriously, since as soon as the opinion or conscience finds outward expression, for example in a joke by one's own fireside, it becomes punishable. See also paragraph 5 below.

PARAGRAPH 2. *First phrase.* The practical application of this rule is that taken together with paragraph 6 it enables those who do not wish to be considered as belonging to the official Churches of their Canton to refuse to pay purely ecclesiastical taxes. The Cantons are permitted to make the presumption that citizens are members until they in due form notify to the contrary; in other words, the citizens must 'contract out'. And taken together with Articles 75 and 51, it enables priests and Jesuits to relieve themselves of their civil incapacities.

The provision is contrary to Catholic canon law, which holds that baptism and ordination are indelible.

Second phrase. See Article 27 (Education), and paragraph 3 below.

Third phrase. This is an important rule. Taken literally it would cut out Sunday as a compulsory holiday, but in practice Cantonal legislation has a fairly free hand as to what it can forbid on Sundays. Federal legislation also recognizes certain other religious feasts as industrial holidays; it is generally agreed that this practice is sensible but unconstitutional. Another consequence is that certain forms of oath calling upon God may not be made compulsory, for example before the Courts, for such an oath is of the nature of a religious ceremony. It would seem that clergy of an unestablished Church could also benefit under this Article, that they could not be forced to administer sacraments, for example, against their convictions: established clergy, on the other hand, may be regarded by Cantonal legislation primarily as officials, bound to obey or resign, and this is constitutional (under paragraph 5).

Fourth and last phrase. Compare Article 58, Ecclesiastical Jurisdiction. The words 'of any sort' represent an ideal unrealizable in a free country—for example they cannot prevent the religious consequences of excommunication, though they might be used to break a boycott resulting from the greater excommunication. It is in fact against any external consequences of ecclesiastical censure that this provision is directed, and in particular against the Cantonal governments, who are thereby forbidden to back up ecclesiastical censure by the apparatus of the State. Paragraph 4 below attains the same object and is sufficient for most cases.

PARAGRAPH 3. The usual age at which a child comes of age is 20, but for purposes of choosing what, if any, religious education he shall receive, a child comes of age at 16. Before that age the matter lies in the free discretion of the father, with consultation of the mother. Proselytism (e.g. attempts to convert an atheist child to Christianity) under the age of 16 is forbidden thereby: in its young days the Salvation Army got into trouble over street meetings at which children under 16 were present without their parents' consent. Contracts to bring up a child in a particular sect are void. See also Article 27, Education.

PARAGRAPH 4. This restrains Cantons from a particular form of persecution, and from backing up ecclesiastical law (e.g. celibacy of the clergy) by the civil power. But by analogy with Article 75 (ineligibility of priests to the National Assembly, &c.) Cantons may exclude priests from certain political rights, including eligibility to offices and councils. The paragraph as a whole is a special case of the last phrase of paragraph 2 above.

PARAGRAPH 5. Thus in spite of the lofty declaration of the inviolability of conscience, a Quaker or Jehovah's Witness may be punished for refusing military service (which in Switzerland is genuinely universally obligatory). Whether connected with this severity, or from the pacific character of Swiss military service, or from the absence of the spirit of nonconformity in Switzerland, or for other reasons, the number of those refusing on conscientious grounds and therefore going to prison is minutely small, even in war-time. Federal legislation, however, excuses clergy from compulsory military service and gives them privileges therein.

PARAGRAPH 6. In a Canton where a Church or Churches are Established, they are financed by taxes levied on, and by, the congregation or 'Church commune'—and these are real taxes properly enforceable, and only to be evaded by relinquishing the Church in due form. It is this provision that makes relinquishment possible for all. The words 'especially' and 'special', however, take much of the sting from the provision. On the one hand Cantons can, and do, pay clergy from public funds—the clergy being regarded in Protestant Cantons as a corps of officials—and taxation to feed the public funds is obligatory; and, on the other hand, where the Church commune raises the taxes, non-members of the congregation can be constrained to pay that part of the Church rate which is not devoted 'specially' to religious purposes—they must pay their share of such things as the upkeep of the churchyard, belfry, and clock.

The Law envisaged has never been passed, and the provision is applied directly.

Religious Freedom as a Freedom-Right. Article 50 'guaranteeing' the externals of religion states also the ends which the Constitution seeks to attain—public order and decency. And the history of Switzerland shows that it is very necessary for the Confederation to protect itself against the Churches. In the first place the State must protect itself from dissolution and must keep the peace between Protestant and Catholic, or cease to exist. In the second place it must protect itself and its subjects from external influences, and in particular from Rome. Before the Revolution the kings of European countries charged themselves with the protection of the Church in their dominions from papal absolutism, and the duty now devolves on the republics their successors. Gallicanism died with the monarchy, but something which might almost (but perhaps not quite) be called Helvetianism still survives, and this is entirely thanks to the Federal and the Cantonal governments. Not all State restrictions on papal power are forced on unwilling Catholics.

But above all, the Constitution protects the individual against the Cantonal Church. In particular, it protects Protestants in Catholic Cantons, a protection which even today is not superfluous. This protection is not only afforded by the Articles expressly claiming to protect religious freedom, it is the tenor of all the freedom-rights—especially the rights of Equality, Press, Commerce, and Settlement—for religion provides the chief motive of intolerance in the Cantons. Localism, Cantonal sovereignty, is the principle threatening the individual's religious freedom; the guaranteed rights, which in a Confederation represent centralism, form the principle protecting it.

And finally, the Constitution protects agnosticism. Parity, or tolerance, is forced on the Confederation, but it goes farther than this and adopts a sort of half-hearted atheism (e.g. Articles 53 and 54, Marriage, &c.); the connexion of atheism with continental liberalism has already been noted. This atheism bears more hardly upon Catholics than upon Protestants.

The question to be asked, however, is not 'Does the Swiss Constitution secure religious liberty?' but 'In what sense of the word "liberty" is religious liberty secured in Switzerland?' In the Confederation it is the individual who is freed, and the Church which is controlled. Cantonal sovereignty, on the other hand, creates a sphere where the opposite is true, where the Church is free to be a Church, and the individual is subject to it. For a Church is only entirely free when it is closely connected with the State, when ecclesiastical sins are civil crimes, and when the sacraments of the Church confer a status that is recognized by the civil power. The Swiss attempt to reconcile these principles is in some ways unsatisfactory, but it secures freedom in a more varied sense than, for example, the American solution. The connexion with the general issue of centralism versus localism should be noted.

The present development is for the Confederation to show more sympathy with religion,[1] and for the Cantons to identify themselves less closely with any particular form of it.

ARTICLE 50. The free practice of religious ceremonies is guaranteed within the limits of public order and decency.

The Cantons and the Confederation may take the necessary measures to maintain public order and peace between adherents of different religious communities, and to combat the encroachments of ecclesiastical authorities on the rights of citizens or of the State.

Conflicts of public or private law arising out of the creation of new religious communities or a schism of old ones may be brought on appeal before the competent Federal authorities.

No bishoprics may be set up on Swiss territory without the consent of the Confederation.

Distinguish Freedom of Conscience, which is guaranteed (in appearance), absolutely, and Freedom of Public Worship, guaranteed subject to two potentially limitless restrictions, 'public order' and 'decency'.

There is a large body of case-law upon the 'Freedom of Worship', i.e. upon the extensive restraints imposed by this Article upon the freedom of worship. But the cases are old, they refer to long-forgotten controversies,

---

[1] And, in particular, less animosity to the Roman Catholic Church. As one of the signs of the times one may notice that whereas before the First World War the Catholic and conservative Appenzell *Inner* Rhodes was always 'odd man out', it is now the liberal and Protestant Appenzell Outer Rhodes which votes with the minority.

such as the once burning question of whether the Cantons could indefinitely forbid the Salvation Army. And the whole balance of power has shifted so sharply since then that the relevance of the pre-1914 case-law to any future dispute is doubtful.

PARAGRAPH 2. This appears to be a direct incitement to violence, for it suffices that the established hierarchy agitates against new-comers for the interlopers to be persecuted by the State as disturbers of the peace. It is not clear what the sinister phrase 'the necessary measures' implies, whether for example it releases the Cantons and the Confederation from all or any constitutional scruples.

The word 'encroachments' indicates that this phrase is a political manifesto or programme, not a rule of law, for the Confederation and the Cantons would at all times have the competence to resist *encroachments*, by definition. One has the impression that nevertheless encroachments have been successfully made, especially by the Roman Catholics, and that religious liberty would benefit if still more were made.

PARAGRAPH 3. The reference is to a split in the Church of Rome as a consequence of the events of 1870. The Old Catholics (or Christian-Catholics) succeeded perhaps to rather more than their fair share of property in some places, notably in Berne, where they were encouraged by Protestant Cantonal governments.

PARAGRAPH 4. This is also a reference to contemporary events of 1874, namely the re-establishment of the Catholic bishopric of Lausanne and Geneva, and a reminiscence of previous disputes over the jurisdiction of the bishopric of Como and the archbishopric of Milan in Ticino. By virtue of this Article, concordats with the Holy See on such matters are within the competence of the Confederation rather than of the Cantons. When the Old Catholics came to set up a bishopric they asked for, and were granted, Federal sanction: it is, however, disputed whether this was legally necessary. The permission does not seem to be required, for example, in the case of the Anglican Church in Switzerland. Roman Catholics, whom the requirement offends, contest its legitimacy.

'The Confederation' in this context seems to mean the Federal Council, under Article 102, s. 2, as it was an Arrêté of the Federal Council which sanctioned the Old Catholic bishopric—though the competence was then disputed. 'The competent Federal authority' of paragraph 3 is the Federal Tribunal.[1]

ARTICLE 51. The order of Jesuits and societies affiliated thereto can be received in no part of Switzerland, and are forbidden to take any part in Church or school affairs.

A Federal Arrêté may extend this prohibition to other religious orders whose activity is dangerous to the State or disturbs the peaceable relationship of religious denominations.

The historical background of this Article is discussed in the note to

[1] In most cases; cf. the famous case of the Mariahilfskirche in Lucerne.

Article 52 below. Unlike the restrictions on monasteries, the prohibition of the order of Jesuits was included in the Constitution of 1848.

The words 'affiliated societies' in the first paragraph are directed against crypto-Jesuits, male and female, and have at various times been interpreted by the Federal Council as applying to various religious orders. The Federal Arrêté envisaged in the second paragraph would presumably not need to be a 'universally binding' one (i.e. challengeable to the referendum) in the sense of Article 89: no such *arrêté* has ever been passed.

The Article is now interpreted as forbidding the Society of Jesus to establish itself as such in Swiss territory, but as permitting individual Jesuits to do everything except teach in schools, act as clergy, or preach in church. Until 1914 the prohibition of Jesuits remained a live issue, but the altered circumstances and interests of modern times have deprived the Article of its importance. The absence of recent cases makes it difficult to determine quite where the present compromise has been struck, for it is doubtful how far the pre-1914 cases are now relevant.

Jurisdiction in this matter belongs not to the Federal Tribunal but to the Federal Council (and, of course, to the Cantons).

ARTICLE 52. The founding of new convents or religious orders, and the re-establishment of those which have been suppressed, are both prohibited.

The Federal Pact of 1815–48 guaranteed monastic houses against Cantonal governments. In defiance of this guarantee, Aargau dissolved monasteries on its territory in 1841. The Catholic Cantons were unable to obtain justice, and Lucerne, where the Catholic party had recently obtained a majority, was provoked to permit the return of the Jesuits, and (in view of the reaction of the Protestant Cantons to this) the Catholic-Conservative Cantons were led to form a 'separate alliance' (Sonderbund). This in turn eventually led to civil war, in which the Sonderbund (Lucerne, Uri, Schwyz, Obwald and Nidwald, Zug, Valais, and Fribourg) were defeated. The Constitution of 1848 was the result. This Article, however, was not in that Constitution.

The Constitution of 1874 was among other things a reaction against the Papal *coup d'état* of 1870. The present Article is a combination of revulsion and memories.

After 1881 and 1901 members of French religious orders sought refuge in Switzerland, and this Article received a temporary importance. The interpretation then placed upon it was unfavourable to *de facto* monasticism. The matter is in the competence of the Federal Council, and not of the Federal Tribunal: the recent practice is to wink at evasions, and this is recognized as being in the true spirit of the Constitution.

ARTICLE 53. Acknowledgement and registration of births, deaths, and marriages[1] is a matter for the civil authorities.

[1] *État civil*, 'Zivilstand', has been translated as 'births, deaths, and marriages', in default of an English equivalent.

Further provisions upon this subject shall be laid down by Federal legislation.

The ordering of cemeteries is the affair of the civil authority, which must see that every deceased person can be decently buried.

The law of marriage is discussed under the next Article. The law of the registration of births and civil names—one can hardly call them Christian names as the baptismal name is not recognized—contains nothing very actively offensive to Christian sentiment. It is characteristic of the paternalism of Swiss bureaucracy that the name chosen for registration is subject to approval by officials: surnames are also strictly regulated, and are nearly, but not quite, unalterable.

The law of burials, on the other hand, is as if to humiliate Catholics. The constitutional provision, applied directly as a rule of law, is interpreted as giving in certain circumstances a right to have suicides buried in consecrated ground, and to have the (Catholic) church bell tolled for them, and as requiring in certain circumstances that Catholic, Protestant, excommunicate, and atheist shall all be buried, mixed up with one grave next the other. This 'right to a decent burial' can be enforced by Appeal in Public Law to the Federal Council.

When a *modus vivendi* is sought on the question of burials, as today seems to be the case, it can always be found. In time of sectarian ill-will, however, it lends Protestants the whole force of the State to attack Catholics at a sensitive point. The question is not a sore one today.

ARTICLE 54. The right to marriage is under the protection of the Confederation.

No bar to marriage can arise from considerations of religious belief or from the poverty of one or other partner, or from past conduct or from other considerations of public policy.

A marriage performed in any Canton or in any foreign country according to the legislation there in force shall be recognized as valid throughout the Confederation.

The wife acquires by marriage the citizenship and the communal citizenship of her husband.

Children born before marriage are legitimized by the subsequent marriage of their parents.

No tax upon admission of one or other partner of the marriage is permissible, nor any similar tax.

Effect was given to the civil-marriage provisions of this and the previous Article by the Law on Registration of Births, Deaths, and Marriages of 24 Dec. 1874, which was challenged to a referendum and passed in the teeth of Catholic opposition by a victorious Protestant and anti-clerical majority. Its provisions were later incorporated in the Civil Code (Articles 105–19). Today Catholics appear to have forgotten the bitterness of their enmity to civil marriage, and do not realize how unnecessary the restrictions on their liberty of conscience in this respect are. To an Englishman, accustomed to civil marriage as an alternative only, the law of marriage appears the least satisfactory part of the Swiss religious settlement. The Civil Code provides that the mock ceremony of marriage by lay officials (Ziviltrauung) must *precede* the religious ceremony. Of the latter, the State takes no account at all, neither forbidding nor recognizing it.

In justice to the present non-Christian system it must be remembered that the old marriage-laws, especially in Catholic Cantons, were extremely harsh in the case of mixed marriages, &c., and that Cantons could, and often did, refuse the certificate which was a necessary preliminary to a recognized marriage on the grounds of poverty. Illegitimacy, which was frequent as a consequence of these laws, led to exclusion from communal and corporate property, and sometimes to 'Heimatlosat'.[1] Moreover, these laws were also repugnant to religious sentiments, and in particular to those of the Papacy itself. Imperfect though the present solution is, it avoids the vast mass of human misery caused by the old system.

PARAGRAPH 6. The 'taxes upon admission' were customary fines, e.g. upon admission of the wife, and hence of the children, to enjoyment of communal or corporate property.

ARTICLE 55. The freedom of the press is guaranteed.

Cantonal legislation shall make appropriate provision against its abuse: such laws must be submitted to the approval of the Federal Council.

The Confederation has the right to take penal measures against improper use of the press directed against the Confederation or the Federal authorities.

The Federal Arrêté which in Dec. 1898 recorded the acceptance in a votation of Article 64 *bis*, and the amendment to Article 64 (Civil Code), added 'when the Penal Code comes into force, paragraphs 2 and 3 of Article 55 of the Constitution go out of effect'. The Penal Code came into force in 1942, and consequently the official editions of the Constitution now omit paragraphs 2 and 3. But the words of the *arrêté* were no part of the project submitted to the referendum, and the constitutional propriety of repealing the actual text of the Constitution by means of a simple Federal Arrêté of merely procedural importance, and not challengeable to a referendum, is questionable. The full text (printed here) moreover makes the history and meaning of the Article comprehensible.

The guarantee of the Freedom of the Press dates from the days when liberalism's only task had been the destruction of legitimacy and established government. Now that liberalism is threatened by sovietism in its turn, more emphasis is laid upon the decent restrictions which must preserve a well-

[1] See page 77.

regulated freedom. It is not quite on all fours to say that communism is using liberalism to destroy liberty itself, for in their day liberals used the characteristic, if unreliable, tolerance of the old régime to destroy that régime itself. The new establishment is defending itself by the old methods, but doing it efficiently.

The wording of the Article gives the Cantons the competence to restrict the freedom of the press, subject to a particular safeguard, namely the censorship of the Cantonal press-law by the Federal executive. The competence it gives the Confederation itself is a limited one, to protect itself and the Federal authorities against improper attacks: one detects a certain sensitiveness here.

The Cantons still possess a not very important residual competence. The greater part of the law is now Federal law, the permanent portion of which is contained in the Penal Code. There is also a certain amount of emergency or makeshift 'legislation', such as the Federal Council's Arrêté on Propaganda Dangerous for the State of 28 Dec. 1948. The ordinary law, however, is sharp enough for most purposes.[1]

The Confederation did not await the outbreak of war to control the press. On 26 Mar. 1934 the Executive 'relying on Article 102, ss. 8 and 9' issued an *arrêté* 'to go into force immediately' conferring upon itself power 'to warn' and 'to suspend' periodicals which in the opinion of the Federal Department of Justice and Police 'exceeded the limits of criticism very severely, in such a way as to threaten the good relations of Switzerland with foreign countries' (that is to say, with Nazi Germany). On 7 Oct. 1938 the *Journal des Nations* was suspended for three months for 'making itself conspicuous by a one-sided anti-fascist viewpoint'. On 5 June 1939 the *Schweizer Rundschau am Sonntag*, which took a similar one-sided viewpoint, was likewise suspended for three months. The Federal Council considered this *arrêté* of so little general interest that it did not publish it in the *Recueil officiel des lois et ordonnances*, in which it has in fact never appeared; indeed at first it did not publish it at all. As a result of protest, however, it printed it in a part of the *Feuille fédérale* usually reserved for the movements of foreign diplomats. It can be found in the Bundesblatt (*Feuille fédérale*) of 26 Mar. 1934 (B.Bl. 86, i. 860). The Socialist party raised a popular initiative 'to modify Article 55, Liberty of the Press', directed against this *arrêté*, which was handed in to the Chancellery in due form with the proper number of signatures on 31 May 1935. It has not yet (Jan. 1953) been submitted to the people and Cantons. The offending *arrêté* itself was repealed at the end of the War.

In view of this record there seems no harm in guaranteeing the liberty of the press in the very fullest terms. It is unlikely to trammel the Executive in any case.

See also Article 67.

The freedom of the press was severely restricted, of course, during the War itself.

[1] For example, a communist (M. Nicole, junior) was sentenced on 1 Dec. 1951 to 15 months' imprisonment for the familiar abuse about subservience to American imperialism.

ARTICLE 56. Citizens have the right to form associations, provided that neither the purpose of the association nor the means it employs are in any way illegal or dangerous to the State. Cantonal legislation shall enact the necessary provisions to prevent misuse of this right.

The freedom to form and join associations, and the freedom of the association joined, is the sign and condition of political liberty. And it is true that freedom is something to be attained by law. Nevertheless it may be doubted whether the aphorism 'Freedom of Association is guaranteed' is the appropriate *rule of law* to attain it. The inviolability of the citizen's house, the safety of corporate funds, and company law, freedom of contract, and equality of *personae fictae* before the law, are all in different degrees capable of definition. But Freedom of Association itself eludes a direct guarantee: like 'freedom of the individual' it is an end-state rather than a rule of law. Indeed this is hardly surprising when we recollect that the word 'association' seeks to include riots, joint-stock companies, shooting-matches, political parties, hunger marches, the Salvation Army, drinking-clubs, conspiracies, learned societies, trades unions and trades union congresses, for each of these desires a slightly different sort of freedom.

The elusive nature of the right makes it difficult to discuss the restrictions upon it in Switzerland, for these restrictions (which on the whole go somewhat farther than in common-law countries) are a part of all sorts of different laws.

The Article itself is now rarely relied upon for an Appeal in Public Law, and still more rarely is an appeal based upon this Article successful. In 1893 appeals against infringements of Religious Liberty, which had hitherto been decided by the political authorities, were transferred by the Law on Judicial Organization of that year to the Federal Tribunal, and in 1912 appeals against infringements of Article 31 were similarly transferred to the Tribunal (which already was competent in the matter of Freedom of Association). The Federal Tribunal ceased thereby to have an interest in extending the meaning of this Article, and consequently it is not now part of the living Constitution as a rule of law constantly applied by the Courts.

The right of public meeting, subject to the same extensive restrictions, is understood to be included in this Article, which, however, only expressly guarantees the right against the State of individuals to form or join associations in certain circumstances.

The word 'citizen' in the Constitution is never a guide as to who is entitled to enjoy a constitutional right. But foreigners, unless beneficiaries of a treaty of settlement, can so easily be expelled from the country (under Articles 69 *ter* and 70) that the problem of whether they can rely on this Article hardly arises; they are lucky if they are tolerated by the police at all.

The Civil Code grants corporate personality freely, but controls the form of the 'association' by laying down for it a single detailed stereotype. Federal law forbids certain classes of persons (e.g. officials, soldiers) from joining special classes of associations.

ARTICLE 57. The right of petition is guaranteed.

This Article contains the rule of law that Cantonal and Federal authorities cannot restrain an inhabitant, or a group of inhabitants, of Switzerland, or Swiss citizens living abroad, from presenting a petition, and that the authorities are bound to receive the petition. The practice is even more generous than the legal requirements, and gives an answer to the petition. The right to petition is classified as a freedom-right, and is therefore in Swiss legal philosophy to be distinguished from rights which are attributes of the people in their capacity as sharers in political power, such as the right of initiative: it is a right *against* the State. It follows that it cannot be exercised by Cantons or towns (communes), which are part of the State, but only by individuals and voluntary ('private-law') corporations.

As to who shall be petitioned in a given case, it must be remembered that, for example, the Federal Assembly is sovereign neither against the Cantons nor against the Federal Executive. A matter within the competence of the Executive will therefore in principle not be entertained by the Assembly. Petition is therefore from the Executive to the Executive. Petitions to the Federal Assembly are referred to a committee (*commission*) by each Council separately, and there they are not treated contemptuously, as in Britain, but if within the Assembly's competence are considered as to their content. The committees recommend a decision, usually rejection, which is taken by each Council. It follows from this Article that the decision *must* be taken by the whole Council, *pro forma*. Such petitions are not numerous; in the autumn session of 1951 there were eight.

There are other restrictions also, numerous but reasonable. In general, what is permitted is all that a benevolent bureaucracy would have permitted its *administrés* had there been no mention of the matter in the Constitution. It is there for historical reasons; petitions were discouraged in the Old Confederation.

Distinguish from the Initiatives (Articles 121, 89), from the Appeal in Public Law (Article 113, s. 3) and for Pardon (Articles 85, s. 7, 92).

ARTICLE 58. No one may be deprived of his lawful judge. Consequently, no extraordinary judicial tribunals may be set up.

Ecclesiastical Courts are abolished.

Constitutional Judge (verfassungsmässiger Richter, *juge naturel*). This provision, with its reminiscence of the French *Chartes* of 1814 and 1830, is not now of day-to-day importance. It was designed to stop Cantons setting up extraordinary tribunals like those of which Liberals had been the victims during the struggles which preceded the Sonderbund war, and was applied in 1853 against Fribourg in this sense ('Ullmer', No. 295). It is now only used against *arbitrariness* in sending people to one tribunal rather than to another or in refusing jurisdiction. It is thus a particular case of Article 4, but it has a procedural advantage over Article 4 in that all the Cantonal possibilities of appeal do not have to be exhausted before bringing a case under Article 58 in front of the Federal Tribunal, whereas all Cantonal possibilities of appeal do have to be exhausted before bringing a case up under Article 4 (Law on Judicial Organization, Art. 86: other constitutional provisions enjoying the same privilege are Articles 45; 46, para. 2; 59, para. 1; 60, and 61).

The abolition of *Ecclesiastical Jurisdiction* means that the decisions of ecclesiastical courts do not have what would now be regarded as civil consequences, e.g. in matters of legitimacy, marriage, divorce, and inheritance. Internal disciplinary tribunals and tribunals deciding purely ecclesiastical matters (as now understood) are left untouched. The paragraph gives institutional effect to the other laicizing provisions of the religious liberty clauses.

ARTICLE 59. Proceedings in personal claims against solvent debtors resident in Switzerland must be brought before the Courts of the debtor's place of residence. A debtor's property shall not be seized or sequestered in personal claims except in the Canton where he resides.

With regard to foreigners, the provisions of international treaties are reserved.

Arrest for civil debt is abolished.

This Article is of practical and historical, but not of constitutional, interest.

PARAGRAPH 1. A reminiscence of the Old Confederation. The qualifications 'personal', 'solvent', and 'resident' have all received their due weight of interpretation. The Courts apply this provision as if it were a guaranteed constitutional right in favour of the debtor, enabling, but not compelling, him to choose the Courts of his Canton of 'residence'—whatever that may mean.

The whole territory of this Article (which is confined to civil debts) is now covered by Federal legislation, in particular by the Civil Code and the laws concerning bankruptcy.

Compare Articles 61, 64, and also 58, para. 1, and 46, para. 1.

ARTICLE 60. Cantons are obliged to treat the citizens of other Confederate States as favourably as their own citizens, in legislation and before their courts of law.

In 1885 a distinguished jurist could still describe Article 60 as 'far and away more important than Article 4' (von Orelli, *Oeffentliches Recht*). This, however, had already ceased to be the case; it was a memory of the 1848 Constitution. In spite of its procedural advantage over Article 4 (see note to Article 58) this Article is now of no importance in the sense that it is now never violated—there has been no (reported) Appeal in Public Law before the Federal Tribunal relying upon it for a quarter of a century. Movement of population, which makes violation more serious, makes it less likely.

The Article forbids a special case of unequal treatment, discrimination by a Canton between those Swiss who do not hold that Canton's right of citizenship and those who do, in favour of the latter. Its application is limited by Articles 43, 44, and 45 (Citizenship, Settlement).

ARTICLE 61. Final judgements in civil cases pronounced in one Canton can be executed anywhere on Swiss territory.

This is a limitation of the sovereignty of one Canton as against another Canton. Each Canton must execute the final civil-law judgements of the properly constituted courts of other Cantons.

There is an Appeal in Public Law to the Federal Tribunal for breach of this provision. Such appeals are infrequent, and turn on the meaning of the word 'final' (rechtskräftig), &c., and on the Law on Suits for Debt and Bankruptcy of 1889 (passed under Article 64), especially Article 81 of that Law.

For criminal law see Article 67; for the Civil Code see Article 64. Other branches of law, e.g. Cantonal public law, are covered by concordat between Cantons, partially or completely.

ARTICLE 62. The custom known as 'traite foraine' is abolished within the confines of Switzerland, and the 'droit de retrait' of the citizens of one Canton against those of other Cantons of the Confederation is also abolished.

ARTICLES 62 AND 63. *Traite foraine* was a fine, a tenth or a twentieth, levied on property when the owner left the community, for example, when property passed by marriage or inheritance out of the Canton or, in some cases, out of the commune. It was anciently widely levied in Switzerland and Germany.

Droits de retrait (Zugrechte) are rights of pre-emption exercised by members of a community, e.g. a family, when real property is sold to a non-member. In such a case a member of the community concerned has the right to substitute himself for the purchaser at the same price. Whereas *traite foraine* is entirely abolished within Switzerland, *retrait* is only abolished when exercisable by all citizens of one Canton against all citizens of other Cantons. As between communities (in particular, the right of a near relative to exercise pre-emption) it is not here abolished, and in some Cantons survives.

Their object having been attained, the force of these two Articles is spent, and in that sense they are antiquarian curiosities.

See Articles 45, para. 6, and 60 (read together), and compare 54, para. 6 (Einzugsrechte), of the Constitution, and Articles 681, 682 of the Swiss Civil Code; cf. also *Code Napoléon*, 726, 912 (*droits d'aubaine* and *de détraction*).

ARTICLE 63. The custom of 'traite foraine' as exercised in respect of those going to foreign countries is abolished, provided the foreign countries concerned do not exercise it against Swiss.

See Article 62. The German text is here misleading.

ARTICLE 64. Legislation upon the following subjects:
Civil capacity of persons;
All the law relating to trade and transactions concerning movable property (law of Contract, including Mercantile law and the law of Negotiable Instruments);
Literary and artistic copyright;
Protection of inventions applicable to industry, including designs and models;
Suits for debt; and Bankruptcy,
is within the province of the Confederation.

The Confederation is also authorized to legislate upon other matters of civil law.

The organization and procedure of the Courts and the administration of justice remain with the Cantons as in the past.

FIRST PARAGRAPH. Since the adoption of the second paragraph of this Article the first has become of minor importance. The rejected Project of a Constitution of 1872 had contained Articles corresponding to the present second paragraph and to Article 64 *bis* (Civil and Penal Codes), but as a concession to the localists both were withdrawn—to be reintroduced some years later. Hence the illogical structure.

Patents. The competence for the protection of inventions was not included in the Constitution of 1874, having been rejected in 1866. In 1882 a project for a constitutional amendment introducing a competence for the Confederation to introduce such protection was submitted to the people and Cantons at the same time as an unpopular Law which had been challenged, and both were rejected. In 1887 the Federal Council tried again, and the Councils submitted a differently worded amendment, which was accepted at a votation. The new wording attempted to secure the same object as the old without appearing to be the same, and was consequently somewhat tortuous. It was also impracticable, since it only protected foreign patents of which a model had been deposited in Switzerland—and it is not easy to submit a model of a process, for example. Furthermore, it became inconsistent with the international obligations the country had assumed. In 1905 the present wording was submitted to a referendum, and accepted: the votation was remarkable in that of the qualified voters of Lucerne only 7·5 per cent. voted, and of Zug 6·5 per cent. Appenzell Inner Rhodes alone rejected the amendment: it had up to that time said 'No' to every compulsory referendum on an Assembly project, except the reintroduction of the death penalty and the introduction of the popular initiative.

Swiss Civil Code.[1] (Second paragraph.) The Federal competence for the unification of civil law was accepted in the votation of 13 Nov. 1898, at the

---

[1] There is an English translation of the Swiss Civil Code by Ivy Williams, Oxford University Press, 1925.

same time as 64 *bis* below. The Federal Council submitted to the Assembly the project of a Civil Code, accompanied by a valuable 'Message' in 1904, and the Law which included the Code was passed in 1907, and came into force on 1 Jan. 1912. The Code has been added to from time to time since.

The Swiss Civil Code is an elegant but drastic document. The following quotation (Articles 161 and 167 of the Code) is a sample: 'The wife stands by the side of her husband with aid and counsel, and must support him in his care for their joint welfare according to her powers. She runs the household. . . . The wife is authorized to exercise a profession or follow a lucrative activity, provided her husband gives his express or tacit approval. . . .' Examples of this spirit of interference could be multiplied. The activities of a citizen's life are systematized, and commanded or forbidden by the State, from the moment of his parents' engagement until his death. At the time the Code was drawn up, great play was made with the claim that it is Germanic rather than Roman in origin, a return to the ancient traditions of the race purified and made logical. It has succeeded in being Germanic in detail, rather as the Palace of Westminster is Gothic.

The Courts in which the Code is applied are Cantonal Courts, which apply Federal law. In certain circumstances cases can come before the Federal Courts, on appeal—see page 125. The fact of a Federal private law exercises a pervasive, but intangible, influence on the life of the country, and seems to have a connexion (the nature of which is difficult to determine) with the centralistic habit of mind that has transformed the whole stuff of public life since 1914.

ARTICLE 64 *bis*. The Confederation is authorized to legislate upon criminal law.

The organization and procedure of the Courts and the administration of justice remain with the Cantons as in the past.

The Confederation is authorized to grant Cantons subsidies for the building of institutions for punishment, labour, or corrective treatment, and for improved methods of carrying out sentences. It is also authorized to assist institutions for the protection of neglected children.

Swiss Penal Code. This competence for the unification of the criminal law was accepted in 1898 in the same votation as the unification of the civil law above, against the same Catholic-Conservative opposition. The present Penal Code survived the challenge to a referendum on 3 July 1938, and came into force on 1 Jan. 1942. Until then the matter had remained in the competence of the Cantons.

The Confederation had passed penal laws for certain 'Federal' offences—for example against smuggling, customs duties being a Federal matter—ever since 1853. This was by virtue of 'general powers', in other words, without constitutional authority. The present Article legitimizes the previous practice, and gives the competence to pass a Federal Penal Code.

There is much in the Penal Code foreign to British ideas. Indeed the cast of mind, as well as the legal vocabulary, is remote from us. The frequency of minimum penalties is particularly striking. Even when the same words are used, such as 'Court' or 'Judge', different functions and offices are described. A lawyer who follows the profession of 'judge' is a cantonal official, who is elected on the proposition of a political party for a fairly short term,[1] and officiates over a fairly small administrative district, where he resides. And the 'inquisitorial' method of obtaining information from the accused in prison forms the basis of an entirely different court procedure in criminal cases.

The following is a sample of the Code:

'Article 266. Anyone who performs an act calculated to infringe or endanger the independence of the Confederation or cause interference by a Foreign Power in the affairs of the Confederation so as to endanger the Confederation's independence, shall be punished with from one to four years' penal servitude or imprisonment.'

PARAGRAPH 2. This paragraph and the corresponding paragraph of Article 64 are not strictly necessary, and are inserted to remove a possible misconception. The Courts for criminal, as for civil, law are Cantonal and their organization and procedure remain Cantonal—subject like all Cantonal acts to the overriding principle of the supremacy of Federal law. The prisons are (in general) likewise Cantonal.

Paragraph 3 is, among other things, a typical concession to localism, 'Referendumspolitik'.

ARTICLE 65. No death sentence may be passed for a political crime.
Corporal punishments are forbidden.

The Constitution of 1848 already abolished the death penalty for political crimes. In 1866 the Federal authorities tried to smuggle into the Constitution a competence to abolish the death penalty and flogging completely, but the attempt failed. Total revision, however, gave the central government another chance, and it succeeded in introducing the Article as it now stands with the exception of the qualifying phrase 'for political crimes', that is to say, in abolishing the death penalty outright. Well-publicized murders, however, stimulated a popular demand for the reintroduction of the death penalty, and in 1879 the Assembly, against the advice of the Federal Council, submitted a project of amendment to the people and Cantons—largely to avoid the threat of total revision, for there was then no popular constitutional initiative. The amendment was accepted, and the Article received its present form, thanks to the rural and Catholic vote. This restored the Cantonal competence, and the Catholic Cantons, led by the primitive demo-

[1] Practice gives the judge both judicial tenure as against the State and against the electorate. But he does not have the spiritual independence which a large income and high public honours give an English judge.

cracies, reintroduced the death penalty. The Swiss Penal Code, however, again (for the moment) abolishes it, and it can now only be imposed by military courts in 'war-time', that is to say, when neighbours are at war. These Courts may try civilians, and in one sense of the word it would be true to say that the death penalty is now *only* imposed for political crimes (treason, &c.) against the Confederation.

'Political crimes' is a large but not clearly defined category. The Article seems to suggest that an ordinary crime merits lighter treatment when it is done from political motives, that assassination is somehow better than murder—though this may be a wrong interpretation. For the use of the word 'political' see Article 7, Treaties, and also Articles 67, Press, and 112, Federal Tribunal.

PARAGRAPH 2. The practice of the Federal Tribunal is to include disciplinary punishments in prison under the prohibition of corporal punishment. The wording appears only to cover punishment, not judicial inquisition. The ordinary Courts and prisons, it will be remembered, are Cantonal, not Federal.

ARTICLE 66. Federal legislation shall determine the circumstances in which a Swiss citizen may be deprived of his political rights.

Thus Federal law can determine that a Canton may (if it wishes) legislate that a bankrupt is to lose his political rights, but that it may not keep him deprived of those rights when he has in due form rehabilitated himself. The Confederation sets the limits within which the Cantonal competence has play. There is no general law covering the whole ground.

ARTICLE 67. Federal legislation shall make the necessary provision for extradition of accused persons from one Canton to another: nevertheless extradition may not be made compulsory for political or press offences.

This rule is of procedural importance, and determines which Canton shall be the Canton of residence of the editor of a paper for the purposes of criminal law.

Until the Swiss Penal Code (Articles 352–8) came into force in 1942, the Law of 1852, and others, saw to this matter. Conflicts about which Canton's Courts shall have jurisdiction are settled by the Court of Accusation (a section of the Federal Tribunal, see note to Article 114).

ARTICLE 68. The granting of citizenship to the *Heimatlos*, and the measures to be taken to prevent new cases of this sort occurring, are subjects for Federal legislation.

At the present day the word 'citizen' means 'subject of a republic'. This usage owes something to absolutism, which saw only one class beneath the sovereign, and something to Revolutionary theory, which saw men as playing stick and doubling round to play donkey in time to receive the blow. This Revolutionary usage itself owes something to what we might call the Swiss system in the form known to Rousseau from Geneva and the Swiss republics.

The Old Confederation was based on privilege, though not on privilege alone. There existed, as it were, concentric circles of privilege in each of the member-States of the Confederacy, at the very centre being the limited number of families who actually exercised sovereignty under the forms of republicanism. Citizenship itself was one of these circles of privilege, not the innermost but within sight of the innermost, and in some cases within reach of the innermost. And the legal theory was often, one might perhaps say always, that sovereignty was vested in the citizenship.

The Restoration of 1814–48 secured to the countrymen who were full members of the communes (including all those communes formerly termed 'subject') the title of citizen of that commune, and thereby of the Canton. The new Confederation of 1848 added to Cantonal citizenship Swiss nationality.

In two respects in 1848 there was a discrepancy between the old 'citizenship', a privilege all but universalized, and the new 'nationality':

1. The old classes of half-citizen (Hintersassen, ewiger Einwohner, *petit-bourgeois, habitant*, &c.) survived. The growth of territorial sovereignty had left them Swiss and Cantonal subjects for lack of another sovereign, and the conservative parochialism of local autonomy had not quite made them citizens.

2. There was a further class of non-citizens who were also in every sense Swiss subjects (for they lived within Swiss territorial sovereignty and were neither subjects of a foreign Power nor properly stateless) but were completely outside the pale of the constitution. These were people who had been deprived of Cantonal citizenship as a punishment, or who were hereditary tramps, or gipsies, and the descendants of such people. Cantonal sovereignty, religious intolerance (which had often punished mixed marriages with loss of citizenship), the system whereby marriage was made dependent upon a licence in order to stop the destitute from breeding, and the desire to keep enjoyment of communal property as narrow as possible, had combined to create a class where misery was a hereditary and indelible status.

The Confederation made use of the competence conferred upon it by this Article to pass the Federal Law on 'Heimatlosat' of 1850, which was to settle the problem by making Swiss nationality and Swiss citizenship coextensive, and giving all Swiss a Cantonal and a communal 'citizenship'.

The first class, the half-citizens, presented no great difficulty. It was the extension of equality before the law to all Swiss nationals. In most cases the half-citizens had a clear local connexion, and in some cases they belonged to Corporations—like the *Corporations françaises* of Vaud, the descendants of Huguenot refugees—which had money. The only difficulty was payment to the accepting communes, which in the last resort the Confederation saw to. The remaining problems of citizenship, such as those of the Bernese Jura, Geneva, and the former principality of Neufchatel, were also settled. The discerning eye can today only detect here and there traces of the old class of half-citizens.

The second class, the *Heimatlos* in the narrower sense, long remained a burden on the Swiss conscience and public purse. Cantons and communes wriggled with inexhaustible resource to avoid receiving *Heimatlos*, for a whole generation. The number was gradually reduced, but at least one *Heimatlos* of this class, the last of the sturdy beggars, survived into the present century. As for the stateless gipsies, their type of freedom was offensive to the Swiss mind, and they were hunted down and were retained in prison or shown the border: gipsies are, however, not quite extinct; the survivors presumably possess a citizenship.

See also Articles 44 and 110. The Law is still partly in force owing to the lack of a *jus soli*, for example, in the case of foundlings. It is said that there still survive some exceptions to the rule that every Swiss citizen is also a citizen of a commune, in Neufchatel and elsewhere.

ARTICLE 69. The Confederation is authorized to make legislative provision for combating diseases which are infectious, very widespread, or especially dangerous to men or animals.

The Constitution of 1874 gave the Confederation the competence to take measures against human and animal epidemics. A Law based upon this competence providing for compulsory vaccination against certain human diseases was challenged to a referendum and rejected in 1882, but another Law of more restricted scope, still in force, was passed in 1886. The present constitutional text dates from an amendment accepted in a votation on 4 May 1913: the Federal authorities wished their powers extended to deal with scourges such as consumption and cretinism which are not strictly epidemics.

The wording of the present Article leaves it uncertain how far the Federal powers extend. The promoters of the revision probably had 'police' measures in mind—vaccination, isolation, water-supply, and milk inspection, &c. But the wording goes farther than this. Does it empower the Confederation to take general social-improvement measures such as milk in schools, holiday camps for children, and so on? The Confederation has gone far in that direction under this Article (e.g. in the laws on tuberculosis) and has also used it as providing a competence to carry out its international obligations in the prevention of the drug traffic (Law on Narcotics of 1924), though one can hardly call opium an infectious or a very widespread disease. Article 31 *bis*, Welfare, probably provides a more plausible competence for the future.

ARTICLE 69 *bis*. The Confederation may legislate upon:
(a) trade in food products;
(b) trade in household goods, &c., in so far as these could endanger life or health.

These Laws are to be executed by the Cantons under the supervision and with the financial support of the Confederation.

The Confederation is responsible for the control of imports at the national frontier.

Accepted in the votation of 11 July 1897 at the same time as an extension of Article 24, Torrents. The division of competences is typical, and, as it were, constitutionally correct.

ARTICLE 69 *ter*. The Confederation is authorized to legislate upon entry, exit, temporary residence, and settlement of foreigners.

Decisions upon permits for temporary residence and settlement are to be made by the Cantons, acting in accordance with Federal law. Nevertheless, the Confederation may make the final decision on the following matters:

(*a*) Cantonal permits for lengthy residence, and permits of 'tolerance'.
(*b*) Violation of treaties of settlement.
(*c*) Expulsions from Cantons which entail expulsion from the Confederation.
(*d*) Refusal of asylum.

Accepted in the votation of 25 Oct. 1925 by a large majority: a typical example of what is called in the note to Article 24 *bis* 'the new patriotism'. The Law of 1931 on Temporary Residence and Settlement of Foreigners now gives effect to this Article. Articles 2 and 25 of the Law delegate important powers of subordinate legislation to the Federal Executive, which has made use of them.

The logical position of the amendment is after Article 70.

ARTICLE 70. The Confederation may expel from Switzerland foreigners who endanger her internal or external security.

This places foreigners not protected by a treaty of settlement, including political refugees, under the free discretion of the Federal Executive. A foreigner cannot appeal against extradition to a court of law on the grounds that his presence does not endanger security. The use the Federal Council made of this power during the recent war has aroused certain criticism. The ordinary permits of tolerance are issued by the Cantonal police, see Article 69 *ter*. The police in such matters, and indeed in general, seem to exercise a freer discretion than in Great Britain.

SECOND SECTION

FEDERAL AUTHORITIES

I. FEDERAL ASSEMBLY

ARTICLE 71. Without prejudice to the rights of the people and Cantons (Articles 89 and 121) the supreme power in the Confederation is exercised by the Federal Assembly, which is composed of two sections, that is to say:
  A. National Council;
  B. Council of States.

This Article contains the statements that the Assembly is the 'supreme power in the Confederation', and that it is composed of two Chambers.

The expression 'the supreme power' can, on the face of it, hardly mean a power supreme against the constitutional rights of the people or the sovereignty of the Cantons—the wording of the Article reserves only the *political* rights of challenge and amendment—for the Article would then virtually constitute an alternative Constitution in itself. On the other hand, the Assembly's practice of granting Full Powers in an emergency to the Federal Council suggests that there is a sense in which the Assembly can claim the powers it effectively delegates. And the rule 'Federal law breaks Cantonal law' and the express constitutional freedom of the Assembly from judicial control (Article 113) do make the Assembly by virtue of the Constitution the supreme power within the territorial limits of the Confederation. And if Article 85, ss. 6, 7, 8, and 9 are read with Article 2, a case can be made out for the constitutional supremacy of the Assembly against the people and Cantons, though it is generally agreed that this interpretation is so dangerous that the whole line of thought must be discarded.

If we take the expression 'the Confederation' in its other sense of meaning 'the central government' and therefore 'the supreme power' as meaning the supreme power as against the Federal Council, then we fall into other difficulties. In the first place, Articles 95 and 102 grant power in almost as large a measure to the Federal Council. And in the second place it is precisely a characteristic of the Swiss Constitution that it establishes a separation of powers and that therefore neither the Legislature nor the Executive is supreme. Nor is the Assembly in practice the more powerful of the two bodies.

'Article 121', i.e. the present Article 123.

Article 92 makes the Chambers separate and Article 85 provides the same competences for each. Neither Chamber has supremacy over the other: the supreme power resides in the process of passing an *arrêté* rather than in a definite body of people.

A. NATIONAL COUNCIL

ARTICLE 72. The National Council is composed of the delegates of the Swiss people. One member is elected for every 24,000 of the total population. A fraction of this number greater than 12,000 is counted as 24,000.

Each Canton, and—in the divided Cantons—each half-Canton, elects at least one delegate.

The figures in this Article have been altered twice to keep pace with the growing population (in 1931 and 1950). It is not one member per 24,000 voters, but per 24,000 inhabitants in each Canton—man, woman, child, foreigner. The inclusion of foreigners weights the representation in favour of certain Cantons, particularly the picturesque Cantons and Vaud and Geneva. Swiss nationality being expensive and reluctantly granted there are, as a consequence, many semi-permanent 'foreigners', whose presence increases the value of the vote of Swiss citizens in the same Canton.

Two hundred is the traditional number of members in several Cantonal Great Councils. It is likely that the number of National Councillors will remain around that number, for which the space and the furnishing of the Assembly building is, by Swiss ideas, suited.[1]

ARTICLE 73. Elections for the National Council are direct. They follow the principle of proportionality, each Canton or half-Canton forming one electoral district.

Federal legislation shall make detailed provision for the application of this principle.

The text of the present Article dates from 13 Oct. 1918. Before 1919 elections were by single-member constituencies, with a second election if an absolute majority was not obtained at the first. This procedure followed from the Federal Law of 1872 (parts of which are still in force) as amended in 1900. The wording of the Constitution before 1918 tacitly permitted the introduction of Proportional Representation: the amended version commands it.

Initiatives in favour of P.R. were rejected in votations in 1900 and 1910. The votation of 1910 is unique in that the popular majority rejected the project while a majority of Cantons accepted it (the small Catholic Cantons being in favour, for in Switzerland the Liberals opposed P.R., while the Catholic-Conservatives and Socialists, who stood to gain, supported it). The only other time when the two majorities had not coincided was in 1866,

[1] In the Thirty-fourth Legislature (Dec. 1951–Dec. 1955) there were 196 National Councillors, divided on the basis of the revised Article and the Federal census of 1950 among the Cantons as follows: Zürich 32, Berne 33, Lucerne 9, Uri 1, Schwyz 3, Obwalden 1, Nidwalden 1, Glarus 2, Zug 2, Fribourg 7, Solothurn 7, Basle-Town 8, Basle-Country 4, Schaffhausen 2, Appenzell Outer Rhodes 2, Appenzell Inner Rhodes 1, St. Gall 13, Grisons 5, Aargau 13, Thurgau 6, Ticino 7, Vaud 16, Valais 7, Neufchatel 5, and Geneva 8. Total 196.

when a popular majority in favour of the decimal system was negatived by the Cantons.[1] A further initiative was handed in during 1913, but voting upon it was postponed because of the war. The temporary desire for a new world which follows a war carried the project to victory in 1918. The 'Proporz Law' (Law on the Election of the National Council, of 1919) was not challenged to a referendum. On 10 Aug. 1919 a temporary consequential amendment (fresh elections on the new basis for the National, and Federal, Councils) was accepted by a large majority and all Cantons—except *Outer Rhodes*. The new Councils met on the first Monday in Dec. 1919, and had been elected for three years. The present term is four years; see Article 76.

Proportional Representation. The system of election introduced by the Proporz Law is the 'list system' with '*panachage*' and 'accumulation'. The parties send printed lists of their candidates through the post to each voter, and an official list which is blank is also sent. On election day the voter can either (1) drop the complete printed list of the party of his choice into the ballot box, or (2) he can scratch out some names, and (3) if he likes he can substitute names from other lists for those he has scratched out (*panachage*), or (4) he can fill the official blank list with his own selection of candidates ('free list'). In 1947 only 3·2 per cent. composed a free list without voting for a party. Of those handing in a party list 67 per cent. adopted the first course, 21 per cent. the second, and 12 per cent. the third. The result is that the selection of individual successful candidates is made by a relatively small proportion of the voters.

The Law also permits 'accumulation', that is to say, two votes may be cast for the same candidate. The result is that a candidate whom his party, but not the voters, particularly wants to have elected can have his name printed twice on the printed list; the device has hitherto always been successful. Parties not at the moment employing it, however, are apt to stigmatize it as undemocratic, and it seems to be losing favour. And the Law also permits 'connected lists', a device whereby the overspill of votes from one party (not enough to secure the election of one more candidate) is transferred to an ally named beforehand. In some large Cantons, notably Berne, parties run two or three lists (in different districts) so as to obtain the advantages of local contacts and to secure a fair representation for regionally grouped minorities. The connected list system ensures that no votes are thereby wasted.

There are normally no by-elections. If a seat is vacated, the next candidate of that party in that constituency steps into the vacant place.

Because the Cantons form the constituencies, the size of the electoral colleges varies greatly. In the smallest Cantons there is only one seat to be filled, while two Cantons have over thirty. The largest Cantons have a proportionately large number of candidates—in Zurich in 1951, for example, there were 304 candidates for 32 seats, and this is about the number to be expected. In the smallest Cantons, on the other hand, the election is often a formality and uncontested.

[1] The majorities have several times not coincided in votations on Laws which have been challenged—where it does not matter since the Cantonal vote is not reckoned.

Results of Proportional Representation.[1] P.R. arouses little enthusiasm in the Swiss people today, and one has the impression that it is only the theoretical difficulty of justifying the majority system that keeps them to the list system. Its effects cannot be clearly disentangled from the other influences which have transformed Swiss public life since 1914. We may notice:

1. That the connexion between the National Councillor and the voter has become extremely tenuous. It is thought bad form for a candidate even to canvass for himself before an election (though sometimes 'an anonymous group of friends' feel impelled to canvass through the post on his behalf), and there are no speeches and no opportunities to heckle the candidate, for he need never set eyes on the voters. And after election he is not worried by constituents, for he represents his party rather than anyone in particular. In the larger Cantons the contact between voter and National Councillor is exhausted by the act of dropping a printed party-list into the ballot box.

2. Another aspect of the same thing is the position of the legislature. The system secures that the strength of parties shall vary hardly at all from one election to another, that no party shall ever be in a majority, and that therefore there is no party 'record'. Even if responsibility for a piece of legislation can occasionally be attributed, responsibility for policy can never be. The Federal Assembly has only a weak hold on the imagination of the people, and the effect of this is to shift the centre of gravity of the Constitution to a point on the civil-service side of the Federal Council. This reflects a universal tendency today, but Proportional Representation on the list system seems to have accelerated it.

3. The immediate result of the introduction of P.R. in 1919 was to create a 'Farmers' Party' (a rather conservative and protectionist group, not now exclusively agrarian), and to abolish the ancient majority of the Liberal parties. The Socialists also gained substantially at the same time. At present there is not a great deal of difference in the strengths of the main parties in the National Council—Liberals 52, Catholic Conservatives 44, Socialists 48, and Farmers 21; other parties 28 (1947–51).[2]

4. The ultimate result has been to shift the parliamentary system from one with a (more or less) party Federal Council and a party majority in the legislative Councils, to one with a coalition Federal Council facing no loyal opposition in a multi-party Assembly. It should be added, however, that the Confederation has never known the two-party system where government alternates with opposition.

ARTICLE 74. Every Swiss aged twenty or more, and not otherwise disqualified for active citizenship by the legislation of the

[1] For statistical analysis of the results of P.R. elections, see the booklets called *Nationalratswahlen — Élections au Conseil national*, published by the Bureau fédéral de statistique, usually about two years after the election concerned. The 1947 election is analysed in the booklet (22e Fascicule, *Contributions à la statistique suisse*) published in 1949. The text is in both German and French.

[2] The figures for 1951–5 are 51, 48, 49, 23, and 25, respectively. There are 5 Communists, as against 7 in the previous Parliament.

Canton where he has his place of residence, has the right to vote at elections and votations.

Federal legislation may regulate in a uniform manner the exercise of this right.

That is to say, in *Federal* elections and votations. The Cantons may have a more generous franchise for Cantonal matters, and could probably even admit women to political rights.

The following categories are excluded from the right to vote:
1. All women. This appears nowhere in the Constitution.
2. Young men under 20, even if they already have a vote in Cantonal matters (as in Schwyz and Zug). Twenty is a younger age in Switzerland than appears at first sight, since Swiss education in general starts and ends a year or two later than in Great Britain. At 20 a young man will only just have entered his university.
3. Those who have been deprived of their civil rights by the Courts or as a consequence of a criminal sentence or, in some Cantons in certain cases, as a result of bankruptcy.
4. Those otherwise deprived of their political rights by the legislation of the Canton where they have their political domicile. In some Cantons paupers, those under tutelage, and those under sentence of exclusion from inns as drunkards, &c., are deprived of political rights.

The Cantons are also free to make voting compulsory, and some of them do, with different degrees of sanction (in particular, Schaffhausen, Inner Rhodes, St. Gall, Aargau, Thurgau, Ticino).

The right includes the right not only to vote for the National Council but also to take part in referendums in the Confederation as well as in the Cantons and communes—and eligibility to the National Council also depends upon it, and hence to the Federal Council and Tribunal. It is a 'constitutional right of the citizen' in the sense of Article 113, that is to say, there is an Appeal in Public Law to the Federal Tribunal (or, in some cases, to the Federal Council) against deprivation of it.

ARTICLE 75. Every lay Swiss citizen possessing the right to vote is qualified to be elected as a member of the National Council.

This means that only those who have the right to vote (which in part depends on Cantonal law, see Articles 66 and 74 above) can be elected to the National Council. It also means that all clergy are excluded from the National Council.

The exclusion of clergy is a restriction of religious freedom, and like most Federal restrictions of religious freedom it bears more hardly on Catholics than on Protestants. The Cantonal Reformed Churches do not have priestly orders in the same sense that the Catholic Church has. The consequence is that whereas a Catholic priest has to relinquish his orders in due form before standing for election, a Protestant minister can be properly elected, and only after election as a National Councillor does he have to decide whether to lay down for the time being his pastoral office or whether to refuse his seat.

The office of Protestant minister in charge of a parish, in other words, is *incompatible* with that of National Councillor, whereas the status of a Catholic priest is a ground of *incapacity*. That a Catholic priest can at any time rid himself of his orders as far as the law of the land is concerned follows from Article 49, paragraph 2; the position in canon law is nearly irrelevant.

The exact status of a Catholic priest as regards the National Council has never been tested in practice. But in 1917 a minister of the Bernese Reformed Church in charge of a parish (Pastor Knellwolf) was actually elected to the National Council, and was required only to give up his parish before taking his seat (see 'Burckhardt', No. 595).

Article 96 extends the disabilities for the National Council to the Federal Council, Article 108 extends them to the Federal Tribunal. Federal law, however, does not extend them to the Council of States, and the restrictions there are a matter of Cantonal law; as far as Federal law is concerned, Catholic priests may be elected to the Council of States.

ARTICLE 76. **The National Council is elected for four years: at the end of that period there is a general election.**

Until 1931 the period for which the National Council was elected was three years. The alteration to four years carried with it that of Article 96 (Term of Office of Federal Council) and Article 105 (Chancellor).

Article 120, Total Revision, provides for a dissolution if necessary before the term of office has expired, for both Councils. Apart from this it is only at the end of the four-year period that there is an election for the National Council, and under the Swiss form of Proportional Representation by-elections can only normally occur in the very small Cantons. The Cantons make their own rules for election to the Council of States, determining both who shall be the electoral college (the people at large, or the Great Council, &c.) and also the term of office, which varies from one to four years—the current situation in the various Cantons is given in the *Annuaire statistique de la Suisse*.

Business is carried over from one session to another, and even from one legislature to another.

The present National Council met for the first time in December 1951.

ARTICLE 77. **Members of the Council of States, or members of the Federal Council or the officials elected by it, may not at the same time be members of the National Council.**

Distinguish between grounds of incapacity and of incompatibility. A person lawfully excluded from the right of voting by his Canton of residence would be *incapable* of election to the National Council. A member of the Federal Council, on the other hand, if elected to the National Council would merely have to decide which of the two offices he preferred: the offices would be *incompatible*.

The expression 'officials elected by the Federal Council' includes even the humblest Federal civil servants. The National Council itself decides upon the eligibility of those elected to it: it appoints a *commission* for this purpose and can, of course, ask the advice of the Federal Council on a point of law. There is no corresponding institution for the Council of States because it is for the Cantons concerned to decide who its representatives are, under Cantonal law.

ARTICLE 78. The National Council shall elect a president and a vice-president from among its members for each ordinary and extraordinary session.

The member who is president for one ordinary session cannot be president or vice-president for the next ordinary session.

No member can be president for two consecutive ordinary sessions.

When the votes are equally divided the president has the casting vote; in elections he votes in the same manner as other members.

The president of one of the Councils is the presiding officer or chairman of that Council. The president of the National Council presides also over the Assembly in joint session.

The word 'session' is interpreted as meaning the annual session provided for in Article 86. The president of the National Council (and of the Council of States) is thus elected for one year. The curious system of compulsory rotation of office is designed to guard against concentration of power in one man, and is used to prevent concentration also in any one party or Canton or linguistic group. The president does not in fact have extensive powers. In spite of this, obstruction is no problem, for there is a time-limit on speeches, business can be carried over from session to session, the Council is small and not very important in the scheme of things, and there are other institutions whereby a minority can delay a decision. The comparison must not be made with a sovereign House of Commons and its Speaker, but with a County Council and its chairman.

The 'elections' mentioned in paragraph 4 are for the *bureau* and for the president, and for the *commissions*. The *bureau* consists of the president, vice-president, and eight tellers (the latter elected for four years). The elections are secret, an urn—a real urn of bronzed tinplate—is taken round, and the ballot papers inserted by the members. Elections for a single officer are by absolute majority, for several together by Proportional Representation (*scrutin de liste*): except for the Finance Committee, the *commissions* are nominated by the *bureau* and sanctioned by the Council.

The president of the Council also presides over meetings of the heads of parliamentary parties to settle the order of business—a procedure in which the right of the private member to debate what interests him appears inadequately safeguarded.

ARTICLE 79. The members of the National Council are indemnified from Federal funds.

Compare Article 83, Council of States. National Councillors are paid 40 francs a day during the sessions when personally present, and they receive the same 'indemnity' for sittings of *commissions* outside the parliamentary session, and a travel allowance. This does not of itself provide a livelihood, and therefore a professional politician must hold another paid political post as well, either in private employ as secretary of his political party, or as secretary of a trade union or pressure-group, or in public employ as an Executive Councillor (Regierungsrat) of a Canton or city. Swiss people often say that politicians in Britain are professional politicians, whereas in Switzerland they are ordinary citizens who serve their country part-time, but this judgement depends on an unduly restrictive definition of 'professional politician'. The security of tenure of a deputy under Proportional Representation makes the lot of the whole-time politician a pleasant one.

B. COUNCIL OF STATES

ARTICLE 80. The Council of States consists of forty-four deputies from the Cantons. Each Canton appoints two deputies: in divided Cantons each half-State elects one deputy.

That is to say, the Cantons determine the franchise, method of election, and duration of office of their deputies to the Council of States, subject to Federal law—e.g. Article 120, Dissolution of both Councils—which will also control any irrationality or arbitrariness of practice.

Most Cantons prescribe the same term of office for Councillors of States as for National Councillors, and the same electorate. The Landsgemeinde Cantons,[1] except Outer Rhodes, elect Councillors of States in the Landsgemeinde; and Berne, Fribourg, St. Gall, and Neufchâtel still elect Councillors of States in the Great Council—the Cantonal legislature. The usual practice is to continue a Councillor of States in office until he retires, but this is by no means invariable.

There is no *Federal* stipulation that the Cantons may not send members of their Executive Councils to the Council of States, and in fact this is frequently done. The Cantons, however, are free to declare the two offices 'incompatible'.

Localism. One of the fundamental facts in Swiss politics is that the two minority interests—the Catholic and the non-German-speaking areas—have a permanent majority in the Council of States if they vote together. Both these minorities have a vested interest in localism. Twenty-three out of forty-four votes in the Council are commanded by French- and Italian-speaking Cantons and the old Sonderbund,[2] together with the Catholic

[1] Both Unterwaldens, Glarus, and both Appenzells.
[2] The Sonderbund was composed of Lucerne, Uri, Schwyz, Unterwalden, Zug, Valais, and Fribourg. Vaud, Neufchâtel, and Geneva are entirely French- and the Ticino entirely Italian-speaking. Valais and Fribourg (both Catholic) have a French-speaking majority.

half-Canton of Appenzell Inner Rhodes. The organization of the parliamentary parties, however, to some extent cuts across the German–Romance dividing line and the division into two Councils. Decisions are taken by the members of the party concerned in both Councils voting together without distinction of which Council they belong to. This is one of the facts on which Swiss political arithmetic is based. It may be added that the Federal Councillors belonging to the party concerned will also normally attend meetings of the parliamentary party. The parties are, on the other hand, only completely 'monolithic' on the Cantonal level—the degree of cohesion on the Federal level varies—and this again must slightly complicate political calculations.[1]

ARTICLE 81. Members of the National Council or of the Federal Council may not at the same time be members of the Council of States.

This is a ground of incompatibility, not of incapacity: see note to Article 77. Article 108 extends it to the Federal Tribunal, Article 12 to those in possession of foreign decorations. Beyond this, the determination of what classes of persons are eligible and ineligible to the Council of States is left to the Cantons concerned. In particular, Cantons are free to exclude Federal officials, Cantonal officials, and residents in other Cantons.

ARTICLE 82. The Council of States shall elect a president and a vice-president from among its members for each ordinary or extraordinary session.

The president or vice-president may not be chosen from the deputies of the same Canton whose representative was president during the ordinary session immediately preceding.

Deputies of the same Canton may not hold the office of vice-president during two consecutive ordinary sessions.

When the votes are equally divided the president has the casting vote; in elections he votes in the same manner as other members.

See note to Article 78 (President of the National Council). The effect of this Article is that the office circulates among Cantons. The position of the half-Cantons is not clear.

ARTICLE 83. The members of the Council of States are indemnified by the Cantons.

Unlike National Councillors, Article 79. Like the Cantonal freedom to determine the tenure and mode of election of their representatives in the

---

[1] See F. Lachenal, *Le Parti politique*, cited on page 104.

Council of States, the principle involved is that of Cantonal sovereignty. For this reason the above Article, and Article 80, are important for the political theory of federalism.

Councillors of States serving on *commissions* outside the legislative session are paid by the Confederation (Law of 6 Oct. 1923).

C. POWERS OF THE FEDERAL ASSEMBLY

ARTICLE 84. The National Council and the Council of States shall handle all business which the present Constitution places within the competence of the Confederation, and which is not allotted to another Federal authority.

The restriction of the Federal Assembly to those matters within the competence of the Confederation which are not allotted to another authority distinguishes the Assembly from a sovereign parliament in two respects—its position against the Cantons, and its position against the executive. The Cantonal parliaments are restricted, *mutatis mutandis*, in the same way, and the Federal Tribunal will ensure the autonomy of the communes against the Cantonal central authority, and the autonomy of the Cantonal legislature, executive, and judiciary against each other.

This Article appears to contain no rule of law. It is not in itself a restriction of the powers of the Assembly—the separation of powers follows from the Constitution as a whole and not particularly from this Article—and it is probable that the allotment of residual competences to the Assembly is not to be deduced from it.

ARTICLE 85. The following are the principal subjects within the competence of the two Councils:

1. Laws on the organization and method of election of the Federal authorities.

2. Laws and *arrêtés* on those matters which the Constitution places within the competence of the Confederation.

3. Salaries and allowances of members of the Federal authorities and the Federal Chancellery: the creation of permanent offices under the Confederation and the determination of their rates of pay.

4. Election of the Federal Council, the Federal Tribunal, and the Chancellor, and of the General-in-Chief of the Federal army.

Federal legislation may confer upon the Assembly other powers of electing and of confirming elections.

5. Alliances and treaties with foreign States, and the sanctioning of the treaties which the Cantons make with each other or with foreign countries. A Cantonal treaty of this type, however,

is only to be brought before the Federal Assembly if the Federal Council, or another Canton, raises objection to it.

6. Measures for the external security of Switzerland, and for the maintenance of her independence and neutrality; declaration of war and conclusion of peace.

7. Guarantee of the Constitutions and territory of the Cantons; intervention consequent upon that guarantee; measures for internal safety and preservation of peace and order; amnesty, and pardon.

8. Measures calculated to secure the observance of the Federal Constitution and the guarantee of Cantonal Constitutions and the fulfilment of Federal obligations.

9. The disposing of the Federal army.

10. The casting of the annual estimates and the approval of the public accounts, and *arrêtés* authorizing loans.

11. The high supervision of Federal administration and justice.

12. Appeals against decisions of the Federal Council in cases of administrative law (Article 113).

13. Conflicts of competence between Federal authorities.

14. Revision of the Federal Constitution.

Bicameralism. Both Councils[1] have the same competences. Laws have to pass both Councils in turn, and therefore the Councils must agree between themselves which shall have 'priority' in any particular business. Annual business, such as the budget, goes one year to one Council first, the next year to the other Council first. Formally, both are equal. In practice the National Council is probably ultimately the more powerful, while the individual Councillor of States is undoubtedly more respected and influential.

The Catalogue of Competences. This list raises several problems:

i. What is the relationship of this list to Article 84? Article 84 allots *subjects* as a whole to the Assembly, whereas section 2 of this Article allots the legislative *stage* of all Federal subjects to the Assembly, with the implication that the executive *stage* of all subjects belongs to the Executive. There is a vertical division and a horizontal division, and the Constitution cannot make up its mind. It is curious in this connexion to note that the original idea, and to a very large extent the present practice, of leaving legislation as a whole (on subject-matters where the Confederation is competent) to the Confederation and *execution thereof to the Cantons*, is nowhere expressly stated in the constitutional document.[2] The principle does not seem to

[1] The Cantonal legislatures are all unicameral: they have a curious procedure (perhaps derived from a misunderstanding of British terminology) of debating laws twice over, so that there is a sort of procedural bicameralism.

[2] That is, in general terms. For a particular example see the new Article 32.

have presented itself in those terms to the constituent: he took it for granted.

ii. Is the list a mere division of competences already granted in Part I of the Constitution between the Legislature on the one hand and the Executive on the other, or can new competences for the Confederation as against the Cantons be grounded upon this Article and upon Article 102?

iii. What is to be understood by the word 'principal' at the head of the list? Are there more not mentioned here? The same word (if we follow the French text) is used in Article 102, so it cannot be an attempt to give residual competences to the Assembly.

These problems are to be accounted for historically. The Confederation in the years before 1848 was not a sovereign State in the modern sense: it was a very special sort of alliance between twenty-five cantons which were themselves in many real senses sovereign. The Liberals, having captured the government of the most important Cantons, wished to give an outward shape to their sense of Swiss nationhood by regenerating the Old Confederation. They did not want to create a new republic, they wished to regenerate an old one by making its central power effective. They wanted to reform the old Diet.

Part I of the Constitution accordingly gives a list of increases in the competences of the old Diet, and gives a more precise form to the procedures of Guarantee and Intervention. When they come to Part II the constituent fathers are faced with the problem of dividing these competences among the appropriate authorities, because they have now decided to establish a régime where the powers are separated—unlike the Diet in this respect. But here the difficulty arises. For by the time Part II is reached it is apparent that something new has been created, the Swiss Republic, different in kind from the Old Confederation. For a state, a republic, has a nature of its own, and is something more than an inventory of competences. The new central power inherits more than an army, a power to mint coin, to issue postage stamps, to appoint ambassadors: it inherits majesty. There is therefore more to be divided among the claimants—Legislature, Executive, and Judiciary—than was mentioned in the list of Part I. The constituent fathers were faced with a difficulty, and wisely refused to meet it. The Constitution after all is not the work of a German professor but of practical politicians and the romantic imagination—and none the worse for that.

SECTION 1. This section has three possible meanings:

i. As a rule of law, that the organization and method of electing the Federal authorities are to be provided for by a 'Law' rather than by any other type of legal instrument. This rule would be an important one under the 1874 Constitution, since Laws in the strict sense cannot be withdrawn from the referendum challenge whereas Federal Arrêtés can be. If this interpretation is followed the problem also arises of what is to be understood by the term 'authorities': in the narrowest sense it includes only the Assembly, the Federal Council, the Federal Tribunal, and perhaps the Chancellor. Does it here include the Federal Civil Service, or the Federal Insurance Court? The practice of the Assembly is sometimes to use instruments subject to the referendum, and sometimes not.

ii. Or is it merely the institutional form of the principle that the Assembly is the supreme authority in the Confederation (Article 71)? Does this clause then exhaust that supremacy? Laws, it goes without saying, are to be issued by the Legislature. Why then mention this class of laws?

iii. The laws on the organization and election of the authorities form a defined category in present-day Swiss jurisprudence ('Staatsrecht'). There appears at first sight to be the possibility that the division between Staatsrecht and administrative law (Verwaltungsrecht) is the same as that between the Assembly and the Federal Council. But the categories do not really correspond: the separation of powers known to the founders of the Constitution was an earlier one derived from Montesquieu, Madison, and Locke.

For the *règlements* of the National Council and Council of States see note to Article 86.

SECTION 2. This seems to embody the opposite principle to Article 84. Under this section the legislative stage of all matters in the Federal competence belongs to the Assembly; under Article 84 the Assembly possesses the whole of all matters not allotted to another authority. The present section makes better sense and approximates more to the practice. It should be noted that the Federal Council passes *arrêtés* as well as the Assembly, both under the powers which the Assembly delegates to it and under powers conferred directly by the Constitution. These Arrêtés of the Federal Council exceed in bulk and number the *arrêtés* of the Assembly: they are never subject to referendum.

SECTION 3. For payment of the National Council, Federal Council, Chancellor, and Tribunal see Articles 79, 99, 105, and 107 respectively. The payment of the Federal authorities in the narrower sense is usually sanctioned by Laws (subject to the referendum), but in recent times this has not invariably been the case. As regards subordinate officials, the times are past when the people could challenge the appointment of a Secretary for Education (as in 1882) or increased diplomatic expenditure in Washington (1884). There is a Law of 1927 on the Status of Officials, but the rest, including the classification of officials in each department and what each class shall be paid, is left to Arrêtés of the Federal Council and to the annual budget (which are not challengeable to referendum).

SECTION 4. These elections are by the Assembly in joint session, under Article 92. Article 107 adds the Deputy Judges of the Federal Tribunal to the list, and Federal legislation has added the election of the Extraordinary Public Prosecutor and the Extraordinary Military Tribunal (neither of which elections has ever taken place, see note to Article 117) and of the Federal Insurance Tribunal. The Assembly also nominates the president and vice-president of the Confederation and of the Federal Tribunal.

This is the only mention in the Constitution of the peculiar office of 'General', discussed in the note to Article 18.

Election of the officers and committees of the Councils (and of the Assembly in joint session) is unaffected by this section.

SECTION 5. *Treaties.* Treaties between the Confederation and other countries are negotiated by the Federal Council: this follows from Article 102, ss. 8 and 9. The draft treaties are then submitted to the two Councils for approval or rejection, and the Councils pass an *arrêté* approving, as the case may be, the treaty, and giving the Federal Council the power to ratify it. The procedure, however, is remarkably unconstant. After 'approval' and before 'ratification'[1] may come the extra stage of the *arrêté* of approval being challenged to a referendum by 30,000 voters (Article 89). Alternatively the Assembly may delegate to the Federal Council power to negotiate and ratify a treaty as a blank cheque, or the Executive may already possess these powers as a part of the 'Full Powers' granted to it upon threat of war.

The Cantonal power of making 'treaties' among themselves and with foreign countries is mentioned in Articles 7, 9, and 10.

SECTION 6. It is not clear what is meant by this dangerously wide competence. It seems in practice that the measures necessary to safeguard neutrality make as great inroads on individual freedom as those to prepare for, and even to prosecute, war.

'Armed neutrality' while neighbours are at war has a certain constitutional status in Switzerland (for example, in Article 39, para. 6) and is usually referred to as 'war'. The Assembly declares neutrality rather as other nations declare war.

When the question arose of seeking admission to the League of Nations, a cautiously worded *arrêté* was submitted to the people and Cantons—as if a compulsory referendum was needed before engaging in a course which might conceivably lead to war. The double precaution of entering the League while expressly reserving neutrality, and of submitting the project to a constitutional referendum on the grounds that neutrality was being imperilled, was nearly, but not quite, insufficient to reassure the voters. The *arrêté* entering the League has never been repealed, but it is not now the practice to print it with the Constitution: it would seem to provide the appropriate constitutional basis for neutrality while preserving the Assembly's right to declare war. See also Article 8.

This and section 9 of Article 102 are the only references to neutrality in the Constitution.

Switzerland has not joined the United Nations.

Comment. Neutrality. During the War of 1914 Switzerland was divided in sympathy; the German-speaking population sympathized strongly with Germany—some even today sympathize in retrospect and teach their children to do so—while the French-speaking population sympathized strongly with France. Neutrality was therefore a condition of survival. The Second World War presented a different situation: the Allies were seen to be right and the fascist Powers wrong—and in a war between right and wrong Switzerland stood neutral. The victory of the Allies was then the condition of national survival. Furthermore, the position of Switzerland in 1939 must be distinguished from the position in 1940 and in 1944, for unlike pacifism (which Switzerland rejects) neutrality is not in itself a moral principle.

SECTION 7. *Guarantee.* See Articles 5 and 6, and 102, s. 3. The mention of territory makes it clear that the Constitution is also thinking of the 'material'

---

[1] This distinction between approval and ratification seems convenient and intelligible. Article 113, para. 3, however, uses *ratifier* for the approval of the Assembly, though Article 114 *bis* uses *approuver* in the same context.

guarantee in Article 5. The only way of guarding the territory of a Canton against force used by another Canton is 'Federal Intervention'.

Intervention. See Article 16. In an emergency the Federal Council would normally be the only authority in a position to order an Intervention; the sanction of the Assembly would have to be obtained later.

Amnesty and Pardon. It is not clear what the difference between these two is, and the question has some importance since Article 92 lays down that pardon shall be exercised by the Assembly in joint session, whereas amnesty is handled by the two Chambers separately. Not only may the party majorities be different in the one case from the other, but also when the matter is handled by the two Councils separately there is the additional chance that they may fail to agree on any decision at all, in which case the amnesty does not take place. There are two main possibilities: (i) that amnesty is a mass measure, and pardon an individual one; and (ii) that amnesty is in advance of sentence, and pardon subsequent to condemnation. By Article 394 of the Swiss Penal Code the cases where the Assembly (sc. in joint session) has the right of pardon are those tried by the Federal Assizes or the Federal Criminal Court, and Federal administrative-penal decisions. It is the last class which really comes in question, and most of the Appeals are against sentences for smuggling, &c. The Assembly appoints a joint committee (9 from one Council and 4 from the other) to consider the cases, and the committee in turn normally follows the recommendation of the Federal Council. The procedure is laid down in the *règlement* for the Assembly in joint session.

Appeals against sentences of military Courts go to the Federal Council only (unless a General has been elected), except for death sentences, which can always go on last appeal to the Assembly. From sentences of Cantonal Criminal Courts (the bulk of the criminal law) appeal for pardon is to the Cantonal authorities.

SECTION 8. *Federal Execution* (Bundesexekution). If a Canton deliberately omits to obey Federal law, then the Confederation is authorized to step in and itself make the legal provisions which the Canton should have made, and these provisions remain in force until superseded by the proper Cantonal legislation in accordance with Federal law. If the Canton goes farther and does not recognize the temporary Federal provisions, then the last sanction of Federal law is Federal Military Execution. This latter has never taken place. It is difficult to see in what circumstances a Canton could nowadays go so far without dissolving the whole fabric of law and order inside its territory (in which case it would be Federal Intervention—to restore law and order—rather than Federal Execution to enforce Federal law, which would be appropriate).

In this connexion, in addition to the normal types of Federal law (treaties, Laws, *arrêtés, ordonnances*, decisions of the Federal Tribunal, &c.), the occasional 'circular letters' (Kreisschreiben) of the Federal Council to the Cantonal governments should be noted: these also are binding upon the Cantons. The theoretical necessity for the concept of Federal Execution arises out of the consideration that the central government commands no army and no police of its own, for these forces are Cantonal.

SECTION 9. It is uncertain what this section means, since legislation on military matters is naturally within the Assembly's competence. Presumably a supreme right of deciding the highest questions of policy in war-time is meant. Compare Article 102, s. 12. Normally this right exhausts itself in the act of appointing the Federal Council's nominee as General when war threatens.

SECTION 10. *The Federal Budget.* The Federal Council submits annually to the Assembly its estimates ('budget') and the Federal accounts (Article 102, s. 14) which each Council debates in turn and eventually sanctions—the National Council and the Council of States having 'priority' in alternate years. Taxes are raised by separate legislation, and until recently were derived from so restricted a number of sources, chiefly customs duties, that a financial *policy* was scarcely possible for the central government. The 'budget' is not used to obtain an effective control over the Executive's administrative policy in the way in which financial procedure is used in other countries—though in the 1920's the Socialist party did use the military estimates as a vehicle of general criticism—for there is no respectable parliamentary opposition and it is considered that the appropriate place for such criticism as is made is not the budget but the debates on the Annual Report of the Federal Council.

The 'budget' does not impose new taxes and rarely undertakes new responsibilities; the main part of financial policy does not come under the budget. It is not used as a method of controlling the Executive. It is not a Law, for it neither supersedes law nor (except rarely) does it create it. What then does it do? The nearest British equivalent is a resolution of the House of Commons: it permits the Federal Council and the Federal civil service to undertake the expenditure, and limits the expenditure to the amount sanctioned. It is therefore best considered as a particular case of the right of high supervision (Articles 71 and 85 s. 11) of the Assembly over the Federal Executive. If the Executive disobeys, the only sanction seems to be the trial of the Federal Councillor concerned before the Federal Assizes (see Article 117, Responsibility).

There is little similarity to British supply and ways and means procedure.

Financial Control. Each Council nominates a Financial Committee to report upon the budget and the accounts, and the two committees each nominate three of their members to form a joint 'Finance Delegation' (Articles 24–27 of the Law on the Relations between the Councils), presided over by a member of the Council which has priority for that year. The Finance Delegation works in close connexion with the Audit Department, a branch of the civil service attached to the Department of Finance, which holds a running book-keeping and economy audit over the whole of the Federal administration. The Finance Delegation sees that the money is spent according to the intentions of the Assembly, and reports to both Finance Committees. Like the two Finance Committees it is assisted by an official of the Audit Department, and has power to send for papers. The report of the delegation is published in the *Feuille fédérale*, but it is short, rather perfunctory and formal, and seldom critical; no minutes of evidence and no details are published. The last sanction of the delegation and the committees is a recommendation by a Finance Committee to its Council not to approve the Federal accounts. The institution is not a lively one, and it works both ways—it is a control by the legislature over the executive, and it gives members of the legislature executive responsibilities and outlooks.

The procedure for debating the budget is the ordinary legislative procedure—Committee, 'Entering upon the business', and 'Article by Article'.

The text of the budget is of some administrative interest, though more secretive than British 'estimates', and is published annually as a separate book (not in the *Feuille fédérale*). The *règlement* of the Audit Department is printed in vol. vi of the *Recueil systématique*, those of the Finance Committees and the Delegation in the *Manuel des Chambres fédérales*. In 1950 the accounts for 1949, and the budget for 1951, were sanctioned.

There is no Federal finance referendum.

SECTION 11. The high supervision over the Federal administration by the Assembly was defined in a report of the Federal Council of 21 Aug. 1925 (Bundesblatt 1925, ii. 781 seq.; reprinted in 'Burckhardt', No. 624) as including 'the right to demand reports from the Federal Council, to criticize its administration, and to give it Instructions for the future. But against this the Federal Assembly cannot itself undertake an act of administration or repeal or vary decisions of the Federal Council . . . and the power of supervision includes no power of appealing to the Federal Assembly against the Federal Council'.

These limited powers are to be exercised by a multi-party bicameral Assembly. The high supervision over the Federal Tribunal very properly amounts to even less, and may normally be said to exhaust itself in the acts of electing the Judges of the Tribunal and of passing Laws on Judicial Organization.[1] The latter are the landmarks of modern Swiss constitutional history.

SECTION 12. The present Law on Judicial Organization (Article 132 of the Law) makes the class of cases that can go to the Federal Assembly on appeal from the Federal Council a small one. Such appeals appear to be extremely rare. This provision has thereby become one of those legal curiosities in which the Constitution abounds, neither a part of the living constitution nor quite dead.

SECTION 13. That is to say, conflicts between the Federal Council and the Federal Tribunal or Insurance Tribunal, or between the two latter. There is no procedure laid down for conflicts of competence to which the Federal Assembly itself is a party. Conflicts which arise over the question of jurisdiction in cases of administrative law are normally settled by an exchange of notes between the authorities (Article 96 of the Law on Judicial Organization) without coming before the Federal Assembly. If the dispute comes before the Assembly it is to be handled in joint session (Article 92 of the Constitution).

SECTION 14. See articles 118-23.

[1] See Article 21 of the Law on Judicial Organization of 1943. The Tribunal submits annual reports to the Assembly, chiefly composed of statistics, which are interesting as far as they go.

ARTICLE 86. Both Councils meet once a year in ordinary session on the day fixed by the Standing Orders.

For extraordinary sessions they may be called together by the Federal Council or on demand of a quarter of the members of the National Council, or of five Cantons.

The first paragraph provides that the Assembly is to meet *at least* once a year for an 'ordinary' session: the practice is to count all the sittings of the Assembly in one year as a single session adjourned.

This is the only passage in the Constitution which can be interpreted as giving the Councils a power to give themselves standing orders (*règlements*); the legal force of the *règlement* of each Council and of the two Councils in joint session is therefore in doubt, and the Councils make a rather timid use of the power they have arrogated to regulate their own procedure. Curiously enough the date of assembling for the ordinary session is not in fact fixed by the *règlement* but by Law, the Law on the Relations between the Councils of 9 Oct. 1902 (printed on pp. 153 seq. of this volume), which now fixes the first Monday in December as the start of the first part of the ordinary session, and the first Monday in June as the start of the second part. The Councils also regularly hold ordinary sittings in March and September.

SECOND PARAGRAPH. An extraordinary session is one not foreseen by the Councils when they adjourned. The Councils have often been called together by the Federal Council for such a session. They have not ever been convened on demand of five Cantons, but they were convened 'on demand of a quarter of the members of the National Council' once, in 1891.

It will be noticed that it is the Cantons which possess this right, not the Council of States. This is consistent with the principle of Article 91, Voting without Instructions. The Cantons themselves determine the procedure to be followed—for example, that the Resolution of the Cantonal Great Council be taken as the demand of the Canton.

ARTICLE 87. A Council may only proceed to business when an absolute majority of members is present.

Effect is given to this provision by Article 32 of the *règlement* of the National Council, and Article 6 of that of the Council of States. The former lays down that the Council shall only 'deliberate' when there is a majority of the total number of members present in the room (and imposes upon the president of the Council the duty of ensuring this, if necessary by roll-call); the latter that the presence of 23 (out of 44) members is necessary for valid decisions.

The rule does not in fact secure the constant presence in the room of more than about one-third of the National Council, unless there is something interesting on, or a Federal Councillor speaking. Neither Council, however, at any time presents the depressing spectacle of the House of Commons on the daily adjournment debate.[1] This is partly because the Council chamber

---

[1] Where five pairs of feet and one head are all the visitor can see.

is a comfortable place for the members to read their papers, chat, and write their letters in, and where there is a sort of privacy—for only members can enter.

The question has been raised (in a theoretical way) whether the Federal Tribunal is bound to enforce a final decision on a matter which concerns the public—for example, an act creating an offence—if the final or a main decision was taken by the Council without a proper majority of members being present. A more possible situation is that the Federal Council would refuse to promulgate such a law. The Article, however, does not give rise to a 'freedom-right' in the sense that the citizen has a right to be governed by Laws and *arrêtés* agreed to by the presence of a majority of Councillors; there is consequently no Appeal in Public Law to the Federal Tribunal for breach of it.

The Constitution only requires the 'presence' in the room, and this would normally be difficult to ascertain unless more than half actually voted.

ARTICLE 88. In the National Council and the Council of States decisions shall be taken by absolute majority of those voting.

The words 'an absolute majority' in Switzerland mean 'more than half', i.e. of those voting, of those present, of the whole Council, &c. The requirement of such a majority follows from the Swiss procedure of voting upon amendments. The procedure in Great Britain is to vote upon amendments before the main question, and to phrase all except one of the motions as amendments to the main question. Voting each time is therefore by Aye and No, and the order in which the questions are put is determined by their form and by certain logical rules. The Swiss rule is similar as regards the order of amendments, but different as regards the main question, for it permits of several—three, perhaps, or more—main questions. In such a case each main question is voted upon by count of hands successively, each deputy only being allowed to vote for one. If none has received an 'absolute majority' the motion which received the smallest number of votes is voted out, and a successive count of hands taken upon the remainder. This continues until one motion receives the 'absolute majority'. When there are only two main questions left, one of them is of course bound to obtain the 'absolute majority' of the votes cast. The procedure as applied to the Councils is described in the *règlement* of the National Council (Articles 79–87) and of the Council of States (Articles 63–71). The clumsy full procedure is not often required to be used.

It will be noticed that the Swiss procedure is suited to a multi-party Assembly, and might tend to produce a multitude of parties (since each shade of opinion can formulate its own main question), whereas the British procedure is that of a government and opposition, and might tend to produce a two-party system. It is possible that there might be a distant connexion between the British method of voting, traditionally by a shout of Aye or No, and the British amendment procedure—and between the method of counting hands[1] (traditional in Switzerland, and even used in the Landsgemeinde) and the procedure of 'several main questions'. The requirement of an 'absolute majority' follows from the 'several main questions' procedure, and only has a meaning in connexion with it. See also Articles 87, 89 *bis*, 92, 100, and 120–3 for similar trains of thought. Where a majority of all members is required, as for the 'urgency clause' in Article 89 *bis*, the president of the Council votes.

ARTICLE 89. Federal Laws and Federal Arrêtés require the agreement of both Councils.

Federal Laws and universally binding Federal Arrêtés shall be submitted to the people for acceptance or rejection on demand of 30,000 Swiss citizens entitled to vote, or of eight Cantons.

Treaties with foreign powers concluded for an undetermined period or for more than fifteen years shall also be submitted to the people for acceptance or rejection on demand of 30,000 Swiss citizens entitled to vote, or of eight Cantons.

PARAGRAPH 1. Taken together with Article 92, this establishes the two-Chamber system for Laws and *arrêtés*, and hence for constitutional revision (Articles 119 and 121). The Federal Council has no right of veto.

There used to be a distinction between Laws and Federal Arrêtés, but since 1874 it has disappeared. Federal Arrêtés have the procedural advantage over Laws that they can be declared 'urgent' or 'not universally binding', and thus be removed from the possibility of challenge by the people. All Laws in the strict sense (Gesetze, *lois*) are subject to the referendum challenge. Laws possess a greater dignity than Federal Arrêtés, and are rather rare—the passage of a new Law is an important event—and on the whole it is still usual to amend Laws by other Laws, and *arrêtés* by *arrêtés*, though it is not necessary to do this.

PARAGRAPH 2. The words inelegantly translated 'universally binding' (allgemein verbindlich, *de portée générale*) have given rise to much dispute, since the French text means something different from the German: the Italian text (*di carattere obbligatorio generale*) is again different, and probably the best one here. The legislative Councils themselves determine whether an *arrêté* is to be furnished with the 'referendum clause', and thus submitted to the possibility of challenge, or whether nothing is to be said, or whether it is to be expressly withdrawn by being labelled 'urgent' or 'not universally binding'. The mere fact of laying a financial burden on the people does not of itself make the *arrêté* '*de portée générale*', for there is no financial referendum in Federal matters: an *arrêté*, for example, creating the Swiss equivalent of the British Council was ruled 'not universally binding'. The bulk of legislation escapes the referendum. All Federal Council Arrêtés escape it, and the greater part of Federal Arrêtés escape it also. Between 1874 and 1950, 620 legislative acts have been liable or subjected to referendum—the figure

---

[1] That is to say, Aye only.

includes constitutional amendments subject to the compulsory referendum, and all acts and treaties liable to the facultative referendum, including in both cases those accepted and rejected. There have been 149 votations in the same period, of which considerably more than half were compulsory referendums. Any statistical data, however, should be used with care, since there were a particularly large number of challengeable acts during the first ten years of the Constitution, and many of these were extremely controversial. In time the Assembly developed a technique of getting legislation passed unchallenged—making the *arrêtés* either too important or too trivial to challenge. After the First Great War the Assembly began to evade the challenge in other, and more dubious, ways, and the consistent misuse of the urgency clause dates from that time. During the same period after 1918 the electorate came of age, and it is not a fair criticism of the institution at the present day to quote cases that happened before 1914.

Procedure. The referendum delay is 90 days after publication of the Law or *arrêté* in the *Feuille fédérale* (Law of 1874 on Votations). The signatures are now often collected by sending reply-paid cards through the post to voters, who merely need to sign and drop the card into a letter-box. The figures occasionally indicate that people who signed in favour of a votation have voted in favour of the Law which was challenged.

The procedure of eight Cantons has never been used. Probably 'Cantons' includes 'half-Cantons', but this is not certain.

Results of the Facultative Referendum. The direct or negative effect of the challenge on the statute book is the most obvious, but certainly not the most important, effect of the institution. The direct negative effect is bound to be conservative, for it is an institution which gives the voters a chance to prevent the *status quo* being altered. In particular it gives opportunity to localism and individualism against central officials and the Welfare State. The indirect effect is more complex and is still unfolding itself:

1. Its effect on the shift of the centre of gravity from local to central is paradoxically rather to accelerate this movement to the centre. Any burden upon the Cantons, especially a financial burden, is avoided in order to escape a challenge from the localists. But in constitutional matters it is more blessed to give money than to receive it; the power follows the burdens. And at the same time, to propitiate Cantonal and other interests, subsidies are given, and given by the central government, which is thereby forced to enlarge its sources of income and its influence.

2. Its effect on the movement of the centre of gravity from Legislative to Executive is to accelerate this process also. In the first place, the Assembly prefers to delegate legislative powers to the Federal Council rather than to legislate itself, for less surface is thereby exposed to criticism: laws are drafted to avoid referendums. And secondly, the Arrêtés of the Federal Council not being exposed to challenge like those of the Assembly, in times of emergency the Federal Council has to do all the legislating.

3. A premium is set upon illegality, since the declaring 'urgent' or 'not universally binding' of *arrêtés* ensures that they will not be challenged.

4. It erodes responsibility—the weak point of the Swiss system—by making the people, an anonymous shifting abstraction, responsible.

5. The high cost per signature of securing the petition of 30,000 for a challenge confines its use to corporate bodies—political parties, trade unions, pressure groups, &c.—and increases their already strong influence on policies. The vitality and influence of these non-public-law bodies appears to a foreigner the most hopeful sign in Swiss democracy, but the Swiss themselves are unanimous in deploring it; perhaps this is because they have deprived themselves of the counterweight of strong political parties divided on issues of public policy.

6. The value of the referendum lies in the fact that it is the 'people' who decide. It is this which gives the institution an educational quality unparalleled by any other political device, and which gives it a moral value. It is this moral value which is first and last the referendum's main justification. The stability of Swiss institutions and the almost exaggerated self-respect of the Swiss people owe much to the noble and not unsuccessful experiment of the legislative challenge. But a House of Lords which acted as irresponsibly as the Swiss people did in the years before 1914 would not deserve to last six months.

PARAGRAPH 3. *Procedure for Challenging Treaties*. The Gotthard Treaty of 1909 made Swiss chauvinists discontented, and a constitutional initiative extending the challenge procedure to treaties was completed in due form. It had not been voted upon by the outbreak of war, and was postponed, but when after the war the votation came the project was accepted (30 Jan. 1921) by a large majority. The procedure has only been used once—though twenty-two treaties have been challengeable—on 18 Feb. 1923, when a 'convention' with France was challenged and rejected (by a majority larger than that which had recently accepted the amendment making challenge possible). The Convention regulated—or rather abolished—the *zones franches* (servitudes of various origins and considerable antiquity upon French territory in favour of Switzerland) and in particular the customs-free French districts around Geneva. The Treaty of Versailles had admitted the competence of the two countries to end this survival, and perhaps went farther. Prolonged bickering followed the Swiss rejection, but today the *zones franches* around Geneva are again customs-free. It is by no means certain that the Swiss people were not right, or at least astute, in being more intransigent than their government. Since then no treaties have been challenged. It is an easy provision to evade and make of no effect.

The German text of the Article reads 'for an unlimited duration', the French 'for an indeterminate duration'. Where the duration is limited, for example, until certain notice is given, but is indeterminate, it is not certain which is meant. The interpretation least favourable to the people is in practice chosen. It is strictly speaking the Federal Arrêté sanctioning the treaty which is the text challengeable. The Law foreseen in Article 90 for Federal votations applies also to the treaty challenge, though this is nowhere stipulated.

The League of Nations amendment was submitted to the people and Cantons as a constitutional amendment, and provided that amendments of it should also be submitted to this double referendum. Nevertheless, by a questionable interpretation of the present Article the alterations to the

Covenant were passed as if they were treaties subject only to the single, facultative referendum: none were in fact challenged.

The former paragraph 3 of this Article was replaced by Article 89 *bis* on 11 Sept. 1949.

ARTICLE 89 *bis*. Universally binding Federal Arrêtés which cannot be delayed may be put into immediate operation if the majority of the total number of members in each Council so resolve: the time for which they are to be in force should be limited.

When a votation is demanded by 30,000 voters or eight Cantons, Federal Arrêtés enacted under the urgency procedure shall go out of force one year from the date on which they were passed by the Federal Assembly, unless they are sanctioned by the people before the end of that period. They cannot be re-enacted.

Federal Arrêtés enacted under the urgency procedure which infringe the Constitution must be sanctioned by the people and Cantons during the year following their adoption by the Federal Assembly. If they are not so sanctioned then they go out of force at the end of this period, and cannot be re-enacted.

This so-called 'Initiative for the Return to Direct Democracy' was accepted on 11 Sept. 1949, and is directed against the practice of withdrawing Federal Arrêtés from the referendum by declaring them 'urgent'. The Assembly recommended the rejection of the initiative, and refrained from submitting a counter-project, as it relied upon the confusion of thought and the bad drafting of the initiative to secure its defeat.

The immediate effect of the Article has been to add to the end of the Constitution a shifting group of 'Temporary Articles'. The ultimate effect will probably either be to extend the power of the Executive by weakening that of the Legislature (the usual result of extensions of popular rights) or to force the Assembly to choose between evasion and frank illegality. It is, however, too soon to judge the results. The impulse to pass the Article is a refreshing sign of the vitality of the spirit of liberty in Switzerland.

The ingenuous mention of '*arrêtés* infringing the Constitution' (in the French text) presumably does not open up a new competence to the Assembly to pass these provided it submits them within a year to a votation. It is likely that the defects of the drafting of this Article will trouble the Swiss people for a longer time than the impulse of passing it will refresh them.

ARTICLE 90. Federal Legislation shall determine the forms to be followed and the delays to be observed for popular votations.

The Federal Law on Votation upon Federal Laws and Arrêtés (Referendumsgesetz) of 1874 gives effect to this Article. It provides that the petition of 30,000 shall be completed within 90 days of the publication of the law concerned in the *Feuille fédérale*.

Other important Laws on this subject are the Law on Federal Elections and Votations (Wahlgesetz) of 1872, the Law on the Procedure for Initiatives and Votations of 1892 (which underwent important modifications in 1950), and the Law on Elections for the National Council (Proporzgesetz) of 1919. All these Laws may be found in vol. i of the *Recueil systématique*.

The Cantons are charged with the execution of the Federal legislation.

ARTICLE 91. **Members of both Councils shall vote without 'instructions'.**

The Diet (Tagsatzung) of the Old Confederation was composed of delegates from the Cantons, and these delegates were bound by the instructions of the Cantons sending them. If a new subject came up they had to 'refer' it back (in most cases) to their Canton for its decision. The present Article abolishes that practice.

The programme which the Article implies is that members should vote from their consciences and not from instructions of their party or other private-law association,[1] and this principle is often, in the abstract, appealed to. There is a curiously universal opinion—by no means only held by the muddle-headed—that members should not represent anything in particular, but just sort of vaguely represent: what a majority composed by adding up the votes of such individuals would mean is unclear. It is perhaps an example of the distortion of thought which arises when the principles of politics and morality are taken, like biblical texts, from the wording of a constitutional document.

An important consequence in political theory of this Article is that members of the Council of States are not, constitutionally speaking, representatives of their Cantons; this diminishes the extent to which the federal principle is formally a part of the structure of the central government. Hence Article 86, Right to summon Parliament not vested in the Council of States but in the Cantons, and Article 93, Cantons' right of Initiative.

ARTICLE 92. **The two Councils sit apart. But for electing the officers mentioned in Article 85, section 4, for exercising the power of pardon, and for deciding conflicts of competence (Article 85, section 13), the Councils shall meet in joint session under the chairmanship of the President of the National Council, and take decisions by majority of members of both Councils voting.**

Although there is an elaborate procedure (described in the Law on the Relations between the Councils, Articles 5–7) for reconciling differences of

[1] For a discussion of the relationships of Swiss deputies with their political parties, see *Le parti politique. Sa fonction de droit public*, by F. Lachenal, Basle, 1944, especially ch. 9.

opinion (*divergences*) between the Councils, there is no procedure whereby an obstinate deadlock can be forced. If after exhausting the procedure of *divergences* neither Council gives way, then the whole project must be dropped, and if reintroduced must start again from the beginning (Article 7 of the Law). Where a decision is essential, therefore, the Constitution provides that the two Councils shall meet and vote together as one. The Assembly in joint session has its own *règlement*, but where this is insufficient it follows the *règlement* of the National Council. For pardons see the note to section 7 of Article 85. The debates on appeals for pardon against sentence of death are held in secret and not recorded.

The Law on Political and other Guarantees of 1934 (reproducing a provision of 1851) provides that when permission to take a legal action against members of the Federal Council or Tribunal is refused there is an appeal to the Assembly in joint session (see note to Article 117): this would appear to be unconstitutional in view of the wording of this Article.

ARTICLE 93. Each of the two Councils and each member of them has the right of initiative.

The Cantons may exercise the same right by correspondence.

The word 'initiative' is used here in two different senses:

1. The 'initiative' of each legislative Council. When the first Council has passed a project of a Law, &c., or motion, the project appears automatically upon the agenda of the other Council. This is what is called the Initiative of one Council before the other Council. If all goes well it is the penultimate stage in the parliamentary history of a law.

2. The initiative of this 'initiative'. In order to get a project adopted by the first of the Councils, it must be introduced into that Council. The right of introduction into both Councils is possessed by each Canton (and half-Canton), and every member of the Assembly may introduce into *his own* Council a project of a law or a motion upon a matter within the competence of the Assembly, and this must first be 'taken up' (*pris en considération*, erheblich erklaert) and then passed by that Council before being sent on to the next one. It is therefore only the *initiative of* an 'initiative of one Council before the other Council'. The present practice is that the project is always first sent to the Federal Council for report, which intercalates another stage between the introduction of the subject (the initiative in sense 2) and the 'taking up' and transmitting to the other Council (the initiative in sense 1).

In general, the word 'initiative' can be used to refer to any stage in the legislative process regarded from the standpoint of the subsequent stage. It is a relative term. Article 121 uses it for the petition of 50,000 for revision of the Constitution.

The reason why the Cantons have this power is that Article 91 prevents the members of the Assembly from voting upon instructions, and therefore the Cantons cannot instruct their member of the Council of States to 'initiate' a project. The decision as to what Cantonal authority (e.g. the Landsgemeinde, the Great Council) is to formulate the Cantonal initiative is left to the Canton. This procedure is still used from time to time, and secures good publicity.

The committees (*commissions*) by custom have the right of initiative before their own Council.

ARTICLE 94. As a general rule the Councils shall hold their sittings publicly.

This gives each Council, and the Federal Assembly in joint session, the power to declare a sitting 'secret'. Article 36 of the *règlement* of the National Council provides that a motion for secret session (*huis clos*) must be presented by a Federal Councillor or at least thirty members, and that the galleries are to be cleared during the debate on the motion. At the same time this Article lays down the rule that such sessions shall be exceptional. This is in contrast to the practice of the Diet, whose debates until 1834 were held in private.

Publicity in the sense of this Article can be extended to mean more than merely allowing the public to listen to debates. It can mean that in principle speeches in either Council may be published without breach of the speaker's possible copyright, that no criminal prosecution follows from the publication of a fair report in a newspaper, that the sale of the *Bulletin sténographique* (the official report of the debates) is similarly privileged, and probably also that there is immunity for such reports from an action for libel. Immunity to the member who makes the speech is given, a little ambiguously, by Article 1 of the Law of Dec. 1850 on the Responsibility of Federal Authorities and Officials (Verantwortlichkeitsgesetz).

II. FEDERAL COUNCIL

ARTICLE 95. The supreme directing and executive power in the Confederation is exercised by a Federal Council of seven members.

This Article raises the question 'Whose executive is the Federal Council?' Is it the Executive of the Swiss Confederation, or is it the executive of the Federal Assembly? The first alternative would establish a separation of powers under the Constitution, to which both Federal Council and Assembly are bound; the second alternative would give effect to the principle that the Assembly was the 'supreme power in the Confederation', and interpret the constitutional provisions concerning the Federal Council not as immutable rules of law, but as merely the arrangements which the founding fathers wanted to start off with. The original intention was probably that the Federal Council should merely be the executive for the Federal Assembly. The present interpretation, under the influence of the idea that *all* the Constitution—and not merely the freedom-rights—is a 'pure ought', is that the Federal Council is the *nation's* Executive. This is an interpretation which in conjunction with the people's rights of referendum leaves only a modest place for the Assembly.

ARTICLE 96. The members of the Federal Council are chosen for four years by the Councils in joint session from among the whole number of Swiss citizens eligible to the National Council. But not more than one member shall be chosen from the same Canton.

After every general election of the National Council there shall be a general election of the Federal Council.

Vacancies occurring in the course of the period of four years are to be filled by the Federal Assembly at its next meeting, for the remainder of the period of office.

The Executive Power in Switzerland. English constitutional history is represented as a struggle against the Executive, and consequently the interesting question for an English student is 'What is the position of the Executive against Parliament and the Judiciary?' The Swiss struggle for freedom, on the other hand, is represented as a struggle of democracy against aristocracy and monarchy; the interest of the Swiss student therefore concentrates upon popular voting rights, initiatives, and the like.[1] His question is neither 'What is the position of the individual against the police power?' nor 'What is the position of the Assembly as against the Federal Council?' but 'What voting and electing rights have Swiss citizens?' English criticism of the Swiss Constitution therefore never meets Swiss praise ('real democracy in action', &c.): the Swiss student points excitedly to the façade, which the Briton maintains is the backyard. The provinciality of the Englishman's standpoint appears with full force when he comes to consider the position of the Federal Council, which seems to him too powerful and too official-minded to be completely compatible with constitutionalism or political liberty. He should in fairness recognize also the stability, cleanness, swiftness, and moderation of the Federal Council, for these are also virtues essential to ordered freedom, and ones in which Switzerland leads the world. It is probably in any case a mistake to praise referendum-democracy or to criticize the position of the Executive independently of one another; they are front and back of the same institution.

Composition of the Federal Council. The Federal Council is elected for the same period of office as the National Council, and so if there is a dissolution for a total revision under Article 120 the Federal Council must also be re-elected for the remainder of the legislature-period. When the term of office for the National Council was raised to four years, in 1931, this Article was also amended in the same sense.

Every fourth year, then (Dec. 1951, &c.), all seven seats in the Federal Council must be filled. Election is by the Assembly, in joint session (Article 92), and each seat is filled in turn, that is to say, there are seven separate elections on the same day. An 'absolute majority' (more than half the number of votes cast[2]) is required. Because it is now the custom to re-elect all the

---

[1] The Swiss are in love with the word 'democracy' rather than with the word 'freedom'.   [2] Voting is by name, not by 'Aye' and 'No'.

Federal Councillors who wish to continue in office, in practice only one or at most two of the seats need to be filled with new members at any one time. It is these new elections that arouse great interest. It is also the custom that there shall be one member from Zurich, one from Berne, and two (usually) from French Switzerland, and that all four parties, both important language-groups, and both confessions, shall be more or less fairly represented. Consequently if the Socialist Federal Councillor from Zurich retires, the effective election of his successor is made by the Socialist party of Canton Zurich—which the Assembly sanctions—and similarly it is the Farmers' party of Canton Berne which in all but form elects the Bernese member. In any case it is expected of a candidate that he will have held high public office, e.g. be or have been a National Councillor or Councillor of States, and perhaps also a Councillor of State (Regierungsrat) in his own Canton: the choice is therefore seldom wide.

Article 9 of the Law on Political and other Guarantees of 1934 (originally of 1851, revised 1947) makes it clear that it is Cantonal citizenship, not settlement, which is meant by paragraph 1 of the Article: this is one of the very few matters where Cantonal citizenship is of account.

There have several times been proposals for direct election of the Federal Council by the people (as there is in all Cantons for the Cantonal Executive Council) and there has twice been a referendum on the subject, both times unsuccessfully (in 1900 and 1942). The point of the proposal for direct election has each time been to secure representation on the Council for an excluded political party or section of the country, and it may therefore be said that the threat of proposing a constitutional initiative for direct election is the sanction behind the custom of having all main parties represented on the Federal Council. The threat has both times attained its object.

That the Executive Council has the same, fixed, period of office as the Legislature is the main institutional originality of Swiss government. The weak executive which is characteristic of countries where the term of office of the Assembly is fixed but the term of office of the Executive is not fixed, is thereby avoided. The ultimate origins of this stroke of constitutional genius seem to lie partly in the Petty-Councils and the plural offices characteristic of the Old Régime, and partly in the Revolutionary *Directoire*. The immediate origin is in the regenerated Cantonal Constitutions of 1830–48.

Political Parties in the Federal Council. The party history of the Federal Council is as follows:

1848–92   All Liberal-Radicals.[1]
1892–1919   6 Liberals and 1 Catholic Conservative.
1919–29   5 Liberals and 2 Catholic Conservatives.
1929–43   4 Liberals, 2 Catholic Conservatives, and 1 Farmers' party.
1943–   3 Liberals, 2 Catholics, 1 Farmer, and 1 Socialist.

The election being by the whole Assembly in joint session, the Liberal and Catholic votes have extra weight; their representation is difficult to justify as against the Socialists'.

---

[1] The homogeneity of the Liberal party in the last century should not be exaggerated.

ARTICLE 97. Members of the Federal Council while in office may hold no other official position either in the service of the Confederation or of a Canton, nor may they follow any other career or exercise any profession.

Article 3 of the Law on the Organization of the Federal Administration of 1914 repeats this provision at a little greater length, but adds nothing of interest except the words '... either directly or through a third party'. The crude personal integrity of Federal Councillors does not ever come under real suspicion. The same Law also provides that near relations shall not be members of the Federal Council at the same time, and that near relations of Federal Councillors shall not hold official positions immediately subject to the Federal Council. Similar provisions apply at other administrative levels, and are duplicated in Cantonal legislation—where they sometimes prove a nuisance.

ARTICLE 98. The President of the Confederation acts as chairman of the Federal Council. The President and the vice-President are elected by the Councils in joint session from among the members of the Federal Council, to hold office for one year.

The retiring President cannot be elected either as President or as vice-President for the subsequent year. The same member cannot be vice-President for two consecutive years.

The Presidency of the Confederation rotates among the members of the Federal Council, the Councillor who was vice-President the year before being customarily (but now always) elected President. New Federal Councillors serve beneath all their seniors before filling the Presidency, and those who have filled the office go to the bottom of the list—otherwise the office is filled by seniority. The Cantons, except for the primitive democracies, follow the same or a similar system of rotation.

The functions of the President of the Confederation are laid down in the Law on the Organization of Federal Administration of 1914, which gives the President certain very limited emergency powers, a general supervisory power, and the responsibility for the Federal Chancellery. It also states that 'the President represents the Confederation at home and abroad'. This formal duty and the chairmanship of the Federal Council are the President's most important functions.

Under a Law of 1849 the office of President of the Confederation was coupled with the headship of the Political (i.e. Foreign) Department, and since this Article provides that the Presidency must be held by a different member each year, the Political Department also circulated among the members of the Federal Council. The Federal Councillors who liked conducting foreign relations would seek to be often President, while those who did not like diplomacy would be satisfied with one turn in the office. The result was that all departments changed hands rather freely, and that because its members were familiar with other departments the Federal Council could be a genuine executive college or presidency-in-commission, carrying out or initiating a policy of the parliamentary majority—whereas now it is a mere 'Staatenbund' of departments.

The rotation of offices had disadvantages, and these were trenchantly expressed by Federal Councillor Numa Droz, who himself had a preference for the Political Department. Under his influence the experiment was tried during the years 1887–94 of dissociating the Presidency from that department—the Presidency continuing to rotate while the Political Department stayed in the same hands. The same arrangement was again tried in 1915–17, and was permanently adopted in 1920. At present a Federal Councillor may well remain in the department to which he was first appointed until he retires. The allocation of Councillors to departments is done by the Federal Council itself: the election of the President and vice-President, now a formality under the seniority system, is made by the Assembly.

ARTICLE 99. The President of the Confederation and the other members of the Federal Council receive a yearly salary from Federal funds.

Under the Federal Arrêté of 29 Mar. 1950 the annual salary of a Federal Councillor is 48,000 francs, and the President of the Confederation has an additional 3,000 francs. There is a credit for certain expenses also, and a pension.

See also Article 85, s. 3.

ARTICLE 100. The Federal Council can only proceed to business when at least four members are present.

The Law of 1914 on the Organization of Federal Administration provides that the deliberations of the Federal Council shall be in private, that decisions shall normally be by count of hands, that there must be at least three votes (and a majority of the Councillors present) on the majority side, and that the President has a casting vote. The Chancellor or a vice-Chancellor acts as secretary (Articles 4, 6, and 7 of the Law of 1914).

ARTICLE 101. Members of the Federal Council may attend the meetings of both sections of the Federal Assembly to give advice, and they have also the right to propose resolutions upon any subject of debate there.

A Federal Councillor is nearly always present during the discussions in each Council: the *règlements* of both Councils permit them to speak 'whenever they judge opportune', and they play in fact an important part in debate, and are heard with respect.

Federal Councillors do not debate with each other in public and they make it their practice to appear before the Assembly as if they were agreed among themselves. The present Article, however, makes it *possible* for them to display their differences to the Councils, and must be distinguished from Article 102, ss. 4 and 16, which provide for a report or a project from the whole Federal Council in its corporate capacity.

In practice, if a Federal Councillor disagrees with a particular project and wishes it to be known that he has been voted down, he publicizes the fact 'unofficially'.

ARTICLE 102. The principal powers and obligations of the Federal Council, within the limits of the present Constitution, are as follows:

1. It conducts the affairs of the Confederation, in accordance with Federal Laws and Arrêtés.
2. It sees to the observance of the Constitution and the Laws and *arrêtés* of the Confederation and the provisions of Federal concordats: it takes the necessary action to see that they are obeyed, either acting on its own initiative or in response to an appeal against a grievance, unless the appeal is of the type which should go before the Federal Tribunal under Article 113.
3. It supervises the guarantee of Cantonal Constitutions.
4. It submits projects of Laws and *arrêtés* to the Federal Assembly, and gives its preliminary advice upon projects which the Councils or the Cantons send up to it.
5. It provides for the execution of the Laws and *arrêtés* of the Confederation and of the decisions of the Federal Tribunal, and of the compromise-agreements and decisions of arbitrators in disputes between Cantons.
6. It undertakes those elections which have not been allotted to the Federal Assembly, the Federal Tribunal, or another Federal authority.
7. It examines the treaties which Cantons make with each other or with foreign countries, and sanctions them if they are allowable (Article 85, Section 5).
8. It acts as guardian of the external interests of the country, paying especial attention to diplomatic relationships, and it looks after foreign relationships generally.
9. It acts as guardian of the external security of Switzerland, her independence and her neutrality.
10. It looks after the internal security of the Confederation, and the maintenance of peace and order.
11. In a case of urgency, when the Federal Assembly is not

in session, the Federal Council is empowered to call up the necessary troops and to dispose them, but it must summon the Councils immediately if more than two thousand men are called up, or if they are embodied for more than three weeks.

12. It has the Federal Army, and all other branches of the Federal administration under, its charge.

13. It examines those Laws and *ordonnances* of the Cantons that have to be submitted for its approval; it supervises branches of the Cantonal administrations, where such supervision is incumbent upon it.

14. It administers Federal finances and prepares the estimates ('budget') and the accounts of Federal receipts and expenditure.

15. It supervises the official conduct of all officials and employees of the Federal administration.

16. It lays before the Assembly at its ordinary session a report on its conduct of business, and a report upon the state of the Confederation at home and abroad, and recommends to it the measures it considers will further the common welfare.

It also submits special reports when the Federal Assembly or one section thereof requires it.

SECTION 1. This sphere of action of the Federal Council as against the other Federal authorities has already been laid down elsewhere in the Constitution (Articles 95 read with 71, 85 s. 11, and 89). The distinction between the Federal Council as a corporate body and its individual departments is dealt with in Article 103. The present section should therefore be regarded as one placed here for logical completeness rather than a rule of law in its own right.

SECTION 2. The words 'inasmuch as' need to be supplied between the phrases 'It sees to . . .' and 'it takes . . .'.

The Constitution does not determine in what circumstances the Federal Council is to intervene on its own initiative and in what circumstances it is only to act on receipt of a complaint or appeal in due form. In practice the question is determined by the nature of the act which is concerned—it is not much good guaranteeing a 'decent burial' if the right can only be enforced by appeal when it is already too late. In the classes of cases reserved for the Federal Tribunal, the Federal Council is presumably entitled to take measures on its own initiative to secure the observance of the Constitution, both to prevent the unlawful action and perhaps to remedy it, but without prejudice to an eventual appeal to the Tribunal (e.g. to secure the voting rights of people who are not prepared to take the case to the Federal Tribunal, or who from procedural obstacles are unable to do so).

For the regular jurisdiction of the Federal Tribunal in cases of 'administrative law' see note to Article 114 *bis*.

This competence to secure observance of the Constitution is understood as being exercisable against Cantonal governments, not against other Federal authorities. This follows from the inclusion of the words 'and the Laws and arrêtés of the Confederation' after the word 'Constitution' and from the terms of the Constitution generally.

SECTION 3. The 'guarantee of Cantonal Constitutions' meant something quite simple in 1848: it meant that the Federal army stood behind the victorious Liberal Cantonal governments. Since then political tolerance and settled conditions have made a wide difference between the 'material guarantee' of Article 5 and the 'formal guarantee' of Article 6.

With respect to the 'material guarantee' this section means that the Federal Council initiates and carries through a Federal Intervention, and obtains the consent of the Assembly (Article 85, s. 7) for this course. With respect to the 'formal guarantee' it means that the Federal Council initiates the Federal Arrêté granting or refusing sanction for revised Articles of a Cantonal Constitution, in the same way as it initiates Laws and arrêtés.

SECTION 4. A message or report from the Federal Council is always accompanied by a draft embodying the action which the Federal Council wishes the Assembly to take, and this draft forms the basis of discussion in the *commission* of each Council and thereafter in the Council itself. It is now the practice of both Chambers that they only debate a project of Law or arrêté when the message and draft of the Federal Council are to hand. The Federal Council initiates, the Federal Assembly amends.[1] Though this central position of the Federal Council in legislative procedure rests on practice alone, the Law on the Relations between the Councils and the *règlement* of each Chamber take it for granted.

The message (or report) and the draft are published in the *Feuille fédérale* and obtain thereby a wide public both in their original form and as interpreted by the daily press. They embody the intentions of the Federal Council in its corporate capacity rather than those of individual members of it.

SECTION 5. Laws and Federal Arrêtés usually contain a clause empowering the Federal Council to execute them and to issue subsidiary rules. This clause would appear to be unnecessary in the light of this section—which would also seem to solve the question of whether it is constitutional for the Assembly to delegate subsidiary law-making powers in view of Article 89, paragraph 1. Both questions are hotly disputed.

The execution of the decisions of the Courts and of many provisions of the Constitution and of much Federal legislation is left to the Cantons. If the Cantons fail to carry out these obligations, then in the last resort appeal can be made to the Federal Council,[2] but this appears to be a special case of the rule in section 2 above that the Federal Council is to see that the Constitution, &c., is observed.

Disputes between Cantons go to the Federal Tribunal in the ordinary way: the wording of the Constitution is a reminiscence of the days before 1848.

---

[1] Legislative procedure is further discussed on page 151.
[2] Article 39 of the Law on Judicial Organization of 1943, Execution of Decisions of the Tribunal.

SECTION 6. The Federal Council in practice delegates its right of appointment in very many cases, and this practice is necessary (e.g. in the case of postmen or railway conductors) and desirable, though probably not envisaged by the fathers of the Constitution. It is not certain to what extent branches of the administration may be set up so as to be independent of the Federal Council (e.g. a Broadcasting Corporation) and appointments thereto transferred to an independent authority: see also section 15 below.

Article 77 provides that officials elected by the Federal Council may not sit in the National Council, and in this sense all Federal officials, including railwaymen and postmasters, are deemed to be appointed by the Federal Council: borderline cases are occasionally of importance.

SECTION 7. See Articles 8, 9, and 10, as well as 85 s. 5. As with the guarantee of the Cantonal Constitution, the approval of a concordat does not save it, or at least does not save actions taken under it, from review by the Federal Tribunal in particular cases for repugnancy to Federal law: 'Federal law breaks Cantonal law.'

SECTIONS 8 AND 9. *Division of Competences between Assembly and Federal Council.* Just as in internal affairs legislation is properly within the competence of the Assembly, while administration (subject to the Assembly's 'instructions') is in the competence of the Federal Council, so in foreign affairs treaties are in the competence of the Assembly, and the day-to-day conduct of foreign relations is in the competence of the Federal Council—subject to the instructions and criticisms of the Assembly. Compare with these two sections ss. 5 and 6 of Article 85, and see also Article 89, Treaty Referendum.

SECTION 10. Actually the maintenance of internal peace and order is a Cantonal competence. If internal order breaks down, then a Federal Intervention takes place—which is supposed to be a matter for the Federal Assembly under Article 85 s. 7 (cf. Article 16). A comparison with Article 85 shows that the Assembly takes 'measures' while the Federal Council 'looks after' it. What is presumably meant is that the Federal Council asks for an *arrêté*, which the Federal Assembly passes and the Federal Council carries out.

Articles 9 and 10 are sometimes interpreted by the Federal Council as conferring a competence upon it as against the Assembly, the guaranteed rights of the citizen, and the Cantons; these two sections must therefore, like Article 2 and the preamble, be considered dangerous.

SECTION 11. This is the only allusion in the Constitution to any special legal order to prevail in a state of 'urgency'. The question whether to introduce a legal concept of 'urgency' into the constitutional document (with all the dangers involved) is often discussed. With short intervals one type of emergency or another has prevailed in Switzerland since 1914, hence the importance of the problem. For the custom of partially suspending the Constitution in favour of decisions of the Federal Council in such times, see page 169.

SECTIONS 12 AND 15. There seems to be no difference between these two sections, except for the mention of the Federal army. It is not certain to what extent these sections exclude the interest of the Assembly in these matters. There is the additional possibility that these sections mean that no branch of the 'administration' may be set up so as not to be under the supervision and within the responsibility of the Federal Council, for example the Technical University, the nationalized railways, or perhaps broadcasting. Compare section 6, where the appointments are the responsibility of the Federal Council.

SECTION 13. Both under the Constitution (Articles 43, para. 6 and—at least until the coming into force of the Penal Code—55, para. 2) and under various Federal Laws.

SECTION 14. That is to say, the 'budget' at the beginning of the year and the accounts at the end of it. Both need the sanction of the Federal Assembly. See note to Article 85 s. 10.

Federal Officials. The principal legislation on the status of Federal civil servants is the Law on the Status of Officials of 1927[1] and the Law on Responsibility of 1850. There are several peculiar features in their position. In particular the language used is always that of 'election' for a particular period, usually three years, after which there is a further election for three years as the case may be. The theory and the façade are of haphazard 'elections' for a short period, the reality is of a highly professional career-bureaucracy, set apart from the people and a dominant factor in public life. There is a claim of a certain nature to re-election, and indeed the whole connexion between vocabulary and reality is rather tenuous. There is usually no pension—a result of the legislative challenge, as it seems—but the purposes of a pension are served by compulsory insurance.

One often receives the impression in Switzerland that the sphere in which the non-bureaucratic frame of mind prevails is smaller there than in Great Britain.[2] There is bureaucracy on the one hand and the political party on the other, and these nearly exhaust public life, even in Switzerland.

Annual Report. Every year the Federal Council submits an Annual Report (*Rapport de gestion*, Geschaeftsbericht) to the Assembly. This report is debated, department by department, and eventually sanctioned—there is a certain faint similarity in this to the House of Commons debates on the departmental estimates in Committee of Supply, although the bulk, incisiveness, and vehemence of criticism is lacking in Switzerland. For the fiction that there is only one ordinary session in the year see Articles 86 and 78.

Messages of the Federal Council. Reports. A 'message' is usually a report which the Federal Council has submitted on its own initiative, accompanied by a draft project, while the word 'report' is usually reserved for one submitted in reply to an express wish of the Assembly, or of one Council ('section'), or of a committee, or in pursuance of a legal obligation. It also is usually accompanied by a draft project. The messages and reports of the Federal Council are published in the *Feuille fédérale*. They are clearer and

[1] There is an English translation of the Law of 1927 in L. D. White, *The Civil Service in the Modern State*, Chicago, 1930.

[2] For example in Church, university, the judicial bench. To a lesser extent it is also the case in Parliament, and even in the civil service itself. The distinction between public and private law made in Switzerland leaves little room for the privileged corporations (such as the universities or the Inns of Court) which play an important intermediary role in Great Britain.

easier to read than British Command and Order Papers, but they are of much less total bulk, and less satisfactory as a source of information: minutes of evidence are not published.

All procedure of both Councils either seeks to elicit a report from the Federal Council or proceeds from one, and in particular no legislative business or popular initiative is considered unless the Federal Council has first submitted a report.

ARTICLE 103. The business of the Federal Council shall be divided into departments and one of its members shall be at the head of each. Decisions shall be under the name and by the authority of the Federal Council.

Federal legislation may empower departments, or branches of the service subordinate to them, to settle certain classes of business themselves, but the right of appeal in such cases shall be preserved.

Federal legislation shall determine in what circumstances this right of appeal shall be exercised before a Federal Administrative Court.

Until the votation of 25 Oct. 1914 this Article read: 'The business of the Federal Council is divided by departments each under a Federal Councillor. The purpose of this division is solely to facilitate examination and dispatch of business; the decision emanates from the Federal Council.'

The Collegiality of the Federal Council. The organization of the Executive sanctioned by this Article is in contrast to the 'directorial' system on the one hand—where the executive power is wielded by a collegiate brains-trust, with the departments run by officers subordinate to the executive college as a whole—and the Cabinet system, where each member runs a department as the subordinate and adviser of a single Prime Minister (or King or President), on the other hand.

The Swiss system, where the executive college is corporately responsible and each member is himself the head of a department, has not worked without difficulties. Indeed it is not clear to what extent the Federal Council as a corporate body exists, and it has long been said that 'there are seven Federal Councillors, but no Federal Council'. It is hard to discover what actually is the case, for the literary habits of Swiss public men do not lead them to gossip about their official life. The arrangements of the room where they meet do not suggest collegiality—since members of four different parties can hardly hammer out a common policy sitting at ornate desks rather far apart in the presence of a Chancellor taking notes—and the indications are that they make set speeches at each other, for this is a favourite means of communication in Switzerland. Decision, moreover, is by majority vote. Yet, on the other hand, the loneliness of very high office and the greatness of the responsibility can hardly fail to engender a corporate spirit; the essential element for obtaining genuine agreement—secrecy of discussion—is after all present. It should be added that Swiss institutions are not calculated to produce a *policy*, and that no clear overall policy is discernible in domestic matters, but just a stable and satisfactory equilibrium of forces.

The Departments of the Federal Council. By virtue of the Law on the Organization of Federal Administration of 1914 the departments of the Federal Council are as follows:

1. The Political Department (foreign affairs).
2. The Department of the Interior (home department).
3. Department of Justice and Police (*see below*).
4. Military Department (includes survey and military education).
5. Department of Finance and Customs (includes alcohol, banks, cereals, and audit and establishment).
6. Public Economy (industry, agriculture, social insurances).
7. Posts and Railways (includes all communications, and water power).

The functions attributed to departments are constantly changing, and the Law of 1914 is not an easy document to use because it is so often amended. Article 23 of the Law gives the Federal Council power to determine what subject-matters are to be delegated to the departments to deal with on their own, and provides for appeals to the Federal Council itself against such departmental decisions in certain circumstances. The Federal Council has taken advantage of this power and issued the Arrêté of the Federal Council of 17 Nov. 1914—an interesting document, also frequently amended.

Department of Justice and Police. This is divided into five divisions, viz. Justice, Police, *Ministère publique* (the division of the Public Prosecutor), Private Insurances, and Patents-and-Copyright.

The Division of Justice is charged with the following duties: Preparation of Federal legislation on civil and criminal law and procedure; the examination of Cantonal Constitutions submitted for guarantee, and of those Cantonal legislative acts which are subject to Federal approval and within the purview of the department; Registers, including those of births, deaths and marriages; the judgement of Appeals under Articles 51 and 53 of the Constitution (Jesuits, Burials); Legal advice to the Federal Council on Appeals made to it, and to the departments; Relations with foreign powers concerning technical legal matters; and the execution of the decisions of the Federal Tribunal.

The Division of Police is charged with citizenship, extradition, naturalization and settlement, and with the preparation of laws on these subject-matters, and with road traffic and gambling. The supervision of foreigners to some extent also comes under this division.

The other divisions of the department do not call for particular comment.

The idea that a Department of Justice is necessary seems to have some connexion with the idea that law is primarily the instrument of the Executive, enabling it to govern.[1] The intention is to bring these matters under the policy of the Executive, not merely as against the Judiciary but also as

---

[1] The continental doctrine of administrative law is also perhaps connected with the idea of law as the instrument of the Executive.

against the Legislature. There would seem to be no particular relevance of the institution of a Department of Justice in Switzerland to a discussion of whether a Ministry of Justice were desirable in Great Britain.

ARTICLE 104. The Federal Council and its departments are authorized to obtain the help of experts for particular items of business.

This Article has no special significance; it merely removes a possible doubt.

III. FEDERAL CHANCELLERY

ARTICLE 105. A Federal Chancellery, at the head of which is the Chancellor of the Confederation, is responsible for the secretarial business of the Federal Assembly and of the Federal Council.

The Chancellor is elected by the Federal Assembly for four years at the same time as the Federal Council.

The Federal Chancellery is under the particular supervision of the Federal Council.

Further details of the organization of the Federal Chancellery shall be determined by Federal legislation.

Under the Federal Treaty of 1815–48 the Chancellor of the Confederation and the Clerk-of-State (Staatsschreiber) were the whole establishment of the Federal civil service. For the rest of its needs the Diet depended upon the services of the Canton in whose capital it happened that year to be sitting. This accounts for the variety of business for which the Chancellor is today responsible: he is the germ of the whole Federal civil service.

The personality of the Chancellor is not important, for his duties are chiefly formal and somewhat mechanical. The office, however, is of considerable dignity, and confers upon its holder a sort of honorary headship of the Federal civil services. There is no British equivalent—but the functions have a faint similarity with those of the Clerk of a County Council, while the prestige is not entirely unlike that of Speaker of the House of Commons.

The office is at present regulated by the Law on the Organization of the Federal Chancellery of 1919 and Articles 19–22 of the Law on the Organization of Federal Administration of 1914, and by various *ordonnances*. By the Law of 1914[1] his duties include:
    (*a*) The Clerkship of the Federal Council, and the 'orientation' of journalists after its meetings.
    (*b*) The office of clerk-at-the-table of the two Councils and of the

[1] As amended by the Federal Arrêté of 19 Feb. 1926.

Assembly in joint session (his deputy acting in one Council while he acts in the other). This includes the supervising of the shorthand report and of the translating, and what we should call the office of serjeant-at-arms.

(c) The supervision of the publication of the *Recueil des Lois* and the *Feuille fédérale*.

(d) The countersigning of Federal acts, and the technical organization of Federal votations.

(e) Certain duties regarding organization and methods of the Federal administration.

The Federal Chancellery is under the superintendence of the President of the Confederation, and the ultimate superintendence of the Assembly. The Chancellor is elected by the Assembly in joint session (Articles 92 and 85, s. 4) and in practice he is continued in office until he retires. The election has a faintly political flavour, and regard is had to the alternation of languages and confessions. The vice-Chancellors are appointed by the Federal Council, and one of them usually acquires a sort of moral claim to the office of Chancellor before the place falls vacant.

The term of office was extended to four years in 1931 to agree with that of the National Council.

IV. FEDERAL TRIBUNAL

ARTICLE 106. There shall be a Federal Tribunal for the administration of justice in so far as this is within the Federal competence.

Juries shall be constituted for criminal cases (Article 112).

This Article contains no rule of law.

The creation of a permanent Federal Tribunal was the chief institutional innovation of 1874. Under the Constitution of 1848 the Federal Tribunal had been a part-time body of little significance. The Tribunal as at present constituted first sat in 1875; since then its jurisdiction has been enlarged several times, chiefly at the expense of the Federal Council.

The Federal Jury is a more or less theoretical institution: see note to Article 112. The institution of the jury has also survived in some of the Cantons, but in general it has not flourished on Swiss soil.

For the Federal Insurance Tribunal see note to Article 34 *bis*.

ARTICLE 107. Members and deputy members of the Federal Tribunal shall be elected by the Federal Assembly, which shall see that the three official languages of the Confederation are represented upon it.

A Law shall provide for the method of organization of the

Federal Tribunal and the sections thereof, the number of its members and deputy members, their term of office and their pay.

These elections are by the two legislative Councils in joint session, under Article 92.

The Law which determines the organization of the Federal Tribunal is the Law on Judicial Organization of 1943, which repeals that of 1893. The term for which the Judges of the Tribunal are elected is six years; they are re-eligible and in practice are nearly always re-elected as often as they wish to be. The original elections have a faintly political character in that the Assembly sees that the main parties and both religious denominations are represented, as well as the three 'official' languages.

The Judges are paid (1949) 30,000 francs a year, with a pension. The President has 2,000 francs extra. The Deputy Judges have an allowance for each day on which they are required to serve. The number of the Judges has several times been raised.[1] It is now fixed by the Law on Judicial Organization as between 26 and 28, and is actually 26.

In 1938 when Article 116, Freedom of Languages, was amended the word 'official' was substituted for the word 'national'.

ARTICLE 108. Any Swiss citizen eligible to the National Council may be appointed to the Federal Tribunal.

Members of the Federal Assembly and of the Federal Council, and the officials elected by these authorities, may not at the same time be members of the Federal Tribunal.

Members of the Federal Tribunal while in office may hold no other official position either in the service of the Confederation or of a Canton, nor may they follow any other career or exercise any profession.

Before 1874 membership of the Federal Tribunal was not incompatible with that of the Federal Assembly nor with following another employment, and in fact was normally combined with one or both of these. The only incompatibility was with employment as a Federal official or membership of the Federal Council.

There is still no incompatibility for the Deputy Judges.

---

[1] In 1875 there were 9 Judges of the Federal Tribunal, in 1893 the number was increased to 14, in 1896 to 16, in 1911 to 24 (on account of the Civil Code and other legislation), in 1928 to 26–28. In addition to the permanent Judges there are now 11–13 Deputy Judges; in 1875 there were 9. The number of Judges who sit on the bench in the various 'Courts' or 'Sections' into which the Tribunal is divided varies: the quorum may be 3, 5, or 7 according to the function performed. In 1949 the Tribunal disposed of 2,376 cases (see *Annuaire statistique*). The Tribunal takes six weeks' holidays in the year.

ARTICLE 109. The Federal Tribunal shall organize its own chancellery and nominate the officials thereof.

The Clerks and Secretaries to the Federal Tribunal are elected by the Tribunal itself for a period of office determined by the Assembly (six years). The Assembly determines the number of such appointments and their pay, but has delegated to the Tribunal the right to determine the functions of each of its officers.

The Tribunal has also a limited delegated authority to determine what business goes to what Section, how large each Bench shall be, and minor procedural formalities. The chief part of the rules of court, however, are laid down by Federal legislation; this is in accordance with the theory of separation of powers.

ARTICLE 110. The Federal Tribunal decides civil law disputes:
1. between the Confederation and a Canton;
2. between the Confederation on the one side and corporations or private persons on the other, provided that the latter are the plaintiffs and the amount in dispute is of the value which Federal law stipulates;
3. between Cantons;
4. between a Canton on the one side and corporations or private persons on the other, at the instance of one or other of the parties and when the amount in dispute is of the value which Federal law stipulates.

The Federal Tribunal further decides cases concerning *Heimatlosat* and disputes upon 'citizenship' between communes of different Cantons.

Articles 41 and 42 of the Law on Judicial Organization of 1943 have fixed the following minimum sums under this Article:
(section 2) 4,000 francs (except for railway, &c., cases);
(section 4) also 4,000 francs, except in cases of expropriation.
Cases under this Article ('first and last instance') are infrequent—there were ten in 1950.

ARTICLE 111. The Federal Tribunal is bound to judge other cases when both parties agree to appeal to it and the amount in dispute is of the value which Federal law stipulates.

The Law on Judicial Organization of 1943 fixes the minimum sum at 10,000 francs. With the Federal Assembly's permission, Cantons may by legislation place classes of civil suits within the competence of the Federal Tribunal.

There were seven cases of 'agreed jurisdiction' in 1950.

ARTICLE 112. The Federal Tribunal decides criminal cases, with the assistance of a jury which pronounces upon the facts:
 1. in cases of high treason against the Confederation, rebellion or violence against Federal authorities;
 2. in cases of crimes or misdemeanours against the law of nations;
 3. in cases of political crimes and misdemeanours which are either the cause or the consequence of troubles which have given rise to an armed Federal Intervention;
 4. when a charge is preferred against an officer nominated by one of the Federal authorities, and this authority seizes the Federal Tribunal.

The Federal Tribunal sitting as a court of first and last instance with the assistance of a jury is called the 'Federal Assizes'. The present law is now contained in Articles 341, 299, and 300 of the Swiss Penal Code (enacted under Article 64 *bis* of the Constitution). The Confederation's criminal jurisdiction without jury is discussed in the note to Article 114.

The Federal Assizes rarely meet. The last time they sat was in 1933, in the Nicole case arising out of the Federal Intervention in Geneva. The panel for the Federal jury is still 'elected' by the people—who seem quite unaware of its existence since election is normally uncontested. The Article in fact has become completely antiquated, and is a constitutional curiosity.

That the Assize offences (high treason, crimes against foreign sovereigns, crimes of the high Federal officers, certain cases of riot) must be Federal is a consequence of Cantonal 'sovereignty'—for the Cantons can only judge offences against the Cantonal powers, not against the Federal.

ARTICLE 113. The Federal Tribunal takes cognizance also of:
 1. conflicts of competence between Federal authorities on one side and Cantonal authorities on the other side;
 2. disputes in public law between Cantons;
 3. appeals against violation of constitutional rights of citizens, and appeals of private persons against violation of concordats or international treaties.

Administrative disputes as determined by Federal legislation are excepted.

In all the above cases the Federal Tribunal shall apply the Laws and the universally binding *arrêtés* passed by the Federal Assembly, and the treaties which it has ratified.

PARAGRAPH 1. Section One. The rule that conflicts of competence between a Federal authority and the authorities of a Canton may be brought before the Federal Tribunal must be read as subject to the qualification in paragraph 3 that Federal Laws and Arrêtés *de portée générale*, and treaties, may not be attacked before that Tribunal—nor may acts 'under' such laws be attacked except on the grounds that the action or the delegated legislation was (as we would say) *ultra vires*: such a plea has not much chance of success. Appeal can be brought by either party (Confederation or Canton) but not by private persons, and the procedure is used to decide cases where it is uncertain in whose competence a task is. It is not primarily of use as a protection of local sovereignty, though on occasion it may serve a Canton against the Federal executive power.

Section Two. Conflicts of civil law come under Article 110; the boundary between civil and public law (Staatsrecht) is not always clear when public authorities are concerned, e.g. in poor-law cases, but is only of procedural importance. Certain classes of cases have been transferred by Federal legislation to the Federal Council for decision, perhaps because considered to be of an 'administrative' nature.

Section Three. 'Appeals of private persons', i.e. not of foreign governments.

Appeal in Public Law (Staatsrechtliche Beschwerde). The original intention of the makers of the Constitution was probably to confine the expression 'the constitutional rights of citizens'[1] to the freedom-rights in the narrower sense (Equality, Freedom of Trade, Religion, Association, &c.), but the practice of the Tribunal has been to include practically every appeal against breach of the Constitution under the heading of guaranteed constitutional rights: the phrase thus now covers also the political rights (voting, &c.) as well as the freedom-rights. It also covers the political and freedom-rights guaranteed either expressly or implicitly[2] in the Cantonal Constitutions.

The Appeal, however, is only open to attack *Cantonal* acts of sovereignty, Federal legislation being exempt from control by virtue of paragraph 3 of this Article. Indeed if we assimilate certain Cantonal norms (Cantonal Constitutions duly guaranteed, and concordats) to the Federal Constitution, we shall not be far wrong if we regard the Appeal in Public Law as simply affording a remedy in a special case of breach of the rule 'Federal law breaks Cantonal law'—the case where the Cantonal act is a breach of the Federal Constitution itself.

In principle any Cantonal act of sovereignty can be attacked, with the doubtful exception of the Cantonal Constitution itself when duly guaranteed, but because of procedural difficulties (and especially of proving sufficient legal interest) the act usually attacked is a particular decision of the Cantonal administration or Courts, for if a Cantonal law is contrary to the Federal

---

[1] It will be noticed that while the term 'Appeal in Public Law' is not used in the Constitution, it nevertheless accurately describes what the appeal is.

[2] The Federal Tribunal considers that certain rights are necessarily 'by implication' guaranteed by a Cantonal Constitution, even if it is silent on the point. These are: 'Separation of Powers', i.e. the autonomy of the Legislature, the Executive, and the Judiciary as against each other or the people; 'Communal Autonomy', i.e. of the communes against the Cantonal authorities; and the 'Right to Property'. The latter has far-reaching economic effects. The autonomy of the *Executive* as against the other powers should be noted.

Constitution, then all its particular applications are illegal and will be voided by the Federal Tribunal. The law therefore may remain formally in effect, but the Canton is practically compelled to repeal it.

Article 4 of the Constitution (Equality) asserts a principle so vague and elastic that the Appeal in Public Law[1] enables every Cantonal act to be attacked on the grounds that it is unjust ('arbitrary'), and in practice more than half of the Appeals arise under Article 4. Other Articles which regularly contribute a substantial number of cases are Articles 31 (Trade); 45 (Settlement); 46, paragraph 2 (Double Taxation); and Article 2 of the Transitory Provisions (Federal Law and Cantonal Law).

In general the Appeal must be against the highest available Cantonal instance, that is to say, all possibilities of appeal within the Canton must first be exhausted: for the exceptions see note to Article 58. The Appeal must be lodged within thirty days of the act complained of; this term is very frequently too short, however, and cases often turn on the question of whether the Appeal was lodged in time. And a sufficient legal interest must be proved, and it is sometimes impossible to do this.

PARAGRAPH 3. *Application of Federal Law by the Tribunal.* The wording of this paragraph only includes Federal Laws, Treaties, and 'universally binding *arrêtés*', and differs slightly from paragraph 3 of Article 114 *bis*. The implication would seem to be that the Tribunal could query the constitutionality of Arrêtés of the Federal *Council*, both those enacted in virtue of the Executive's original and of its delegated powers: as far as delegated powers are concerned the Tribunal has in fact repeatedly claimed to be able to challenge Arrêtés of the Federal Council for, as we would say, *ultra vires*. In every case, however, the Federal Tribunal (as opposed to the Federal Insurance Tribunal) has found that in fact the delegation was perfectly proper; the real constitutional position appears therefore in doubt, since there is no clear precedent, but only opinions and *obiter dicta*. In particular the Federal Tribunal has always found itself unable to question the Full Powers Arrêtés of the Assembly or the *ordonnances* made under them. The question whether to introduce an Article empowering the Tribunal to challenge Federal legislation for its constitutionality is a favourite one for academic speculation. The failure of the Constituent to separate the powers of government at this vital point gives a distinctive character to the whole Constitution.

ARTICLE 114. Federal legislation may, in addition to the subjects mentioned in Articles 110, 112, and 113, transfer other cases to the competence of the Federal Tribunal, and may in particular grant it the powers necessary to ensure the uniform application of the laws provided for in Article 64.

Since 1875 the centre of gravity of this part of the Constitution has shifted. Nearly 95 per cent. of the cases which come before the Federal Tribunal

---

[1] Appeals in those subject-matters of law traditionally considered 'administrative' used to go to the Federal Council: some still do, see note to Article 114 *bis*.

come there now by virtue of Federal legislation, or by virtue of an extensive interpretation of the first phrase of the third section of the first paragraph of Article 113, or under 114 *bis*. Articles 110, 111, 112, and the rest of Article 113 are of some ultimate importance and some sections of them produce a few cases regularly, but they are not now the daily bread of the Constitution. The Constitution as it stands is therefore somewhat misleading, and the legislation under it of great importance.

The principal legislation is contained in the Law on Judicial Organization of 1943, the Laws on Federal Civil Procedure (1947) and Criminal Procedure (1934, much amended since), the Law of 1889 on Suits for Debt and Bankruptcy, and the Civil and Penal Codes.

(*a*) *Civil Jurisdiction of the Federal Tribunal*. Nine-tenths of the civil cases (in 1950, 460 cases) heard by the Tribunal are appeals (*recours en réforme*, as opposed to *recours en nullité*; the difference is procedural) from decisions of Cantonal Courts, and may therefore be regarded, like the Appeals in Public Law under Article 113, para. 1, s. 3 and the appeals in criminal law considered below, as particular applications of the rule 'Federal law breaks Cantonal law'. The purpose served by these appeals is the unity of civil law —since the Civil Code is applied by the Cantons in their own Courts. The other tenth of cases is a 'mixed bag' arising out of Articles 110 and 111 of the Constitution, and Article 68 of the Law on Judicial Organization.

(*b*) A special section of the Federal Tribunal deals with suits for debt and bankruptcy on appeal from Cantonal Courts under the Law of 1889 passed under the old Article 64 before it was revised.

(*c*) *Criminal Jurisdiction of the Federal Tribunal*. This consists of:

1. The Federal Assizes with jury, as described in Article 112.

2. The Federal Criminal Court. The Federal Assizes are in practice rarely held. The original criminal jurisdiction of the Federal Tribunal, for example in cases of forgery of (Federal) money or of forcible resistance, is exercised in the Federal Criminal Court. For the classes of offences which go to this section of the Tribunal see the Swiss Penal Code, Articles 340 and 342 (and also Article 10 of the Law of 1934 on Federal Criminal Procedure, and Article 18 of the same Law). Only three or four cases a year come before this Court in this way: the jurisdiction is of ultimate but not daily importance—it is the mailed fist in the Federal glove.

3. The Court of Accusation (Anklagekammer). This (i) prepares business for the Federal Criminal Court and decides if there is a prima facie case, and (ii) decides disputes as to the place of criminal jurisdiction, i.e. in which Canton. This Court now receives up to 60 cases a year, of which 55 are conflicts of jurisdiction.

4. The Court of Cassation, which since the coming into force of the Penal Code in 1942 has been increasingly important. A Cantonal decision which is contrary to Federal law is null—'Federal law breaks Cantonal law'—and this applies to (most) Cantonal decisions under Federal criminal law, and particularly to Cantonal decisions under the Penal Code. The method of annulling the Cantonal decision is by an appeal 'in nullity' (Nichtigkeitsbeschwerde) to the Court of Cassation. Such an appeal 'in nullity' can only be made for breach of Federal law by a Cantonal decision (Article 269, as

revised, of the Law of 1934 on Criminal Procedure). If the Federal law broken is the Federal Constitution itself, however, the appeal is not to the Court of Cassation in nullity, but there is an Appeal in Public Law to another section of the Tribunal (all these Courts with different names being sections of the one Federal Tribunal). The jurisdiction of the Court of Cassation plays an important part in the unification of Swiss penal law: the annual number of cases was around 60 or 70 before 1942, since then it has increased every year, and is now (1951) around 550.

5. From the Assizes, the Criminal Court, and the Court of Accusation an appeal may lie to an Extraordinary Court of Cassation of seven Judges.

IV *bis*. FEDERAL ADMINISTRATIVE AND DISCIPLINARY JURISDICTION

ARTICLE 114 *bis*. The Federal Administrative Court takes cognizance of those classes of Federal administrative conflict which Federal legislation shall transfer to it.

The Administrative Court also has jurisdiction in those disciplinary cases which Federal legislation refers to it, unless they are referred to a special tribunal instead.

The Federal Administrative Court shall apply Federal legislation and treaties approved by the Federal Assembly.

Subject to the approval of the Federal Assembly, the Cantons may transfer their own Cantonal administrative conflicts to the jurisdiction of the Federal Administrative Court.

A Law shall provide for the organization of Federal administrative and disciplinary jurisdiction and for the procedure to be followed.

The Federal Administrative Court. This Article was introduced by the votation of 25 Oct. 1914. The Law which gave effect to it was that of 1928 on Federal Administrative and Disciplinary Jurisdiction, and this was repealed by the Law on Judicial Organization of 1943, which is now in force.

The Administrative Court is not a separate Court like the Insurance Tribunal, but it is a section of the Federal Tribunal. In the early days after 1874 Appeals in Administrative Law (e.g. education, religion, freedom of trade and industry) went to the Federal Council. Successive new Laws on Judicial Organization transferred classes of cases to the Federal Tribunal, and this tendency has continued. The administrative law jurisdiction of the Federal Council (under Article 113, paragraph 2, above) is now confined by Article 125 of the Law on Judicial Organization to the following main classes of cases:

(1) Appeals under Federal legislation, other than the Constitution itself, unless the law concerned determines otherwise;

(2) Appeals under certain classes of international treaties;
(3) Appeals under the following Articles of the Constitution: 18, para. 3 (free military equipment); 27, paras. 2 and 3 (primary schools); 51 (Jesuits); 53, para. 2 (cemeteries).

Concept of Administrative Law. The term 'administrative law' is used in three senses in Great Britain: (i) 'Dicey's sense', (ii) delegated legislation, and (iii) the sort of law which local government officers need to know. In order to understand the sense in which the term is used in Switzerland it is necessary to clear one's mind of the English senses.

Swiss lawyers classify law as 'public' and 'private'. These are historical categories, from Roman Law, rather than logical ones. 'Public law' (oeffentliches Recht) deals with 'the relationships of citizens to the State'. Strictly speaking it deals with the public-law relations of citizens to the State only—and this involves a circular definition. Public law in turn is divided into two parts: State-law (Staatsrecht)[1], and Administrative Law (Verwaltungsrecht). Criminal law may be reckoned as a third category of public law or may be a category of its own; it is best defined as 'the contents of the Penal Code'.

State-law includes the law on the organization of the State, the structure of the high authorities, and the voting rights of the people. It also includes some of the guaranteed constitutional rights of the citizen. All the rest of public law which is not State-law is called *Administrative law*, which includes, for example, the relations of Church and State, the registration of births, deaths and marriages, citizenship, poor-law, health, education, traffic, weights and measures, industry, agriculture, and trade. Administrative law is therefore primarily a class of law rather than a stage of it, but it is *also* used to describe a stage of law. The *règlement* of a legislative Council might, for example, be described as a sort of administrative law, or the very detailed rules concerning elections might be called administrative law (while the broad outlines of the same process would be State-law).

In principle the general rule is that cases in the subject-matter of law called administrative law go to a political tribunal rather than to a judicial one; for example, in the Cantons they would usually go to the Cantonal Executive Council, and in the Confederation they *used* to go to the Federal Council. The result is that much of what in Great Britain would go to a court of law goes to a political or civil-service tribunal in Switzerland, while nearly all that in Britain would go to a 'specialized' tribunal goes to a political, &c., tribunal in Switzerland, and also to the same tribunal appears to go a certain amount of what in Britain would not receive any sort of quasi-judicial treatment at all but would be settled by correspondence with a government office. Without administrative experience in both countries a true comparison between them is hardly possible, however.

It must also be borne in mind that Swiss courts in general do not satisfy Anglo-Saxon prejudices as to what a court of law should be, nor is even the status of a Judge easily comparable there and here.

---

[1] Elsewhere in this book 'Staatsrecht' is translated also as 'public law'.

V. MISCELLANEOUS PROVISIONS

ARTICLE 115. All decisions relative to the place of session of the Federal Authorities shall be made by Federal legislation.

Since 1848 the seat of the Federal administration and Assembly has been Berne. The Federal Tribunal has sat at Lausanne since 1875. The Federal Insurance Tribunal (which is not a Federal authority within the meaning of this Article) sits at Lucerne.

The Law on Political and other Guarantees in favour of the Confederation of 1934 (repealing that of 1851) gives the authorities a sort of extraterritoriality as against the Canton where they happen to be. The most important consequence of this Law, the exemption of Federal property from Cantonal direct taxation, is referred to in the note to Article 22 above.

ARTICLE 116. German, French, Italian, and Romanche are the national languages of Switzerland.

German, French, and Italian shall be deemed the official languages of the Confederation.

French, German, and Italian. The greater part of the inhabitants of Switzerland and a majority of the Cantons are German-speaking. That is to say, they speak both High German and also one of the sub-dialects of 'Swiss German'. Swiss German is not now merely a peasant language, and all classes of the population (as a rule) speak it at home as their mother tongue. Its natural development would be to form an independent minor literary language, like Dutch, but in practice it cannot do this, if for no other reason than because the French Swiss cannot reasonably be expected to learn Swiss German as opposed to the literary language. Swiss German, the language of the majority, may not be spoken in the Federal Assembly, but it is spoken, in varying degrees of robustness, in most Cantonal parliaments.

The dialects of French Switzerland, of considerable linguistic interest, are peasant languages, dying out, and so are those of the Italian valleys of the Grisons. To a much less extent this is also the case in the Ticino.

The language frontier between German and Italian is a sharply defined one, following the main line of the Alps, and except for one tiny enclave (Bosco-Gurin) of German in Ticino, presents no difficulties. The German-French boundary is a zigzag line running approximately north and south, through Biel, Fribourg, and Sierre. It is an invisible line, strolling through town and country, so that one farm speaks French and the next farm, and all to the east of it, speak German. It is independent of the religious boundary, and sometimes runs along it and sometimes cuts right across it. Historically it represents the boundary between Allemanni and Burgundians, and has on the whole moved little during the last thousand years—here one language gains a little, and there the other, but each language has its own sources of strength and the general balance of forces is a surprisingly stable one. Politically, the linguistic differences are less important than the religious ones—apart from anything else, an individual can learn to be bilingual, but to be bi-confessional is not possible. The fact that the religious and the linguistic minorities together form a majority in the Council of States is mentioned in the note to Article 80.

Romanche. In parts of Grisons another tongue is widely spoken, Romanche, which itself is divided into sub-dialects. It (or a dialect of the form of Romanche called Ladine) is also spoken outside Switzerland, in Italian South Tirol and the Carnic Alps, as a peasant dialect. Within Grisons it is now an official Cantonal language in two dialects, and an amendment of this Article in 1938 makes Romanche a 'national language', while promoting German, French, and Italian to 'official languages'. This gives it a certain nuisance value in Federal affairs, soothes the sensibilities of local patriots, and stakes out the claim that Romanche is a 'language' and not a 'dialect', in order to strengthen the hand of Switzerland against Italian cultural aggression. Romanche looks like a sort of germanized Italian: it is much farther removed from literary Italian than are the dialects of northern Italy. Romanche-speakers normally speak German also.

'*Freedom of Languages.*' Swiss writers often include the 'Freedom of Languages' in the catalogue of freedom-rights, but in the strict sense it is not one, for it is not a guaranteed constitutional right of the citizen in the sense of Article 113, and there is no Appeal in Public Law for breach of 'Freedom of Languages'. In this it resembles the guarantee of the secrecy of the post, Article 36. The phrase describes the practice of the Federal Authorities of (1) permitting where possible citizens to talk with officials in the language of the *district*—for example in French Switzerland to talk with postmen and railway officials in French—and (2) of permitting every citizen to correspond with the central government in Berne in his own mother tongue, and to plead before the Federal Tribunal in one of the three official languages. The Cantons follow the same practice, which errs rather on the side of absurdity than that of oppression, for the rules concerning language are obeyed nearly as meticulously as the rules of accountancy.

In the Assembly, speeches are usually made in French or German, with simultaneous translation in earphones. Speeches are also made in Italian from time to time, and appear to be listened to as attentively as other speeches—the audience read newspapers and write letters without any sign of annoyance from the unintelligible language. But Laws, &c., usually only have French and German original texts, the Italian text is a translation made after the law has left the Assembly. In Federal 'jobs' an arithmetical proportion of speakers of the official languages, with a slight bias in favour of minorities, is the rule. This is an advantage to those Ticinese who do not float of their own buoyancy.

There is no Italian-speaking university on Swiss territory, and this leads to difficulties, especially in the case of Italian-speaking Swiss who wish to qualify as doctors and practise medicine in Switzerland—but the Confederation mitigates these difficulties as far as is possible.

The only other reference to the large-minded generosity to linguistic minorities which is the rule in Switzerland, and which makes Swiss language-federalism possible, is in Article 107, Elections to the Federal Tribunal.

ARTICLE 117. Those who hold Federal office are responsible for their official conduct. A Federal law shall determine what is to be included in this responsibility.

The Law which carries out this competence is that on the Responsibility of the Officials and Authorities of the Confederation of 1850 (Verantwortlichkeitsgesetz), which is supplemented by the Law on the Status of Officials of 1927 and by other legislation.

The rather vague concept of 'responsibility' includes:

(i) A method of proceeding against the high officers of the Confederation elected by the Assembly and responsible to it, under Article 112 s. 4 of the Constitution and Articles 20–31 of the Law of 1850. This procedure, a sort of romantic reminiscence of impeachment, has never been used. There is also for the trial of the Federal General and of certain high military officers an Extraordinary Military Court, which is described in Articles 20–22 of the Law of 1889 on Military Penal Procedure, and which has also never been used. The Extraordinary Public Prosecutor for the former, and the Extraordinary Military Court for the latter, are to be elected by the Assembly in joint session. The institution is a legal curiosity.

(ii) Looked at in another way, the procedure to be used against the high officers of the Confederation can be regarded as a device to secure them special privileges before the Courts.[1] For if a private person wishes to prosecute one of them, he may only do so with the officer's consent, or that of the Federal Council, or that of the Assembly in joint session if their consent is refused (the Law on Political and other Guarantees of 1934, Articles 4 and 5, gives the precise details). The members of the legislative Councils also have certain procedural privileges, and parliamentary immunity for speeches and votes in their Chamber.

(iii) It includes a check on the illegal conduct of subordinate Federal officials. Such a check postulates: (1) disciplinary action within the civil service; and (2) the possibility of taking criminal action against an official (a) on the initiative of the Confederation, and (b) on the initiative of a private person; and (3) the possibility of taking civil action for damages against an official on the initiative (a) of the Confederation, or (b) of a private person.

The ideal law would provide all these remedies in the same measure against the State as between two private persons or as the State enjoys against the subject. Swiss Federal law falls short of this ideal—that goes without saying—and the impression one receives is that it also falls short of English law in this respect. A comparison of the two systems of law, however, on this point would need a separate study and would face very considerable difficulties in translating from one legal system to the other. The best method of approach is not to enumerate the remedies open to the subject but to measure the extent to which these remedies fall short of the 'ideal' law. The present writer is by no means convinced that Dicey's

---

[1] The legislation of the Cantons may do the same for the corresponding Cantonal civil authorities.

adverse judgement of continental legal systems is wrong, but would himself prefer to ascribe the defects of these systems not primarily to the existence of a category of 'administrative law' but rather to the juristic distinction between 'public law' and 'private law'—with the corollary of 'one law for the State and another for the private person'. English law, in attempting to assimilate the relations of sovereign to subject to private-law relations, is at least attempting the right task. The note to Article 114 *bis*, Administrative Jurisdiction, discusses these matters further.

THIRD SECTION
REVISION OF THE FEDERAL CONSTITUTION

ARTICLE 118. The Federal Constitution can at any time be revised, totally or in part.

The Constitution as passed in 1874 did not speak of 'total' and 'partial' revision, but only of 'revision'. It was therefore disputable whether the referendum-petition of 50,000 voters could or could not propose a partial revision—the revision of a particular Article in a particular sense. In August 1880 National Councillor Joos accordingly handed in a popular initiative duly signed by 50,000 demanding the submission to the people and Cantons of a revised Article 39 (Banknotes) 'relying on Article 120' (which then lacked the qualification 'total' before 'revision'). The Councils, however, did not interpret the then Constitution in this sense, and submitted, to the *people* only, the question 'Shall the Federal Constitution be revised?' The voters replied 'No'. That the Councils possessed the right of proposing partial revisions had been decided by the precedent of 1866. The wording of the Constitution as it had then stood neither expressly conferred the right on the Councils nor deprived the people of it, and the merit of Herr Joos's case—that either the right was possessed by neither or by both—must be admitted. The matter was set at rest in 1891 when the people and Cantons accepted an amendment expressly conferring upon the voters the right of initiating also *partial* revisions.

The whole of Articles 121 and 122 date from 1891, and the expressions 'partial' and 'total' in Articles 118, 119, 120, and 123.

Constitutional Revision since 1874. There have been two proposals for *total revision*—in 1880 when partial revision by petition of 50,000 was not yet recognized, and a project of Swiss Nazis, right-wing Catholics, and others in 1935.[1] Both were rejected. If the decision for total revision were at any time accepted, it is difficult to see how in modern conditions the Assembly could neglect the normal business of the country for the long period necessary to work out a text of a new Constitution. There have therefore been proposals for a separate Constitutional Assembly to be elected if total revision were ever decided upon.

There have been numerous *partial revisions*. Comparatively few of these

---

[1] This was rejected by a majority greater than 5:2. The Cantonal vote was not reckoned, but the Cantons in which there was a majority for total revision were Obwalden, Fribourg, Valais, and Appenzell Inner Rhodes (by one vote). These are all Catholic-Conservative Cantons.

have altered the constitutive parts of the Constitution; the vast majority have extended the competences of the central government—particularly in restriction of the Freedom of Trade and Industry. Other amendments impose upon the citizens the exacting standards of morality in matters of drink, gaming, and the receipt of foreign orders which democratic professional politicians everywhere feel compelled to advocate in public. Amendments to *constitutive* parts of the Constitutional document have been:

1891. Popular Constitutional Initiative, Articles 18–123.
1914. Administrative Jurisdiction, and Delegation to Departments, Articles 103 and 114 *bis*.
1918. Proportional Representation, Article 73.
1921. Treaty Referendum, Article 89, paragraph 3.
1931. 1950. Figures altered in Article 72, Number of Inhabitants per National Councillor.
1931. Term of Office of National Councillor, and hence of Federal Councillor and Chancellor, raised to four years, Article 76, &c.
1939. Rules for declaring *arrêtés* 'urgent' amended, Article 89.
1949. Urgency Rules again altered, Articles 89 and 89 *bis*.

Among the amendments which extend *Federal competences* may be particularly noted the Federal Civil and Penal Code Articles of 1898 (64 and 64 *bis*) and the Economic Articles of 1947.

ARTICLE 119. Total revision shall follow the procedure laid down for enacting Federal legislation.

The *drafting* of the new constitutional document 'follows the procedure for enacting Federal legislation', that is to say, the two Chambers debate it separately (Article 89). The same is the case when the Assembly drafts a partial revision (Assembly initiative) of the Constitution, and when it has to formulate the text of an 'unformulated' popular initiative (Article 121, paragraph 5).

Unlike Federal legislation the completed document *must* be submitted to the people *and* Cantons (Article 123).

ARTICLE 120. When one section of the Federal Assembly passes a resolution that there be a total revision of the Constitution, and the other section does not assent to it, or when 50,000 Swiss citizens entitled to vote demand total revision, then the question of whether there should be such a revision shall, in the one case as in the other, be submitted to a votation of the Swiss people by Aye and No.

If in the one case or in the other the majority of Swiss citizens taking part in the votation decide in the affirmative, then both

Councils shall be elected anew to take in hand the work of total revision.

This Article provides two alternative procedures for a total revision of the Constitution:
1. *The Popular Procedure. Initial Stages.* These resemble the stages of the unformulated initiative for partial revision:
    (i) Initiative petition of 50,000 in proper form, sent to the Federal Chancellery;
    (ii) Publication of the result of the scrutiny in the *Feuille fédérale* and a report from the Federal Council. *Arrêté* of the Assembly ordering a votation;
    (iii) Votation of *people* only;[1]
    (iv) If a majority for revision, then a new election of both Councils.
2. *The Assembly Procedure. Initial Stages.* This starts when one of the two Councils passes a draft *arrêté* in favour of total revision. The second Council then has a choice of two procedures:
    (a) It may decide to disagree with the first Council and reject the draft *arrêté*. The Constitution in such a case envisages that there should then be a votation of the people (only). If the project of a total revision is accepted by the people, then there is a new election of both Councils for the remainder of the legislature-period;
  or (b) The second Council may agree, or it may privately disagree and decide to adopt different tactics. For if it did privately disagree, course (a) would be extremely ill advised, as entailing the possibility of a popular majority for revision and a double dissolution. If it formally *agrees* (hypocritically or genuinely), then there is no dissolution and no popular vote. The project for a new Constitution must then be elaborated, 'following the procedure for enacting Federal legislation'. By Article 7 of the Law on the Relations between the Councils (carrying out Article 89, para. 1 of the Constitution) if the two Councils cannot agree 'the project is to be deemed rejected'. If the second Council decides on a total revision in principle, but against any given text, it apparently wins the day.
3. *Later Stages.* The Constitution provides (Article 123) that when the text is ready there shall be a votation of the people and Cantons upon it. But in the case of a total revision this expectation might in some circumstances be somewhat optimistic, for example, if there were a revision abolishing the equality of the Cantons or giving voting rights to women.

If the first project of a new Constitution is rejected, then presumably the Assembly works out a second one. This would more certainly be the case if the people had already answered 'Yes' to the question 'Shall a total revision take place?'

It will be noticed that in one respect a total revision is easier to set on foot

---

[1] This is one of the two cases where a compulsory Referendum is of the people only, without the Cantons. The other case is the unformulated popular initiative, Article 121.

than a partial revision, for any group of 50,000 can force a vote upon the question 'Shall a total revision take place?' and either Council can do the same. And if successful in the popular vote (whatever the majority of the Cantons) there is a double dissolution. Such a double dissolution entails a re-election of the Federal Council.[1]

ARTICLE 121. Partial revision can follow either the procedure of a popular initiative, or that laid down for enacting Federal legislation.

The popular initiative consists of a demand handed in by 50,000 Swiss citizens entitled to vote requiring the adoption, or the repeal or amendment, of particular Articles of the Federal Constitution.

If two or more subject-matters are proposed for an amendment of the Constitution by a popular initiative, each one of them must form a separate project of initiative.

The project of initiative may take the form of a proposal couched in general terms, or of one worked out in detail.

When the project is couched in general terms, the Federal Chambers shall, if they are in agreement with it, undertake a partial revision in the sense proposed by the initiants, and submit it to the people and Cantons for acceptance or rejection. If, on the other hand, the Federal Chambers are not in agreement with the project, the question of a partial revision shall be submitted to a votation of the people. If a majority of the Swiss citizens taking part in the votation decide in the affirmative, then the Federal Assembly shall undertake the revision in the sense of the people's decision.

If the project is one worked out in detail and the Federal Assembly is in agreement with it, it shall be submitted to the people and Cantons for acceptance or rejection. But if the Federal Assembly is not in agreement with the project, it may work out its own separate version, or it may recommend the people to reject the project, and submit its own version, or its recommendation of rejection, together with the text

---

[1] Article 96, para. 2, but cf. para. 1 of the same Article. Both Burckhardt (*Kommentar der BV*, 2nd ed., p. 736) and Giacometti (*Bundesstaatsrecht*, p. 573, n. 27) come to the conclusion that the Federal Council also is to be re-elected. Until the circumstances have actually arisen, however, the matter must remain in doubt. In both cases the re-election is for the remainder of the period of office only, not for the full period of four years.

of the popular initiative, to the votation of the people and Cantons.

This Article provides two alternative procedures for a partial revision—the popular and the Assembly procedure.

    1. *The Popular Procedure.* There are two forms of this, the formulated and the unformulated initiative:

    (*a*) *The Formulated Initiative.* The group who decide to launch the petition of initiative work out the text, and then try to collect signatures for it; this is expensive but not difficult to do—see note to Article 89. The method of doing this is laid down in the Law on the Procedure for Popular Initiatives of 1892 (printed in vol. i of the *Recueil systématique*[1]) which lays down *inter alia* that only those signatures dated within the six months preceding the handing-in of the initiative are to be counted. The signatures collected, the petition is handed in to the Federal Chancellery who forward it to the Statistical Department to count and classify the valid signatures. The result is published in the *Feuille fédérale*. The initiants now await the report to the Assembly of the Federal Council. The eventual report of the Federal Council contains a project of *arrêté* submitting the text to the people with a recommendation to accept or reject it, as the case may be, or to reject it in favour of a counter-project. The Councils now debate this. If they agree on a decision, then the project and their recommendation is submitted to a votation of people and Cantons, and by Articles 8 and 9 of the Law as revised, even if they do not agree and can formulate no decision, the project is nevertheless to be submitted three years after the receipt of the Initiative by the Chancellery.

    (*b*) *The Unformulated Initiative.* In this case the initiating group do not work out a complete legal text of a revised Article of the Constitution but content themselves with a general wish that certain Articles should be revised in a certain sense. If the Assembly on receipt of the report of the Federal Council agrees to the general wish, they set to work to elaborate a text. If they cannot agree on a text within two years, or if they disagree with the general wish, the project is submitted to a simple referendum (of the people only). If the majority are in favour of the wish expressed, then the Assembly is to conform to the wish and work out a project in that sense. It is, however, impossible to coerce two chambers into agreeing on a text, and if they can work out no text then presumably this is a snake in the game of legislative snakes-and-ladders. The text eventually worked out is submitted to the double referendum. An unformulated initiative has twice been submitted, in 1937 and 1946.[2]

    2. *The Assembly Procedure.* The Assembly agrees upon a text in the same manner as agreeing upon a law, and the text in the form of an *arrêté* altering the wording of the Constitution is automatically submitted to a referendum

---

[1] But the text was revised in 1950, and is therefore not now that of the *Recueil systématique*. The Articles revised were Arts. 4, 7, 8, and 9 of the Law.

[2] From 1891 to the end of 1951 fifty-nine Federal initiatives were launched. Seven only were successful.

on the next convenient date; the referendum is the double one, of people and Cantons.

The weakness of both these procedures lies in the relationship between the Assembly and the Federal Council, for it has now become the custom that the Councils will enter upon no business without the preliminary report of the Federal Council, and the Federal Council makes it its practice to withhold its report for tactical and political reasons, if necessary indefinitely. An initiative of 1935 designed to safeguard the liberty of the press still awaits the report of the Federal Council, though the executive act against which it was aimed has now, after a dozen years, been repealed. In the last few years, however, most of the initiatives that still remained, at the Executive's discretion, in the cocoon stage for ten or twelve years, have been withdrawn by their promoters—an action which recent amendments to the law have facilitated. The suspensive veto of the Federal Council is now an important part of the Constitution, even if an unofficial one, and was used perhaps justifiably during the period of danger from Germany. The Legislature does not possess this power.

Paragraph 3 establishes the principle known as 'unity of material', that is to say, an initiative must only propose a single alteration in the Constitution (although other alterations may legitimately be made consequent upon the one alteration; for example, if the term of office of the National Council is altered, that of the Chancellor may be changed to correspond with it). The Constitution, however, provides no means of enforcing the principle: if a popular initiative is completed, and the initiating committee refuse to withdraw it, the Assembly cannot alter its text—though they may submit their counter-project to the referendum at the same time. It is not easy to determine the limits of the principle of unity: some of the Articles of the Constitution can hardly be said to observe it very strictly.

PARAGRAPH 6. When there is an Assembly counter-proposition, then the questions submitted to the voter are 'Do you want to accept the proposition contained in the popular initiative?' and 'Do you want to accept the Federal Assembly's project?' The voter can answer 'No' to both, or 'No' to one and 'Yes' to the other, but not 'Yes' to both.

There is no Federal popular initiative for legislation.[1]

'*Unconstitutional*' *Initiatives*. Swiss jurists have raised the question of whether a properly completed project of initiative which struck at the root of the Constitution would be legal. The conclusion they have usually reached is that an anti-liberal initiative would be void and there would be no obligation to submit it to the people and Cantons. This conclusion is a sign that Swiss democracy is healthy and capable of defending itself against a wolf in constitutional clothing, though perhaps the arguments as arguments are rather weak.

The discussion is not purely speculative because the problem has actually arisen in the case of a Cantonal Constitution. In 1935 an initiative to amend

---

[1] But a Federal legislative initiative has several times been proposed. See the Report of the Federal Council of 5 Dec. 1952 (*Feuille fédérale*, 1952, iii. 761). There is a legislative initiative in all the Cantons.

the Constitution of Basle-Country was duly completed, proposing the reunion of the half-Canton with Basle-Town. The Cantonal Executive Council refused to accept the initiative, and the case was argued before the Federal Council on the issue whether a proposal to abolish the existence of the half-Canton could lawfully be the object of a constitutional amendment under the Cantonal Constitution: the Tribunal decided it could not.[1]

ARTICLE 122. A Federal Law shall determine the procedure to be followed for popular initiatives and for votations upon revision of the Federal Constitution.

The Law of 1892 concerning Initiatives, and the Law of 1872 on Federal Elections and Votations, can be found in vol. i of the *Recueil systématique*.

ARTICLE 123. The revised Federal Constitution, or the revised part of the Constitution, comes into force when it has been accepted by the majority of the Swiss citizens taking part in the votation and by the majority of States.

To reckon the majority of States, the vote of a half-Canton is counted as a half-vote.

The result of the popular vote in each Canton is counted as the vote of the State.

Majority of States, i.e. 11½ Cantons.

---

[1] *Arrêts du Tribunal fédéral*, 1935, i. 169. There were other issues and the decision did not turn upon this point. The amendments later came before the Federal authorities, who refused their guarantee on general grounds of policy: see note to Article 6.

TRANSITORY PROVISIONS

ARTICLE 1. The receipts from the Posts and customs shall be distributed on the basis of the arrangements now in force, until such time as the Confederation undertakes the effective burden of the military charges now borne by the Cantons.

Federal legislation shall further provide that any Cantons which suffer a financial loss in consequence of the changes effected by Articles 20, 30, 36 para. 2, and 42 (*e*), taken as a whole, shall not incur the whole loss at once, but only after a period of years has elapsed.

Those Cantons which are in arrears with their military commitments under the old Constitution at the time when Article 20 comes into force are obliged to carry them out, at their own cost.

The Confederation took over the responsibility for the army, and the Cantons sacrificed the sums they were receiving under the Constitution of 1848 as compensation for the abolition of Cantonal customs-duties, in 1875. The only Canton which lost over the deal was Basle-Town, which received diminishing annual sums as compensation for five years.

ARTICLE 2. Those provisions of Federal Laws and of concordats, and of Cantonal Constitutions and Laws, which are in contradiction with the new Federal Constitution cease to have effect when the present Constitution, or the Laws under it, come into force.

The legal tag 'Federal law breaks Cantonal law' (which has become attached to this Article, in rather the same way that 'denial of justice' has anchored itself to Article 4) has been given the status of a freedom-right by the Federal Tribunal, in that an Appeal in Public Law can be brought against any Cantonal act of sovereignty on the ground that it is contrary to Federal law.

The rule is that any Cantonal act of sovereignty, from the Cantonal Constitution to an administrative decision, which is, or becomes, repugnant to any Federal act, is void. The expression 'Federal act' includes the Federal Constitution, Laws and Arrêtés, the Arrêtés of the Federal Council, and the *arrêts* of the Federal Tribunal. In the practice of the Courts there are no doubt certain hesitations and ambiguities—a Court will clearly treat a Cantonal Constitution with the greatest respect—but the principle, that Federal law prevails over Cantonal law, is well established and of daily application.

There are certain logical difficulties about this rule. In the first place, is it right to regard the Constitution as Federal law, and thus to assimilate it to acts of the central government? And in the second place, how can any conflict of Federal and Cantonal law arise? The Confederation has competences, the Cantons have competences, and there is an area where the two overlap and where the Confederation legislates and the Cantons execute, but there is no area where a conflict can arise. The only case of possible difficulty is that provided for by this Article, which determines that the new Constitution is to be taken as repealing the old law, Cantonal and Federal, either at once or (as in the case of a new Federal competence to legislate) when the laws which the Constitution envisages come into force. It is in fact because the Constitution is regarded as Federal law, because anything the Confederation does is presumed to be under the Constitution, because (to take the matter a stage farther back) there is no judicial review of Federal acts, that we have the maxim 'Federal law breaks Cantonal law'. To consider the right to make an Appeal in Public Law against a Cantonal act (on the grounds that the Cantonal act infringes Federal law) as a freedom-right is, if anything, to underestimate the importance of it. It is rather a principle arising from the very nature of the Swiss State, above and behind the constitutional document, all of which (including, for example, Article 4) must be read as commands enforceable by the Confederation against the Cantons.

Federalism. The legal tag is so all-embracing that one wonders at first sight whether it is necessary to say anything more about the juridical side of Swiss federalism. The opposite maxim 'Local law breaks central law' (compare 'Landesrecht bricht Reichsrecht' of the Holy Roman Empire) is the mark of the loose Confederacy—such as the Thirteen Colonies under the Articles of Association or Switzerland before 1798 and from 1814 to 1848. For the question 'Which prevails, central law or local law?' is decisive—perhaps too decisive, since it permits neither Confederacy nor Confederation but only indivisible sovereignty: Confederacy is local sovereignty, ornamented on the outside, while Confederation is central sovereignty, qualified within. It is doubtful whether a separation of powers within the supreme power (e.g. calling one aspect of it the Supreme Court) does anything more than mask the central power's supremacy. The question 'Which prevails?' is in fact the wrong question, for Switzerland *is* a Confederation, and the Cantons are in a sort sovereign, and a line of argument which disproves this is false.

Interest in the relationship of central to local government must in any case not encourage the student to think that the antagonism is always present to the consciousness of Cantonal authorities and officials. The Cantonal governments face the people, and have their backs to the Federal authorities.

ARTICLE 3. The new provisions concerning the organization and competences of the Federal Tribunal shall only come into force when the appropriate Federal laws have been passed.

The Federal Tribunal entered upon in its new functions in its reorganized form on 1 Jan. 1875.

ARTICLE 4. The Cantons are granted a delay of five years for the introduction of gratuitous primary education (Article 27).

ARTICLE 5. Persons following a liberal profession who, before the legislation provided for in Article 33 comes into force, obtained a certificate of competence from a Canton, or from an authority representing several Cantons set up by concordat, may exercise their profession throughout the Confederation.

This Article is still in force, in particular as regards professional qualifications of lawyers. On the other hand, Federal legislation has been passed concerning certain professions, in particular, medicine. See note to Article 33.

Article 6 of the Transitory Provisions was repealed in the votation of 6 July 1947 (Economic Articles). It had been introduced in 1885, and had gone out of effect in all its provisions by 1895. Its subject-matter was duties upon alcohol, in connexion with the old 32 *bis*.

RESOLVED by the National Council. To be submitted to the people and Cantons.

    Berne, 31 Jan. 1874

              President: ZIEGLER
              Secretary: SCHIESS

RESOLVED by the Council of States. To be submitted to the people and Cantons.

    Berne, 31 Jan. 1874

              President: A. KOPP
              Secretary: J. L. LUTSCHER

(Accepted by a majority of voters and of Cantons on 19 Apr. 1874; declared in force as from 29 May 1874. The number of voters was 340,199 in favour, and 198,013 in opposition. Of the Cantons 14½ accepted, while Lucerne, Uri, Schwyz, Obwald, Nidwald, Zug, Fribourg, Valais, and Appenzell Inner Rhodes rejected the project. These are the Cantons which formed the old Sonderbund (though, because of its small size and isolation, Inner Rhodes was not able to do more than sympathize with that alliance and its campaign). The French- and Italian-speaking Cantons, which had voted against the Project of 1872, voted in favour of that of 1874—with the exception, of course, of the Catholic Fribourg and Valais.)

ADDITIONAL PROVISIONS

(From time to time additional Articles of temporary duration are added to the Constitution, having been accepted at a votation of people and Cantons. These are now usually (i) concerning temporary financial expedients, permitting the central government to levy direct taxation, or (ii) under the new Article 89 *bis*. The ones now in force are not printed here, but can be found in the German text of the Constitution, on p. 208.)

ALPHABETICAL ANALYSIS OF THE FEDERAL CONSTITUTION

The figures refer to the *Articles* of the Constitution. (The more remote references are in parentheses)

Absinthe, 32 *ter*.
Accident insurance, 34 *bis*.
Administration, Federal, 85 s. 11, 102 s. 12. *See also* Administrative Law; Officials, Federal.
Administrative law, 113, *114 bis*, (50), 103, 102 s. 2, 85 s. 12, (117).
Agriculture, 31 *bis*, 23 *bis*, 25, 29, 32 *bis*, 34 *ter*, (69).
Alcohol, 32 *bis*, 32 *ter*, 31 *ter*, 32 *quater*; 34 *quater*.
Alpine districts: corn, 23 *bis*, (31 *bis*); (torrents, 24); game, 25; roads, 30, 37.
Amendment of the Constitution, *see* Revision.
Amnesty, 85 s. 7.
Arms: and munitions, supply of, 20; monopoly of, 41; of the soldier, 18.
Army, Federal: conscription, 18; Federal and Cantonal competences, 13, 19, 20, 21, 22, t.p. 1; Federal authorities and, 85 s. 4, s. 9, 102 s. 11, s. 12; exemption tax, 18, 42, t.p. 1; arms retained by soldier, 18; military insurance, 18, 34 *ter*; miscellaneous, 14, 15, 16, 17, 23, 11, 12. *See also* War; Arms and munitions.
Arrest for civil debt, 59.
Arrêtés of the Federal Council, 35, 41.
—, Federal, 89, 89 *bis*, 32, (34 *ter*), 113; 85 s. 2, 102 s. 1, s. 2, s. 4, s. 5, 51.
Assizes, Federal, 106, 112.
Association, right of, 56, 34 *ter* (31 *bis*). *See also* Associations, religious.
Associations, religious, 49, 50, 51, 52.
Asylum, right of, for foreigners, 69 *ter*, 70.
Authorities, Cantonal: incompatibilities for, 12, 97, 108; conflicts of competence, 113.
— Federal: election and pay, 85 s. 1, s. 3, s. 4, 92; conflicts of, 85 s. 13, 92, 113; violence against, 112; seat of, 115. *See also* Federal Assembly; Federal Council; Federal Tribunal; Chancellor, Federal.
Aviation, 37 *ter*.

Banishment, 44, (69 *ter*, 70). For Extradition, *q.v.*
Banks, 31 *quater*; Cantonal, 31 *quater*; Swiss Federal, 39.
Births, deaths, and marriages, registration of, 53.
Bishoprics, 50.
Budget, *see* Estimates.
Burials: 'decent', lay, 53; of paupers, 48, (53).
Butchery, Jewish, 25 *bis*.

Cafés and restaurants, 31 *ter*, 32 *quater*.
Capacity, civil, 64.
Capitulations, military, 11.
Casting vote of president, 78, 82.
Cemeteries, 53.
Challenge, legislative, 89, 89 *bis*, (90), 71; 32, 34 *ter*.
Chancellor, Federal, 105, 85 s. 3, s. 4, 92. (For signature of Chancellor Schiess, see the end of the Constitution.)
Children, 34, 64 *bis*, (34 *quinquies*), 44, 49, 54. *See also* Education.
Citizenship, 43, 44, 54, 68, 110. *For the words* 'Swiss citizen', *q.v.*
Civic rights, deprivation of, 45, 66, 74.
Civil law, 64, 114, 46, 47, 50, 59, 60, 61, 110, 111.
Coinage, 38.
Collective contracts, 34 *ter*.
Commerce, freedom of: *see* Trade and Industry, freedom of.
Commissioners, Federal, 12.
Communes, 43, 44, 45, (54), (68), 110.
Concordats, 7, 85 s. 5, 102 s. 7, 113, t.p.2, t.p.5, (24 *bis*), (102 s. 2).

Conflicts between Cantons, *14*, 110, 113, 102 s. 5, (7).
— of competence, 85 s. 13, 113.
'Constitutional judge', 58.
Constitutional rights of citizens, *see* Freedom-rights.
Constitutions, Cantonal: guarantee of, 5, 6, 85 s. 7, 102 s. 3; and the Federal Constitution, *t.p.*2, 3, 6.
Consultation of interests, 32, 34 *ter*.
Contingents, Cantonal: money, 42; soldiers, 19.
Convents, 52, (51).
Convocation of Federal Assembly, *86*, 16, 102 s. 11.
Corn, 23 *bis*. *See also* Agriculture.
Corporal punishment, 65.
Council of States, 80–83, 71. *See also* Federal Assembly.
Courts: Cantonal, 64, 64 *bis*; ecclesiastical, 58; 'extraordinary', 58.
Criminal law, *64 bis*, 65, 55, 56, 58, 67, 112, (106, *114*, 117), 45.
Crises, economic, 31 *quinquies*, 32, (29).
Customs duties, *28, 29*, 30, 42, 8, 23 *bis*, t.p.1, (31 *bis*, 69 *bis*).

Death penalty, 65.
Debt and bankruptcy, 64, 59, 114. *See also* Civil law.
Decent burial, right to, 53.
Decorations, foreign, 12.
Departments of the Federal Council, 103, 104.
Derogatory force of Federal law, *t.p.* 2, *113*; 3, 5, 6; 7, 9; 14, (24 *bis*), 27.
Disputes, *see* Conflicts.
Dissolution of Federal Assembly, 120, 76.
Domicile: civil law, 46, 59; political rights, 43, 74; taxation, 46; poor law, 45; foreigners, 44. *See also* Settlement; Constitutional judge.
Double Taxation, 46.
Droit de retrait, 62.
Duration of mandate for National Council, 76; for other authorities, 96, 105, 107, (120).

Education: primary, 27, 27 *bis*, t.p.4; military, 20; religious, 27, 49, 51; higher education, 27; professional, 31 *bis*, 34 *ter*, (27). *See also* Professions, liberal.
Elections: for National Council, 72–76, 120, 85 s. 1; of Council of States, 80, 120; of other Federal authorities, *see* Federal Council; Federal Tribunal; Chancellor, Federal; General, Federal; Officials, Federal; President, of a Council; other elections, 102 s. 6, 85 s. 4. *See also* Incapacity; Incompatibility.
Electricity, 24 *bis*, (26).
'Emergency', 'extraordinary circumstances', &c., special provision for, *19*, 29, 86, *89 bis, 102 s. 11*, 16, 17, 31 *bis*, *32*, (34 *ter*), 39, *58*, (9, 14, 15, 30, 31 *quinquies*).
Emigration agencies, 34.
Equality before the Law, *4*, 60, 34 *ter*, (43, 45, 58).
Estimates (budget), Federal, 85 s. 10, 102 s. 14.
État civil, 53.
Execution, Federal, 5, 85 s. 8, 102 s. 2, s. 3, s. 5, s. 10, (27).
Experts, 104.
Expropriation, 23, (22).
Extradition from Canton to Canton, 67, (46, 61).

Factory law, 34 *ter*, 34.
Family, the, 34 *quinquies*.
Federal Assembly, 71–94; competences of, *85*, 84; joint session, 92, 85 s. 4, s. 13, s. 7; elections by, 85 s. 4, 92, 96, 105, 107, 102 s. 6. *See also* Challenge, legislative; Convocation; Dissolution; Federal Council; Chancellor, Federal; Incompatibility.
— Council, 95–104; competences of, *102*; election of, 96, 85 s. 4, 92; incompatibility for, 77, 81, 97, 108, 12; judicial powers of, 85 s. 2, 103, (113, 114, 114 *bis*); other mention of, 10, 16, 85 s. 5, 86, 105, 35, 41, 43, (117).
'Federal law breaks Cantonal law', *see* Derogatory force of Federal law.
Federal Tribunal, *106–114 bis*, t.p.3, 85 s. 4, (92), 85 s. 11, 102 s. 2, s. 5, s. 6, (12).
Finances, Cantonal, *see* Taxation, Cantonal.

Finances, Federal: for Federal income, *see* Property, of the Confederation; Customs duties; Monopolies, Federal; Military exemption tax; Contingents, Cantonal: money; Stamp duties; Tobacco; Gambling. For Subsidies, Federal, *and* Estimates, Federal, *see* those words.

Fishing and shooting, 25.
Foodstuffs, 69 *bis*.
Foreigners, 69 *ter*, 70; 59; naturalization, 44.
Foreign relations, 85 s. 5, s. 6, 102 s. 8, s. 9, s. 16. *See also* Treaties; War; Neutrality; 'Independence'.
Forests, 24, (25).
Freedom-rights: in general, *113*, 5, (16), 102 s. 2, (*t.p.2*); particular rights: equality, 4; trade, 31; settlement, 45; belief, 49; worship, 50; press, 55; association, 56; constitutional judge, 58; to primary education, 27; from double tax, 46; to decent burial, 53; marriage, 54; petition, 57; judge of domicile for debt, 59; from corporal punishment, 65; to postal secrecy, 36; to asylum, 69 *ter*, 70; of languages, 116. *See under those words for further references. For Political rights, of individuals, q.v.*

Gambling, 35.
General, Federal, 85 s. 4, 92, (12). (*See also* Army, Federal, Federal authorities and.)
Grisons, 1, 30, 37.
Guarantee of Cantonal Constitutions, 5, 6, 85 s. 7, 102 s. 3.
Gunpowder, 41, 42.

Half-Cantons; 1, 13, 72, 73; 80, 123; (82, 86, 89, 89 *bis*, 96).
Health, public, 69, 69 *bis*, 34. *For* public health insurance, *see* Insurances, social. *For* Alcohol, *q.v.*
Heimatlos, 68, 44, 110.
Heimatschein, 45.
'High supervision', 24, 24 *bis*, 37, 85 s. 11.
High treason, 112, (65).
Hunting, 25.

Incapacity: political, of priests, 75, (49), (96, 108); other incapacities for certain offices, 78, 82, 96. *See also* Civic rights, deprivation of; Incompatibility.
Incompatibility: with National Council mandate, 75, 77; Council of States, 81; other authorities, 96, 97, 98; 108; for holders of foreign decorations, 12.
'Independence', 'security', &c., as against foreign nations, 2, 16, 70, 85 s. 6, 102 s. 9, (preamble), (23).
Industrial relations, 34 *ter*.
Infectious diseases, 69.
Initiative: popular, 120–2, 71; parliamentary, 93, (91).
'Instructions', 91.
Insurances: private, 34, (41 *bis*): social, against accidents, illness, 34 *bis*; unemployment, 34 *ter*; age, disability, widowhood, 34 *quater*, 32 *bis*; maternity, 34 *quinquies*; military, 18, 34 *ter*.
International personality of Cantons, *see* Treaties, Cantonal, with foreign countries.
Intervention, Federal, 16, 17, 85 s. 7, (2, 5, 102 s. 10).

Jesuits, 51.
Jews, (25 *bis*).
Judge: 'constitutional', 58, (59); Federal, *see* Federal Tribunal.
Judicial organization, Cantons, 64, 64 *bis*.
— review: of Federal legislation, 113, 114 *bis*; of Cantonal legislation, *see* Derogatory force of Federal law.
Jury, Federal, 106, 112.

Kursaals, 35.

Languages, *116*, 107.
Law, civil, criminal, *see* Civil law; Criminal law.
Legitimation by subsequent marriage, 54.
Loans, public, 85 s. 10.
Lotteries, 35.

Majorities, special, required: in Assembly, 87, 88, 89 *bis*, (32, 34 *ter*), 92; in Federal Council (100); in votations, (citizens) 120, 121, 123, (cantons) 123; in Cantonal votations, 6.

Mandate, *see* 'Instructions'.
Marriage: right to, 54, (49); registration of, 53; and citizenship, 54, 44.
Maternity insurance, 34 *quinquies*.
Messages of the Federal Council, 102 s. 4, s. 16.
Military exemption tax, 18, 42.
Monopolies, Federal: posts, *36*, 42, t.p.1; coinage, 38; gunpowder, 41, 42, (flour, 23 *bis*; railways, 26; brandies, 32 *bis*; National Bank, 39).
— Cantonal, 31, (31 *quater*).
Motor-cars and bicycles, 37 *bis*.

National Council, 71–79, 86. *See also* Federal Assembly; Incompatibility.
Nationality, *see* Citizenship.
Natural judge, the, 58.
Navigation, 24 *ter*, 24 *bis*; aerial, 37 *ter*.
Neutrality, 102 s. 9, 85 s. 6.

Officers: commissioned by Cantons, 21; and Foreign decorations, 12.
Officials, Federal: appointment, pay, 102 s. 6, 85 s. 3, s. 4, 109; responsibility of, *117*, 112, 114 *bis*; incompatibilities, 77, 97, 108, 12; supervision of, 102 s. 15, s. 12, 85 s. 11.
Order, public, *see* Public order.
Orders, foreign, 12.

Parade-grounds, 22.
Pardon, 85 s. 7, 92.
Patents, 64.
Paupers, 45, 48, (44, 54).
Payment: of members of Federal authorities, 85 s. 3, 79, 83, 99, 107; of officials, 85 s. 3.
Penal law, *see* Criminal law.
People, the: as an organ of the Federal power, 32, (34 *ter*), 89, 89 *bis*, 90, 71, 120–3, concluding formula of the Constitution; as an organ of the Cantonal power, 5, 6, 1.
Petition, right of, 57.
Police, 13, (9).
'Political', word used, 6, 43, 47, 49, 66; 65, 67, 112, (55, 70); 7, (8).
Political crimes, 65, 67, 112.
— rights, Federal, (of individuals), (2, 5), (4), 6, 43, 47, 49, 66, (113); Federal, of challenge, 89, 89 *bis*; of initiative, 118–22; to referendum, 119–23, (89 *bis*); to elect, 72–76, 85 s. 1, (91), 106, 112; to be elected, 75 (*see also* Incompatibility; Incapacity); (of Cantons), 89, 89 *bis*, 80, 83, (91), 93, 121–3.
Poor law, *see* Paupers.
Posts, 36, 42, t.p.1, (37 *bis*, 37).
President: of the Confederation, 98, 99; of a Council, 78, 92, 82, (*see also* concluding formula of the Constitution).
Press, Freedom of, *55*, 67.
Prisons, 64 *bis*.
Procedure, civil and criminal law, 64, 64 *bis*.
Professions: liberal, *33*, t.p.5; others, 31 *bis*, 31 *ter*, 32, 32 *quater*, 34 *ter*. *See also* Trade and Industry, freedom of.
Property of the Confederation, 42.
Public accounts, 85 s. 10, 102 s. 14.
Public health, *see* Health, public.
Publicity of debates, 94.
'Public order', 2, 50, 85 s. 7, 102 s. 10, (5, 16, 51, 54, 55, *56*, 70, 112).
Public welfare, *see* Welfare, public.
Public works, 23.

Railways, 26.
Referendum: compulsory (Constitutional), *120–3*, 71, 85 s. 14, (89 *bis*); facultative, legislative, *see* Challenge, legislative.
Registers of births, deaths and marriages, 53.
Règlement (Standing Orders) of Council, 86.
Religion, freedom of, 49, 50, 27, (preamble); qualifications of this freedom, 27, 49, 50, 25 *bis*, 51, 52, 53, 54, 58, 75.
Reports of Federal Council, 102 s. 4, s. 16.
Representation: basis of, 72; proportional, 73.
'Residence', place of, various uses of term, 43, 45, 46, 47, 59, 74.
Responsibility of officials, *117*, (112, 114 *bis*).
Revision of the Constitution, 118–23, 85 s. 14, 90, (89 *bis*, 71).
Rights: political, *see* Political rights; civil, *see* Freedom-rights.

ALPHABETICAL ANALYSIS 147

Roads, 37, 30, t.p.1, 37 *bis*, (23, 36).
Romanche, 116.

Sanction, Federal, 7, 24 *bis*, 35, 41, 43, 50, 55, 102 s. 13. *For* guarantee of Cantonal Constitutions, and ratification of treaties, *see* Guarantee; Treaties.
Seat of Federal authorities, 115.
Settlement, 43, *45*, 46, 47, 69 *ter*.
Social services, *see* Insurances, social; Factory law; Paupers; Children; Welfare.
'Sovereign', word used, 1, 3, 5, 24 *bis*.
Stamp duties, 41 *bis*, 42.
'Subjection', 4.
Subsidies, Federal, 23, 24, 27, 27 *bis*, 64 *bis*, 69 *bis*, (20, 23 *bis*, 30, 37, 31 *bis*, 31 *quinquies*, 34 *quinquies*, 44).
'Supervision', 20, 23 *bis*, 34, 40, 69 *bis*, 102 s. 13, s. 15, 105. *See also* 'High supervision'; Sanction, Federal.
'Swiss citizen', 'Swiss', 'citizen', use of these words, 4, *18*, 43, 45, *56*, 60, 74, 75; 5, 6, 19, 31 *bis*, 34 *bis*, 34 *quater*, 44, 47, 66, 89, 89 *bis*, 96, 108, 113, 120, 121, 123.

Taxation, Cantonal, 31, 39, 46, (41 *bis*, 45, 49, 54; 24 *bis*, 31 *bis*, 32 *quater*, 62, 63, t.p.1; 4, 60).
— Federal, *see* Finances, Federal.
Technical High School, 27.
Ticino, 1, 30, 37.
Titles, foreign, 12, (4).
Tobacco, 41 *ter*, 34 *quater*.
Torrents, 24.
Trade and Industry, freedom of, *31*; qualifications of this freedom, 31, 31 *bis*, 31 *quinquies*, 32, 32 *quater*, 34 *ter*; 23 *bis*, 24 *bis*, 24 *ter*, 26, 28, 31 *ter*, 31 *quater*, 32 *bis*, 32 *ter*, 32 *quater*, 33 t.p. 5, 34, 34 *bis*, 34 *quater*, 34 *quinquies*, 35, 36, 37 *bis*, 37 *ter*, 38, 39, 41, 64, 69 *bis*.
Trade unions, 34 *ter*, (56).
Traite foraine, 62, 63, (54).
Transport (36), 24 *ter*, 26, 37 *bis*, 37 *ter*, 24 *bis*. *See also* Roads.
Treason, 112, (65).
Treaties, Federal, 8, 29, 85 s. 5, 113, 114 *bis*, 11, 59, 69 *ter*, 112; referendum and, 89; Cantonal, with foreign countries, 9, 8, 10, 11, 85 s. 5, 102 s. 7; with other Cantons, *see* Concordat. *For* Foreign relations, *q.v.*
Tribunals, *see* Courts; Federal Tribunal.
Troops, *see* Army, Federal.
Trusts, 31 *bis*.

Unemployment, 31 *quinquies*, 34 *ter*.
University, Federal, 27.
Urgency, 89 *bis*, 32, 34 *ter*, 102 s. 11, (31 *bis*, 39).
Uri, 1, 30, 37.

Valais, 1, 30, 37.
Vice-president: of Confederation, 98; of a Council, 78, 82.
Votations, mentioned, 43, 74, 89 *bis*, 90, 120, 121, 122, (32, 34 *ter*, 89, 123).
Voting rights, *see* Political rights.

War, 8, *85 s. 6*, *19*, 31 *bis*, *39*, 41, (14–17). *See also* Army, Federal.
Water power, 24 *bis*.
Weights and measures, 40.
'Welfare', 2, *31 bis*, 31 *ter*, 32 *quater*, 102 s. 16, (24 *bis*, 35, 41, 69 *bis*).
Worship, freedom of, 50. *See also* Religion, freedom of.

II
PARLIAMENTARY PROCEDURE

The procedure of the Federal Assembly differs radically from that of the United Kingdom Parliament. In particular:
1. The Assembly is not sovereign, it is one of two powers which are in principle co-ordinate. The Assembly has competences, the Federal Council has competences, and there is an area where the two overlap and where the Assembly 'supervises' the Federal Council; but the Executive is not the creature of the Legislature, it is a power co-ordinate with it.
2. There is no conflict in principle between Executive and Legislature. Composed of the same parties, both representing the people, both equally under the Constitution, the two powers are intended to co-operate and not to war with each other. English procedure, based upon the dualism of government and opposition, and of front bench and back bench, is inapplicable to Swiss circumstances.

The procedure of the two Councils (the differences between the National Council and the Council of States are interesting, but inconsiderable) centres round the message or report of the Federal Council: all debate either leads up to a Federal Council report or away from it.

(a) Procedures leading up to a Report

There are four ways in which the Assembly may elicit a report from the Federal Council:

(i) *Motion.* A motion is a politely phrased command to the Federal Council to submit a report or a project or to take certain action, upon which *both* Councils agree.[1] The motion is finally 'settled' when the report is submitted, or when the motion is withdrawn or lapses. The first signatory of the motion may withdraw it, but the other signatories in succession may take it up again if they do not agree to the withdrawal. Although the motions are mandatory, in practice the Federal Council does not always comply with those which are tiresome, and it is to save the annoyance of printing the same motion every year for twenty years or more that motions are deemed to lapse when the signatories cease to be members of the Council, or if the motion is not discussed at all within two years, or is not answered by the Federal Council within four years.[2] To those accustomed to a sovereign legislature Swiss practice appears rather casual.

---
[1] Art. 14, Law on the Relations between the Councils (printed below).
[2] In 1946 ten motions were struck off as being unanswered: five dated from 1919. This is exceptional; in most years one or none is struck off.

The following is an example of a motion:

'*National Council, 12 June 1951*

'The Federal Council is invited to lay before the Chambers a project revising the Federal Laws on Subsidies to Public Primary Education in the following sense:
(1) The subsidy to the Cantons shall be based on the number of children liable to compulsory education;
(2) The supplementary subsidy provided for by Article 4 of the Law of 1930 shall be granted to mountainous Cantons *pro rata* to the number of schoolchildren in those regions.

'*Signed* (7 Members of the Council of States)

'*2 Oct. 1951. Decision of Council of States: This Motion of the National Council is taken up* (prise en considération).'

[The Assembly now awaits the Report of the Federal Council.[1]]

(ii) *Postulate*. A postulate, unlike a motion, is not mandatory. It is adopted by *one* Council only, not by both, but it has the same intention as a motion, namely the eliciting of a report from the Federal Council. A postulate habitually contains the words 'The Federal Council is requested . . .' Like motions, postulates are in writing, and lapse if ignored—in 1951, a typical year, 31 were struck off. They deal with the same sort of subject-matter as motions, asking for closer supervision of foreigners, protection from foreign competition, or more subsidies, &c. In 1950 there were 55 postulates, and 5 motions, handed in to the Federal Chancellery.

(iii) *Interpellation*.[2] An interpellation is a question in writing addressed to the Federal Council, countersigned by a certain number of deputies (in the National Council 10, in the Council of States 3). There is no need, as there is for a motion or a postulate, for the matter to be 'taken up' by the Council. The interpellant can deliver a short lecture in support of his question, and the Federal Councillor can, immediately or at a later date, answer it verbally in the Chamber. The interpellant can then declare himself satisfied or not; a debate can only take place by a resolution of the Council, and there is no vote. The following is an example of an unusually incisive interpellation:

'How long will the Federal Council tolerate that Swiss milk is liable to competition from imports of powdered and condensed milk from countries which have devalued their currency, or practise dumping?' (*21 signatures*.)

(iv) *Question*. (National Council only.) Written questions are handed in to the president of the Council, and the Federal Council is supposed to reply to them, orally or in writing, before the end of the next session. There is no opportunity for subsidiary questions. Like motions, postulates, and interpellations, unanswered questions are superannuated. There is also in every session a so-called 'Question Hour' in the National Council. It frequently happens that only one question is asked, couched in the form of a postulate, and with no bite to it. The Question Hour is an interesting demonstration of how different the position of the Swiss Assembly *vis-à-vis* the Executive is from that of the United Kingdom Parliament. About 400 written questions are asked during a legislature-period.

[1] (The Law of June 1953 is based on this motion.)   [2] Art. 22, LRC.

(b) Procedure deriving from a Report of the Federal Council

The Federal Council, either on its own initiative or in reply to a motion, &c., submits messages (in the first place) and reports (in reply to motions, &c.) to the Assembly.[1]

At the beginning of each session the presidents of each Council settle between them the 'priority' of business, i.e. which Council shall deal with a particular business first. They then submit the agreement each to his own Council, and the Councils either agree or decide by lot.

The Council which has priority in the business automatically refers it to a *'commission'* for prior consideration. These *commissions*, standing or *ad hoc*, are composed proportionately to the groups in the council—a 'scale' is drawn up beforehand, determining, for example, that in a committee of 17 the Catholic Conservatives will have 5 representatives, in a committee of 19 they will have 6, &c. The *commissions* sit independently of the sessions of the Assembly, touring to attractive hotels or symbolic places at will, and calling in front of them Federal officials, or requesting the presence of Federal Councillors. They take as their basis the project of the Federal Council, but amend it freely, and print majority and minority projects of their own, which they lay before the Council concerned. The majority on the *commission* appoints two *rapporteurs*, one German and one French, and the minorities appoint *rapporteurs* as they need them.

When a project of a Law (or *arrêté*) comes before one of the Councils there is first what would be called in Britain a 'second-reading debate' upon the question of 'entering upon the matter' (eintreten), and this is followed by an 'Article by Article' debate (which corresponds to the 'committee stage' in Great Britain), and this by a vote on the whole. The project is then sent to the other Council, who go through the same procedure. If agreement is not at first obtained between the two Councils, the project is shuttled backwards and forwards until they either do, or finally cannot, agree. The procedure of *'divergences'*, when they cannot agree, is described in Articles 5 and 6 of the Law on the Relations between the Councils.

Laws and *arrêtés* almost always delegate powers to the Executive in sweeping terms. If they are furnished with the 'referendum clause' they are first published in the *Feuille fédérale*, where they are subject to challenge for three months. If unchallenged, or if accepted, they are then published in the *Recueil des lois fédérales*.

A large proportion, perhaps three-quarters, of the Assembly's time is spent on legislation. The only opportunity for a methodical criticism is the debate on the Annual Report of the Federal Council, but because there is no need for opposition, the use made of this opportunity is not very great. The effective organs of control of the Executive—or rather, of collaboration with the Executive—are the *commissions*; they are the operative part of Swiss parliamentary government.

Character of the Debates: General Impressions

It seems probable that the Swiss concept of an ideal legislature is a Roman Senate as seen through the eyes of the early nineteenth century. The

[1] Art. 20, LRC; Article 102, s. 4 of the Constitution.

National Council meets in a large, dignified, and appropriately 'classical' (as opposed to Gothic) room, which is arranged for oratory rather than for discussion, and for decorous attention by listening lawgivers.

But, as it happens, the Swiss temperament, while scorning informality, does not rise to rhetoric—nor are the acoustics (microphones) of the room adapted to it—and human nature is not equal to the task of sustainedly listening to Swiss speech-making. To the student of government, however, to watch a debate from the public gallery (Tribüne) is exceedingly interesting and revealing. In the centre of the long side of the room where the debate is proceeding is a desk, a little raised, from which an *orateur* reads a speech into a microphone. The president of the Council, behind him, consults his watch, then continues to read his newspaper. To the president's right are members—the *doyen d'âge*, an old peasant in a dark suit, and others —to his left is the Chancellor (busy writing) and other officers. In front of the orator sit the tellers, and on each side are the six ornate chairs, three and three, for the members of the Federal Council. On one of them is a Federal Councillor, looking quietly distinguished. All these face the public gallery. With their backs to the gallery, their seats arranged in wide, flat semi-circles, are the members of the Council. Each has his own desk, with ear-phones in which a simultaneous translation can be heard. Many desks are empty, but the members present are all busily engaged, writing letters, reading documents or newspapers, and chatting. A messenger brings a member a parcel, he undoes it, and rolls the string up carefully to add to a little collection in his desk. The orator stops speaking, there is a quick vote by standing and sitting, and then the 'debate' continues, the speakers addressing the Council in the order in which they had, before the debate started, handed in their names to the president. All read carefully prepared lectures.

The reports in the daily papers of the debates are full and good.

The Council of States, being smaller, seems more purposeful, and holds the attention better. The Cantonal legislatures, especially when their council-chamber has not been too radically 'restored', are often impressive, for they meet in historically evocative surroundings. The 'Landsgemeindes' have even considerable beauty, and are visually and emotionally memorable. Apart from the Landsgemeindes, however, there is no effort to stress the aesthetic functions of government. And the *procedure*[1] is nearly the same throughout Swiss democracy—dignified, uninteresting, and ineffective.

[1] For further description of the procedure of the Federal Assembly see K. Eichenberger, *Die oberste Gewalt im Bunde* (part II), Berne thesis, Zürich, 1949, and also P. Cron, *Die Geschäftsordnung der schw. Bundesversammlung*, Fribourg thesis, Fribourg, 1946. The latter work does not entirely fulfil the promises of its title-page, though it contains passages of value.

LAW ON THE RELATIONS BETWEEN THE COUNCILS

(GESCHAEFTSVERKEHRSGESETZ)

FEDERAL LAW

ON THE RELATIONS BETWEEN THE NATIONAL COUNCIL, THE COUNCIL OF STATES, AND THE FEDERAL COUNCIL, AND ON THE FORM OF PROMULGATION AND OF PUBLICATION OF LAWS AND ARRÊTÉS

(of 9 October 1902)

THE FEDERAL ASSEMBLY

OF THE

SWISS CONFEDERATION

Having Regard to the Message of the Federal Council of 30 March 1899

DECREES

I. RELATIONS BETWEEN THE NATIONAL COUNCIL AND THE COUNCIL OF STATES

ARTICLE 1. The National Council and the Council of States meet on the first Monday of December for the first part of the ordinary session, and the first Monday of June in the year following for the second part of the same session.

The Councils may be called together for an extraordinary session by the Federal Council, or on the request of one-quarter of the members of the National Council, or of five Cantons.

For times of meeting, and convocation of extraordinary sessions, see page 98.

ARTICLE 2. At the beginning of each session the presidents of the two Councils shall agree as to which Council shall handle which subject of debate first. Each shall submit the decision which is reached to the approval of the Council over which he presides, at its first or second sitting.

If, at a time before the Councils have met, the Federal Council declares a subject specially urgent, the presidents of the two Councils shall come to an agreement on the allocation of priority before the session starts, and this agreement does not require the sanction of the Councils.

In such a case, the presidents are permitted to require the *bureaux* to nominate committees, and to allow these committees to start work.

'Priority', see also page 91; 'bureaux', see page 87. The National Council itself decides on the credentials of its own members, so in order to break what would otherwise be a deadlock after a general election, the oldest presumed member (*doyen d'âge*) nominates six tellers (*scrutateurs*) and he and the tellers compose the 'provisional bureau'. This in turn nominates a provisional committee to examine the credentials of those who claim to have been elected. The Council can 'constitute itself' when a quorum—half the total number—have been declared elected. The members then take the oath, or make an affirmation, and the Council can proceed to business. Its first act is to set up its regular bureau.

In the Council of States the Cantons decide on the credentials of their representatives, so no problem arises there.

ARTICLE 3. If the Councils (or, in the case provided for by Article 2, paragraph 2, the presidents of the Councils) are unable to agree upon the question of priority, the presidents shall decide by casting lots.

ARTICLE 4. When one Council has passed a resolution upon a project of Law or *arrêté*, the president and the secretary are to sign it in the form in which it is at the end of the debate, and send it with a covering letter to the other Council: this shall normally be done within two days.

But in exceptional cases, and when the text of the Law is long and can be split into sections, each Council may, with the assent of the other Council, break the text of the project of Law into sections for the first discussion, and send the parts as completed to the other Council. If this is done, members of both

Councils still have the right to move 'that the whole project be examined anew'—until the project reaches the stage where 'differences' are discussed.

If one of the Councils at its first discussion decides 'not to enter upon the matter' when a project has been submitted by the Federal Council, or has been sent to it by the other Council, it must inform the other Council of its decision.

If one of the Councils decides 'not to take into consideration' a project of Law or *arrêté* submitted in the form of a motion, or if it rejects the motion after debate, no further action is taken upon the project, and the decision taken is not communicated to the other Council.

Following the French text a distinction is made between 'entering upon the matter' (eintreten) and 'taking into consideration' (erheblich erklaeren). The German here uses the word 'eintreten' for both, but the distinction follows from the *règlements* of the Councils. 'Eintreten' is the decision of a Council to hold a debate, while 'erheblich erklaeren' denotes acceptance and transmission to the second Council.

ARTICLE 5. If the second Council disagrees with the first Council's decision, it shall send its own decision back to that Council for it to debate the points of difference.

Further debate shall be restricted to the points at which there is disagreement, except when the amendments that have been adopted make a fresh debate from the start necessary, or when the *commissions* of both Councils agree upon a recommendation to do so.

The Councils shall repeat this procedure until they either come to an agreement or pass a resolution to persist in their disagreement.

This is the procedure of 'differences' (*divergences*, Differenzen). Projects are often bandied to and fro between the Councils several times, and do not lapse at the end of a session (or even of a legislature), as Bills do in Great Britain. The deadlock seldom reaches the stage of a conference or of rejection. If one of the Councils dislikes the whole project, then Article 11 of this Law presumably provides a more decisive procedure.

ARTICLE 6. If the Councils resolve to persist in their disagreement, then the remaining points of difference between them shall be submitted to a conference composed of the *commissions* of both Councils: this conference shall try to secure agreement.

If the *commission* of one Council has fewer members than that of the other, then members shall be added to make both of them the same size.

The chairman of the Conference is the member who was chairman of the *commission* of the Council which had 'priority' in the matter concerned.

ARTICLE 7. The proposals for agreement which the Conference makes shall go first to the Council which had 'priority' in the matter concerned.

If the Conference does not succeed in formulating a proposal, or if the Councils are unable to agree to the proposal it makes—a matter which each Council shall decide outright—the project is to be deemed rejected, and can only be reintroduced by the procedure laid down for initiating legislation.

ARTICLE 7 *bis*. When a project of a universally binding *arrêté* contains the 'urgency clause', the clause shall not be debated until the debates on 'differences' between the Councils is finished. The same procedure is to be followed when a member of one of the Councils proposes the addition of the urgency clause.

'Urgency' can only be declared by a majority of the total number of members of each Council—the vote of the president of each Council being reckoned in the same manner as the votes of other members for this purpose. The motion to introduce the clause must be expressly inserted in the Order Paper.

When the decision of one of the Councils on this matter does not agree with that of the other, the latter Council shall transmit this decision to the former, which shall vote again upon the question. If the Council which has voted against urgency reaffirms its decision, then this decision is final, and the referendum clause is substituted for the urgency clause.

Introduced by an amending Law in 1939. The importance of a declaration of 'urgency' is that it removes the *arrêté* from the referendum: see Article 89 *bis* of the Constitution. Article 38 of the present Law is an example of the 'referendum clause'.

ARTICLE 8. Laws and universally binding *arrêtés* shall go to the Committee of Revision when the Councils have finished debating them, unless the Councils themselves decide otherwise, before the final decision is taken. This committee shall determine the final German and French texts, especially from the standpoint of seeing that the two texts agree, and shall make any purely verbal alterations necessary to bring them into line with enactments already in force. The committee has no power to alter the substance of decisions taken by the Councils.

ARTICLE 9. This Committee of Revision consists of the *rapporteurs* of the *commissions*, of the second vice-Chancellor, and of the Interpreters of both Councils. It may call for the attendance of other Federal officials, and experts. It shall be called together by the *rapporteur* of the *commission* which had priority in the debates on the project, and he shall act as chairman.

The secretaries of both Councils may attend the meetings of the committee, and submit remarks and suggestions in writing.

ARTICLE 10. The corrected text is sent back to both Councils. If they both approve it, they both proceed to a final vote on it.

ARTICLES 8, 9, AND 10. The Councils now as a matter of routine resolve not to send the finished project to the Committee of Revision: the institution therefore leads a more or less theoretical existence.

ARTICLE 11. A final vote shall always be taken even when the project has not been sent to the Committee of Revision.

If the project is rejected on the final vote in both Councils or in one Council, it is deemed to be totally rejected and can only be reintroduced by the procedure laid down for initiating legislation.

This Article acquires a particular importance in the light of Articles 119 and 121 of the Constitution, that both total and partial revision follow the formalities (in certain circumstances) of Federal legislative procedure.

ARTICLE 12. The Italian text of laws and universally binding Federal Arrêtés is revised by a committee consisting of one Italian-speaking member from each Council, and the second vice-Chancellor or another high office-holder who speaks Italian, and the Translator of the project.

The members of the committee from the National Council

and the Council of States are nominated by the presidents of their respective Councils for the whole legislature-period.

The Italian version of the text of a Law or *arrêté* is thus an inferior text to the French and German versions, since it is a translation, whereas both German and French are original texts.

ARTICLE 13. Each Council is obliged to debate the matters sent up to it from the other Council as promptly as possible.

ARTICLE 14. Resolutions of one Council inviting the Federal Council to submit a report and a project do not require the agreement of the other Council. The agreement of both Councils is necessary, however, when the submission of a project of Law or *arrêté* is demanded, or when a resolution contains instructions upon the substance of projects to be submitted, or requires the Federal Council to adopt a particular course of action.

'Resolutions inviting the Federal Council to submit a report', &c., are postulates. The other sorts of resolutions described in the second sentence are motions. A postulate is the work of one Council and is a request; a motion is the work of both Councils, and commands.

ARTICLE 15. When both Councils meet in joint session in accordance with Article 92 of the Federal Constitution, the president of the National Council provides for their convocation, and is in charge of the proceedings.

The procedure which the Federal Assembly is to follow for debates and elections is that of the National Council.

That is to say, the president of the National Council acts as president of the Federal Assembly in joint session. The Assembly in joint session has a short *règlement* of its own supplementing that of the National Council.

ARTICLE 16. Neither Council can dissolve itself or adjourn without the consent of the other Council.

Suspension of three sittings does not count as adjournment for this purpose.

ARTICLE 17. Debates on Federal Laws and universally binding *arrêtés* are recorded in shorthand in both Chambers.

Each Council may also have other proceedings recorded in shorthand.

The *Bulletin sténographique* is submitted to each orator before going to press. Speakers may request improvements of an editorial character provided they do not affect the meaning of the speech.

Differences of opinion concerning the accuracy of the editing are decided by the *bureau* of the Council concerned.

The debates of both Councils are recorded in shorthand, but all that is published in the *Bulletin sténographique* are the debates on Laws and universally binding *arrêtés*—though occasionally other debates are included by a special resolution of one or other of the Councils.

II. RELATIONS WITH THE FEDERAL COUNCIL

ARTICLE 18. The Federal Council shall send each member of the legislative Councils an individual letter of convocation. Enclosed with this there shall be a list of all new and pending business of the Federal Assembly, indicating in each case what stage the debate has reached.

A supplementary list shall be sent of any matters which arise in the course of a session.

The Order Paper of the first sitting as agreed by the presidents of both Councils shall be included in the Federal Council's letter of convocation.

Important 'Messages' shall as far as is possible be sent to members of the Federal Chambers eight days before the beginning of the session.

ARTICLE 19. The Federal Council shall send all communications to be debated by the Federal Assembly simultaneously to the presidents of the two Councils.

The relevant documents shall be deposited for the time being in the Federal Chancellery for the use of the Council which is to deal with the matter first.

The relations of the Federal Chancellery with the *commissions* and with members of the Councils shall be governed by a *règlement* to be issued by the Federal Council.

PARAGRAPH 3. This *règlement* was issued by the Federal Council on 5 Nov. 1903 (revised 1947). It can be found in vol. i of the *Recueil systématique*—as can the *règlements* of the two Councils.

ARTICLE 20. The Federal Council may be asked to submit a report on any subject before a debate upon it is held. The *commissions* of both Councils are empowered to request the attendance of members of the Federal Council to give them information.

As the procedure of both Councils either leads up to a demand for such a report of the Federal Council, or is derived from a report or message submitted by the Federal Council, this Article must be regarded as extremely important.

The attendance of Federal Councillors, or, more usually, their permanent departmental officials, at the sittings of legislative committees gives these committees their distinctively 'executive' outlook. The *commissions* are thereby the chief channels of compromise between the civil service and the political parties.

ARTICLE 21. Complaints against its arrangements or decisionare to be transmitted to the Federal Council before being debated.

ARTICLE 22. Every member of the Federal Assembly has the right to require information from the Federal Council upon any matter which is a subject of interest to the Confederation ('interpellation'). A member who desires to exercise this right must first inform the president [of his Council] in writing. The interpellation must be seconded by at least ten members in the National Council, or by at least three in the Council of States.

The president informs the Assembly and the Federal Council of the interpellation, and unless the latter wish to reply at once, puts the interpellation down for a day in the near future.

The member speaks in support of his interpellation, and a representative of the Federal Council answers it.

When an interpellation has been replied to, the interpellating member is entitled to declare that he is, or that he is not, satisfied with the reply. Further debate can only take place if the Assembly so resolves.

The use of the word 'Assembly' in paragraph 2 is confusing. Its meaning can only be 'the Council concerned'. An interpellation is the work of one Council, or rather, of any ten (or three) members in either Council. A postulate needs a majority in one Council, a motion a majority in both. An interpellation is thus (apart from the Question) the least weighty of the procedures for extracting information from the Federal Council. The British equivalent would be the half-hour adjournment debate, but the similarity is not great.

ARTICLE 23. At the June session the Federal Council shall lay its Annual Report on its Conduct of Business (Geschaeftsbericht), together with its accounts for the past year, before the Federal Assembly, and at the December session it shall submit its estimates for the coming year. These documents are to be printed and sent to the *commissions* at least one month before the opening of the session.

The two Councils must designate the members of their *commissions* appointed to examine the Annual Report not later than the December session, regardless of which Council has priority in the matter.

The word here translated by 'estimates' is the French word *budget*, which is also colloquially used in German. As explained on page 96, the Confederation is in no position to have a financial policy—or at least according to the Constitution is in no position to have a financial policy.

The debate on the Annual Report could be made the vehicle of thoroughgoing criticism of the Executive, department by department, but it seems never to be so used.

ARTICLE 24. The estimates, the supplementary credits, and the public accounts for any one administrative period must all be sent to the same *commission* (the Finance Committee) for examination and report.

Each Council designates its own Finance Committee. No one may belong to the Committee more than six years running. Vacancies occurring in it during the course of an administrative period should be filled as quickly as possible.

The Finance Committees appoint their own chairmen.

The Finance Committee is thus extremely important. Its existence naturally moderates public criticism in the Councils.

ARTICLE 25. The Finance Committees of the two Councils shall each elect three of its own members to sit together and form a Delegation for an administrative period. This Delegation shall elect its own officers.

ARTICLE 26. This Delegation is responsible for examining and controlling the whole field of Federal finance.

It shall meet whenever the need arises, and at least once in every three months.

It has at all times an unrestricted power to examine the accounts of the various departments and divisions.

The Audit Department (*Contrôle des finances*) shall afford the Delegation all information and assistance it requires, and to this end shall place at its disposal all minutes of evidence and decisions upon cases,[1] all correspondence between the Finance Department and other departments or the Federal Chancellery or Federal Tribunal [*or Insurance Tribunal*], and all Arrêtés of the Federal Council that have to do with supervision of credits and with Federal finance in general.

Any official staff required by the Delegation for special inquiries and checks is to be placed at its disposal: the Delegation may in addition obtain advice from experts upon points requiring specialist technical knowledge.

The reports of the Finance Delegations leave one in doubt whether the Federal administration is unnaturally blameless, or whether the control is totally ineffective. Perhaps the main problem facing the student of Swiss government is whether to regard its placidity with satisfaction or with extreme disquiet. Is there nothing to criticize, one wonders, or are the springs of criticism dry?

ARTICLE 27. The *commissions* appointed by the National Council and Council of States to examine the estimates and the accounts of the Alcohol Administration designate in the same manner a Delegation to examine these estimates and accounts. The Alcohol Administration shall lay before the Delegation printed quarterly reports on the whole field of its activities.

ARTICLE 28. The Chambers may designate further *commissions* for the whole of a legislature period.

The National Council appoints the following permanent *commissions*: Contested Elections, Finance, Conduct of Business, Alcohol, Petitions, Pardons, Railway Concessions, Railways, Customs, Foreign Affairs, Army, and Posts-and-Telegraphs. The Council of States does not appoint so many.

ARTICLE 29. The combined *bureaux* of both Councils are empowered to nominate *commissions* for affairs which are urgent, or which are of minor importance, that are due to come before the Federal Assembly in joint session, and, in particular, for consideration of appeals for pardon.

[1] *tous les procès-verbaux et les censures.*

Article 30. The presidents of the two Councils are charged with seeing that the *commissions* prepare each session a sufficient number of items of business.

Article 31. All decisions of the Councils shall be brought to the cognizance of the Federal Council, which shall provide, as the case may be, for execution thereof.

The Council which shall do this is the Council which first considered the item of business concerned.

III. FORM OF PROMULGATION AND OF PUBLICATION OF LAWS AND ARRÊTÉS

Article 32. When a Law or *arrêté* has been passed by both sections of the Federal Assembly, the Federal Chancellery shall prepare an official text, which shall be signed in the name of the Federal Assembly by the presidents and secretaries of both Councils, and shall bear the date on which it was passed, and shall then be dispatched to the Federal Council for publication and, as the case may be, for execution.

The end of this present Law is an example of how this is done.

Article 33. All Laws, *arrêtés*, and *ordonnances* of general importance, and treaties with foreign States after exchange of ratifications, shall be published in the *Recueil officiel des lois et ordonnances* of the Swiss Confederation.

The provisions of the Law of 17 June 1874 apply with respect to the Laws and *arrêtés* subject to referendum.

That is to say, Laws, &c., subject to referendum, are first published in the *Feuille fédérale*. See Article 38 below.

Article 34. *Arrêtés* concerning grant, amendment, or transfer of railway concessions shall be published in the *Recueil des pièces officielles relatives aux chemins de fer suisses* (Railway Gazette).

Article 35. The *Recueil officiel des lois et ordonnances* of the Swiss Confederation shall whenever possible be published simultaneously in German, French, and Italian, and the Railway Gazette in French and German.

A copy of the *Recueil officiel* shall be sent free of charge to Cantonal governments, to their departments or services, to the *préfets* (Regierungsstatthalter) or district authorities, to the Cantonal Courts, and to the political communes.

The Cantonal authorities are obliged to keep bound copies of them. Citizens have the right to consult them in the offices of the communes.

The Statthalter here mentioned incidentally is an official whom the student of Swiss local government would be well advised to investigate. In their talk of Cantonal sovereignty and communal autonomy Swiss constitutional writers are apt to pay little attention to the 'Statthalter', considering him of mere administrative interest. He is a sort of Regional Commissioner, and is either appointed by the government of the Canton, or is nominated by a political party ('elected by the People'), according to the Canton. In either case he is the servant of the Cantonal government, and he exercises administrative supervision over the communes in his district. He is the other side of the medal of communal autonomy.

Where (as today is less frequently the case than formerly) he also holds the office of local judge—the judge being also a government servant, and also 'popularly elected'—the 'Statthalter' and Judge is the direct successor of the Vogt (Bailiff, governor, district officer) of the old régime, and he frequently has his office or place of business in the same castle (Amtsschloss) as his predecessors of the Old Confederation. Nothing is more curious than the continuity of offices under different names and theories.

The terminology of offices and districts varies widely from Canton to Canton, the same word being often used to describe different institutions—even where the institutions are themselves the same.

Political communes. See page 53.

ARTICLE 36. If the date on which a Law, Federal Arrêté, or *ordonnance* is to come into force is not mentioned in the text of the legislative act itself, it shall be fixed by the Federal Council and published at the same time as the Law, Federal Arrêté, or *ordonnance*.

This date shall normally be not less than five days after publication.

If the date on which the legislative act is to come into force has not been fixed, then it shall come into force five days after the date of publication. If the various texts are not published simultaneously, then the delay of five days runs from the date of the text last published.

ARTICLE 37. The Federal Law of 22 Dec. 1849 on the Relations between the National Council, the Council of States and the Federal Council, and on the Form of Promulgation and of Publication of Laws and Arrêtés, and all other provisions contrary to the present Law, are hereby repealed.

ARTICLE 38. The Federal Council shall publish the present Law and fix the date on which it comes into force, in accordance with the provisions of the Law of 17 June 1874 on Votations upon Federal Laws and Arrêtés.

RESOLVED by the National Council.

> Berne, 7 October 1902
> President: DR. ITEN
> Secretary: RINGIER

RESOLVED by the Council of States.

> Berne, 9 October 1902
> President: CASIMIR VON ARX
> Secretary: SCHATZMANN

(*Date of coming into force:* 20 Jan. 1903, except Articles 17, 35, and 36 which came into force at various dates within the next year.)

[The revisions of 1928 (para. 2 of Article 4) and of 1939 (Article 7 *bis*) have been incorporated in the text.]

ALPHABETICAL ANALYSIS

(The figures in parentheses refer to Articles of the Federal Constitution)

Accounts, public, 23, 24, 26, (102 s. 14, 85 s. 10); of the alcohol monopoly, 27.
Adjournment, 16.
Alcohol, *commission* of, 27.
Annual Report of Federal Council, 23, (102 s. 16).
Amtliche Sammlung, see *Recueil officiel*.
Arrêtés, Federal, *see* Laws and Arrêtés; Motions; 'Urgency'; Railway Gazette.
— of the Federal Council, 26. See also Ordonnances; *Règlement*.
Audit Department, 26.

Budget, *see* Estimates; Accounts, public.
Bulletin sténographique, 17.
Bureaux, when nominate *commissions*, 2, 29; and shorthand report, 17.

Cantons: five, may convoke Assembly, 1, (86); governments of, 35.
Chairmen of *commissions*, 6, 24, 25.
Chancellery, Federal, 19, 26, 32, (105). *See also* Secretaries; Vice-Chancellor.
Commissions: Alcohol, 27; Annual Report, 23; Finance, 24, 25, 23; Italian laws, 12; Pardon, 29; of Revision, 8, 9, 11; general power to nominate, 28; when nominated by *bureaux*, 29; preparation of business for, 30; and divergences, 5, 6, 7; and Federal Council, 20; and Chancellery, 9, 12, 19.
Communes, 35.
Conference: divergences and, 6, 7, 5.
Contrôle des finances, see Audit Department.
Convocation of sessions, 1, 18, (86, 16, 102 s. 11).
Council, Federal, *see* Federal Council.
Councils, legislative, *see* Federal Assembly, joint session; Secretaries of, *see* Secretaries.

Delegation: Finance, 25, 26; Alcohol, 27.

Departments, 26; of Finance, 26; Audit, *q.v. See also* Officials, Federal.
Dissolution of Chamber, 16.
Divergences, 5, 6, 7, 4; on priority, 3; on 'urgency', 7 *bis*; on final vote, 11; on shorthand report, 17.

'Entering upon the matter', 4.
Estimates: submission of, 23; examination of, 24, 25, 26, (102 s. 14, 85 s. 10); of alcohol monopoly, 27.
Experts, 9, 26, (104).

Federal Assembly, joint session, 15, (92); *commissions*, 29.
— Council, convokes Chambers, 1, 18, (86, 16, 102 s. 11); prepares business and submits reports, 2, 18, 19, 20, 23, (101, 102 ss. 4, 16); members reply to interpellations, 22; attend *commissions*, 20; is informed of Assembly's decisions, 31, 32; executes them, 31, 32, (102 s. 5); fixes date of application of laws, &c., 36, 38: Arrêtés &c., of, 26, 19, 33, 36.
— Tribunal, 26.
Final vote, 10, 11.
Finance, *see* Estimates; Accounts, public; *Commissions*: Audit Department; Supplementary credits.

Interpellation, 22.
Interpreters, 9, 12; see Languages; Italian.
Intervals: sending projects to other Chamber, 4, 13; interpellations, 22; dispatching 'Messages' to members, 18; Estimates, &c., 23; Laws, &c., after publication, 36.
Italian, 12, 35, (116).

Joint Delegation, *see* Delegation.
— session, of Federal Assembly, *see that word*; of *bureaux*, 29; of *commissions*, 6. See also *Commissions*: of Revision.

Languages: German and French, 8, 35, (116); Italian, *q.v.*

Laws and Arrêtés, Federal: projects of, 4–13; especially long, 4; submitted as motions, 4, 14; reports of debates, 17; Italian version of, 12, 35; publication, 33, 32, 38; date of application, 36, 38; urgency clause, 7 *bis*, (89 *bis*).

Lots, casting of, 3.

Majorities, special, for 'urgency', 7 *bis*, (89 *bis*); other purposes, (87, 88, 92).

Messages of Federal Council, 18.

Motions, 14; laws based upon, 4, 14.

Officials, Federal, 9, 12, 26.

Ordonnances, 33, 36, 35. *See also* Arrêtés of the Federal Council; *Règlement*.

Pardon, *commission* for, 29, (85 s. 7, 92).

Postulates, 14.

Presidents of *commissions*, see Chairmen.

Presidents of the legislative Councils: Federal Council and, 19, 22; and *commissions*, 30, of revision, 12, determine priority, 2, 3, 18; and joint session, 15, (92); interpellations and, 22; sign documents, 4, 32; vote in elections, throw casting votes, (78, 82).

Priority, 2, 3, 31, 6, 7, 9, 19, 23.

Publication of Laws, &c., 32–38; of debates, see *Bulletin sténographique*.

Railway Gazette, 34, 35.

Rapporteur of *commission*, 9.

Recueil officiel des lois, 33, 35.

Referendum clause, 7 *bis*, 33, 38.

Règlement of legislative Council, 15, (86); of Federal Council, 19.

Repeal clause, 37.

Revision, committee of, see *Commissions*: of Revision; of speeches, by members, 17.

Secretaries, of legislative Councils, 4, 9, 32, and signatures at the end of this Law (*cf.* the signatures to the Constitution itself). *See also* Chancellery, Federal.

Sessions, 1, 18, 16, (86).

Shorthand report, 17.

Standing order (*règlement*) of Councils, 15, (86).

Supplementary credits, 24.

Treaties, 33.

'Urgency', declaration of, 7 *bis*.

Urgent matters, 2, 3, 29.

Vice-Chancellor, second, 9, 12. *See also* Secretaries; Chancellery, Federal.

III

EMERGENCY FULL POWERS

Powers to take any action that might be necessary to preserve neutrality were granted by the Assembly to the Federal Council in 1849, 1853, 1859, and 1870—but they were never used. On 3 August 1914 powers similar to those granted in 1939 were conferred: they were extensively used, and the grant was repealed in 1919. When war was imminent in 1939 the *arrêté* printed below was passed by the Federal Assembly. Disregard for the Constitution, however, has not been confined to war-time. During the economic crisis of the early 1930's, and under the shadow of the political threat from Germany and Italy of the later 1930's, the Federal Assembly conferred extraordinary economic powers upon the Executive, and the Federal Council took further extraordinary political powers upon itself.

The text of the Federal Constitution contains no mention of special emergency provisions except in Article 102, s. 11. The competence to take the measures foreseen by the Full Powers Arrêté can only be deduced from Article 2 (and perhaps the preamble) read with Article 71, the Supreme Power, Article 85, ss. 6 and 7, and Article 102, ss. 8, 9, and 10. It can hardly be contended with honesty, in fact, that the grant of Full Powers is constitutional.[1] A written Constitution has by its nature the disadvantage that, because it cannot be completely followed in war-time, all checks on the executive power tend to disappear during such emergencies. Few free countries at war, however, have gone as far as Switzerland—and Switzerland was not at war. Yet there is no hint of a suggestion of a *coup d'état*, no doubt at all that the country remains a free country and would, if it could, return to the Constitution of 1913 tomorrow—nor any doubt at all that in all future emergencies the Constitution will again be joyfully thrown overboard.

The action taken under the Full Powers Arrêté was unconstitutional in three respects: powers belonging to the Cantons were exercised by the central government, powers belonging to the Legislature were exercised by the Executive, and guaranteed constitutional rights of the citizen were suspended. It is the last point which is the important one.

---

[1] For a discussion of the constitutional aspects of the *régime des pleins pouvoirs* see Giacometti, *Das Vollmachtenregime der Eidgenossenschaft*, Zürich, 1945. The foremost Swiss juristic writer here attacks Full Powers all along the line. Other writers (e.g. Dr. Hans Marti) take a different attitude. For a general discussion see Muenci Kapani, *Les Pouvoirs extraordinaires de l'exécutif en temps de guerre et de crise nationale*, Geneva, 1949 (Geneva thesis), which was reviewed by Sir C. Carr in the Spring 1951 number of *Parliamentary Affairs*. Dr. Kapani's book is not confined to Switzerland.

FEDERAL ARRÊTÉ OF 30 AUGUST 1939

ON MEASURES TO SECURE THE SAFETY OF THE COUNTRY AND THE MAINTENANCE OF ITS NEUTRALITY

THE FEDERAL ASSEMBLY

OF THE

SWISS CONFEDERATION

Having Regard to the Message of the Federal Council of 29 August 1939

DECREES

ARTICLE 1. The Swiss Confederation asserts its firm determination to maintain its neutrality in all circumstances and against all States.

The Federal Council is empowered to bring this declaration of neutrality to the notice of the States concerned.

ARTICLE 2. The Federal Assembly takes notice of the mobilization ordered by the Federal Council, and approves it.

ARTICLE 3. The Federal Assembly grants to the Federal Council the power and the duty to take the measures necessary to maintain the security, independence, and neutrality of Switzerland, to safeguard the credit and economic interests of the country, and to secure its supply of food.

ARTICLE 4. The credits necessary for this purpose are granted to the Federal Council. In addition, the power is granted to the Federal Council to contract the necessary loans.

ARTICLE 5. The Federal Council shall furnish the Assembly at its July and December sessions with a report upon the measures it has taken in pursuance of the present *arrêté*.

It is for the Federal Assembly to decide whether such measures shall continue in force.

ARTICLE 6. Both Councils shall appoint permanent *commissions* for preliminary examination of the reports of the Federal Council.

The Federal Council shall if possible consult the *commissions* of both Councils before issuing important measures.

ARTICLE 7. The present *arrêté* comes into force immediately.

[The enacting formula, '*Resolved* by the National Council', &c., is the same as for a Law, and is not reprinted here.]

The Arrêté of 30 August 1939. The Full Powers Arrêté was passed without debate through the two Councils at a special session at a time when it seemed the highest patriotism to confer all possible powers upon the Executive. The Federal Council no doubt planned that this should be so; it is certainly remarkable that the country went into a state of armed neutrality with full military, but no legislative, preparations made. The first enthusiasm for bureaucratic government soon faded, and had changed by the end of the war into discontent at the continuance of unconstitutionality. On 6 Dec. 1945 the Councils passed another *arrêté* 'restraining the extraordinary powers of the Federal Council', which called on the Executive to rescind all measures 'not really necessary' and only to pass new measures in exceptional circumstances and subject to the right of the Assembly to decide if they are to remain in force. It also restored the normal budget procedure. A further Federal Arrêté of 18 Dec. 1950 provides that acts passed under emergency powers are to go out of force at the end of 1952, unless continued by the procedure laid down in Articles 89 or 89 *bis* of the Constitution. The tactics of the authorities seem to be to present the people with a choice between chaos or the continuance of emergency legislation.

ARTICLE 2. See Article 102, s. 11 of the Constitution.

ARTICLE 3. This is a limitless delegation.

ARTICLE 6. This safeguard is an improvement on the 1914 Arrêté. It was introduced largely because the Socialist party were then unrepresented in the Federal Council, and wanted their say. The appointment of *commissions* was no part of the Federal Council's plan, and was added by the Assembly.

ARTICLE 7. This phrase withdraws the Arrêté from the referendum challenge. It is not the normal 'urgency' formula.

GERMAN TEXT OF THE FEDERAL CONSTITUTION

THE German text of the Constitution is given here in the orthography which printed versions at the present day normally follow.

The usual method of referring to the Constitution is to give the number of the Article (together with the letters BV—Bundesverfassung, or Cf—*Constitution fédérale*) and the number of the paragraph (Absatz, *alinéa*). But the paragraphing of the German version in a few cases varies from that of the French version, and so it may very occasionally be necessary when referring to paragraphs to state which version is being employed. The Articles where this difficulty arises are numbers 78, 98, and (due originally to a misprint) 29. The question of what to include in Articles 55 and 64 *bis* respectively is discussed on page 68 above. The course followed here is not the usual one; the last two paragraphs of Article 55 are usually omitted.

The original official version contained a misprint (the omission of the word 'von' in Article 16) which has here—following the usual practice—been corrected.

The text is that of the Constitution as amended to 1 July 1953.

BUNDESVERFASSUNG
DER
SCHWEIZERISCHEN EIDGENOSSENSCHAFT

IM NAMEN GOTTES DES ALLMÄCHTIGEN!

Die Schweizerische Eidgenossenschaft,

in der Absicht, den Bund der Eidgenossen zu befestigen, die Einheit, Kraft und Ehre der schweizerischen Nation zu erhalten und zu fördern, hat nachstehende Bundesverfassung angenommen:

ERSTER ABSCHNITT
ALLGEMEINE BESTIMMUNGEN

ART. 1. Die durch gegenwärtigen Bund vereinigten Völkerschaften der zweiundzwanzig souveränen Kantone, als: Zürich, Bern, Luzern, Uri, Schwyz, Unterwalden (ob und nid dem Wald), Glarus, Zug, Freiburg, Solothurn, Basel (Stadt und Landschaft), Schaffhausen, Appenzell (beider Rhoden), St. Gallen, Graubünden, Aargau, Thurgau, Tessin, Waadt, Wallis, Neuenburg und Genf, bilden in ihrer Gesamtheit die schweizerische Eidgenossenschaft.

ART. 2. Der Bund hat zum Zweck: Behauptung der Unabhängigkeit des Vaterlandes gegen aussen, Handhabung von Ruhe und Ordnung im Innern, Schutz der Freiheit und der Rechte der Eidgenossen und Beförderung ihrer gemeinsamen Wohlfahrt.

ART. 3. Die Kantone sind souverän, soweit ihre Souveränität nicht durch die Bundesverfassung beschränkt ist, und üben als solche alle Rechte aus, welche nicht der Bundesgewalt übertragen sind.

ART. 4. Alle Schweizer sind vor dem Gesetze gleich. Es gibt in der Schweiz keine Untertanenverhältnisse, keine Vorrechte des Orts, der Geburt, der Familien oder Personen.

ART. 5. Der Bund gewährleistet den Kantonen ihr Gebiet, ihre Souveränität innert den Schranken des Artikels 3, ihre Verfassungen, die Freiheit, die Rechte des Volkes und die verfassungsmässigen Rechte der Bürger gleich den Rechten und Befugnissen, welche das Volk den Behörden übertragen hat.

Art. 6. Die Kantone sind verpflichtet, für ihre Verfassungen die Gewährleistung des Bundes nachzusuchen.

Der Bund übernimmt diese Gewährleistung insofern:
- *a.* sie nichts den Vorschriften der Bundesverfassung Zuwiderlaufendes enthalten;
- *b.* sie die Ausübung der politischen Rechte nach republikanischen (repräsentativen oder demokratischen) Formen sichern;
- *c.* sie vom Volke angenommen worden sind und revidiert werden können, wenn die absolute Mehrheit der Bürger es verlangt.

Art. 7. Besondere Bündnisse und Verträge politischen Inhalts zwischen den Kantonen sind untersagt.

Dagegen steht ihnen das Recht zu, Verkommnisse über Gegenstände der Gesetzgebung, des Gerichtswesens und der Verwaltung unter sich abzuschliessen; jedoch haben sie dieselben der Bundesbehörde zur Einsicht vorzulegen, welche, wenn diese Verkommnisse etwas dem Bunde oder den Rechten anderer Kantone Zuwiderlaufendes enthalten, deren Vollziehung zu hindern befugt ist. Im entgegengesetzten Falle sind die betreffenden Kantone berechtigt, zur Vollziehung die Mitwirkung der Bundesbehörden anzusprechen.

Art. 8. Dem Bunde allein steht das Recht zu, Krieg zu erklären und Frieden zu schliessen, Bündnisse und Staatsverträge, namentlich Zoll- und Handelsverträge mit dem Auslande, einzugehen.

Art. 9. Ausnahmsweise bleibt den Kantonen die Befugnis, Verträge über Gegenstände der Staatswirtschaft, des nachbarlichen Verkehrs und der Polizei mit dem Auslande abzuschliessen; jedoch dürfen dieselben nichts dem Bunde oder den Rechten anderer Kantone Zuwiderlaufendes enthalten.

Art. 10. Der amtliche Verkehr zwischen Kantonen und auswärtigen Staatsregierungen, sowie ihren Stellvertretern, findet durch Vermittlung des Bundesrates statt.

Über die im Art. 9 bezeichneten Gegenstände können jedoch die Kantone mit den untergeordneten Behörden und Beamten eines auswärtigen Staates in unmittelbaren Verkehr treten.

Art. 11. Es dürfen keine Militärkapitulationen abgeschlossen werden.

Art. 12.* Die Mitglieder der Bundesbehörden, die eidgenössischen Zivil- oder Militärbeamten und die eidgenössischen Repräsentanten oder Kommissarien sowie die Mitglieder kantonaler Regierungen und gesetzgebender Behörden dürfen von auswärtigen Regierungen weder Pensionen oder Gehalte, noch Titel, Geschenke oder Orden annehmen. Handeln sie dem Verbote zuwider, so hat dies das Ausscheiden aus ihrer Stellung zur Folge.

Wer solche Pensionen, Titel oder Orden besitzt, ist als Mitglied einer Bundesbehörde, als eidgenössischer Zivil- oder Militärbeamter, als eidgenössischer Repräsentant oder Kommissar, oder als Mitglied einer kantonalen Regierung oder gesetzgebenden Behörde nur wählbar, wenn er vor Amtsantritt auf den Genuss der Pension oder das Tragen des Titels ausdrücklich verzichtet oder den Orden zurückgegeben hat.

Im schweizerischen Heere dürfen weder Orden getragen, noch von auswärtigen Regierungen verliehene Titel geltend gemacht werden.

Das Annehmen solcher Auszeichnungen ist allen Offizieren, Unteroffizieren und Soldaten untersagt.

Art. 13. Der Bund ist nicht berechtigt, stehende Truppen zu halten.

Ohne Bewilligung der Bundesbehörde darf kein Kanton oder in geteilten Kantonen kein Landesteil mehr als 300 Mann stehende Truppen halten, die Landjägerkorps nicht inbegriffen.

Art. 14. Die Kantone sind verpflichtet, wenn Streitigkeiten unter ihnen vorfallen, sich jeder Selbsthilfe, sowie jeder Bewaffnung zu enthalten und sich der bundesmässigen Entscheidung zu unterziehen.

Art. 15. Wenn einem Kantone vom Ausland plötzlich Gefahr droht, so ist die Regierung des bedrohten Kantons verpflichtet, andere Kantone zur Hilfe zu mahnen, unter gleichzeitiger Anzeige an die Bundesbehörde und unvorgreiflich den spätern Verfügungen dieser letztern. Die gemahnten Kantone sind zum Zuzuge verpflichtet. Die Kosten trägt die Eidgenossenschaft.

Art. 16. Bei gestörter Ordnung im Innern, oder wenn [von] einem andern Kantone Gefahr droht, hat die Regierung des bedrohten

---

* *Temporary provision to Article 12:*

Wer vor dem Inkrafttreten des abgeänderten Artikels 12 erlaubterweise einen Orden oder einen Titel erhalten hatte, darf als Mitglied der Bundesbehörden, eidgenössischer Zivil- oder Militärbeamter, eidgenössischer Repräsentant oder Kommissar, Mitglied einer kantonalen Regierung oder der gesetzgebenden Behörde eines Kantons gewählt werden, wenn er sich verpflichtet, für seine Amtsdauer auf das Tragen der Titel oder Orden zu verzichten. Die Zuwiderhandlung gegen diese Verpflichtung zieht den Verlust des Amts nach sich.

BUNDESVERFASSUNG

Kantons dem Bundesrate sogleich Kenntnis zu geben, damit dieser innert den Schranken seiner Kompetenz (Art. 102, Ziff. 3, 10 und 11) die erforderlichen Massregeln treffen oder die Bundesversammlung einberufen kann. In dringenden Fällen ist die betreffende Regierung befugt, unter sofortiger Anzeige an den Bundesrat, andere Kantone zur Hilfe zu mahnen, und die gemahnten Stände sind zur Hilfeleistung verpflichtet.

Wenn die Kantonsregierung ausserstande ist, Hilfe anzusprechen, so kann, und wenn die Sicherheit der Schweiz gefährdet wird, so soll die kompetente Bundesbehörde von sich aus einschreiten.

In Fällen eidgenössischer Intervention sorgen die Bundesbehörden für Beachtung der Vorschriften von Art. 5.

Die Kosten trägt der mahnende oder die eidgenössische Intervention veranlassende Kanton, wenn nicht die Bundesversammlung wegen besonderer Umstände etwas anderes beschliesst.

ART. 17. In den durch die Artikel 15 und 16 bezeichneten Fällen ist jeder Kanton verpflichtet, den Truppen freien Durchzug zu gestatten. Diese sind sofort unter eidgenössische Leitung zu stellen.

ART. 18. Jeder Schweizer ist wehrpflichtig.

Wehrmänner, welche infolge des eidgenössischen Militärdienstes ihr Leben verlieren oder dauernden Schaden an ihrer Gesundheit erleiden, haben für sich oder ihre Familien im Falle des Bedürfnisses Anspruch auf Unterstützung des Bundes.

Die Wehrmänner sollen ihre erste Ausrüstung, Bekleidung und Bewaffnung unentgeltlich erhalten. Die Waffe bleibt unter den durch die Bundesgesetzgebung aufzustellenden Bedingungen in den Händen des Wehrmannes.

Der Bund wird über den Militärpflichtersatz einheitliche Bestimmungen aufstellen.

ART. 19. Das Bundesheer besteht:
a. aus den Truppenkörpern der Kantone;
b. aus allen Schweizern, welche zwar nicht zu diesen Truppenkörpern gehören, aber nichtsdestoweniger militärpflichtig sind.

Die Verfügung über das Bundesheer mit Inbegriff des gesetzlich dazu gehörigen Kriegsmaterials steht der Eidgenossenschaft zu.

In Zeiten der Gefahr hat der Bund das ausschliessliche und unmittelbare Verfügungsrecht auch über die nicht in das Bundesheer eingeteilte Mannschaft und alle übrigen Streitmittel der Kantone.

Die Kantone verfügen über die Wehrkraft ihres Gebietes, soweit sie nicht durch verfassungsmässige oder gesetzliche Anordnungen des Bundes beschränkt sind.

Art. 20. Die Gesetzgebung über das Heerwesen ist Sache des Bundes. Die Ausführung der bezüglichen Gesetze in den Kantonen geschieht innerhalb der durch die Bundesgesetzgebung festzusetzenden Grenzen und unter Aufsicht des Bundes durch die kantonalen Behörden.

Der gesamte Militärunterricht und ebenso die Bewaffnung ist Sache des Bundes.

Die Beschaffung der Bekleidung und Ausrüstung und die Sorge für deren Unterhalt ist Sache der Kantone; die daherigen Kosten werden jedoch den Kantonen vom Bunde nach einer von ihm aufzustellenden Norm vergütet.

Art. 21. Soweit nicht militärische Gründe entgegenstehen, sollen die Truppenkörper aus der Mannschaft desselben Kantons gebildet werden.

Die Zusammensetzung dieser Truppenkörper, die Fürsorge für die Erhaltung ihres Bestandes und die Ernennung und Beförderung ihrer Offiziere ist, unter Beachtung der durch den Bund aufzustellenden allgemeinen Vorschriften, Sache der Kantone.

Art. 22. Der Bund hat das Recht, die in den Kantonen vorhandenen Waffenplätze und die zu militärischen Zwecken bestimmten Gebäude samt Zugehören gegen billige Entschädigung zur Benutzung oder als Eigentum zu übernehmen.

Die Normen für die daherige Entschädigung werden durch die Bundesgesetzgebung geregelt.

Art. 23. Dem Bunde steht das Recht zu, im Interesse der Eidgenossenschaft oder eines grossen Teiles derselben auf Kosten der Eidgenossenschaft öffentliche Werke zu errichten oder die Errichtung derselben zu unterstützen.

Zu diesem Zwecke ist er auch befugt, gegen volle Entschädigung das Recht der Expropriation geltend zu machen. Die nähern Bestimmungen hierüber bleiben der Bundesgesetzgebung vorbehalten.

Die Bundesversammlung kann die Errichtung öffentlicher Werke untersagen, welche die militärischen Interessen der Eidgenossenschaft verletzen.

Art. 23 *bis*. Der Bund unterhält die zur Sicherung der Versorgung des Landes nötigen Vorräte von Brotgetreide. Er kann die Müller verpflichten, Brotgetreide zu lagern und seine Vorräte zu übernehmen, um deren Auswechslung zu erleichtern.

Der Bund fördert den Anbau von Brotgetreide im Inland, begünstigt die Züchtung und Beschaffung hochwertigen inländischen Saatgutes und unterstützt die Selbstversorgung unter besonderer

Berücksichtigung der Gebirgsgegenden. Er übernimmt gutes, mahlfähiges Inlandgetreide zu einem Preise, der den Getreidebau ermöglicht. Die Müller können verpflichtet werden, dieses Getreide auf Grundlage des Marktpreises zu übernehmen.

Der Bund sorgt für die Erhaltung des einheimischen Müllereigewerbes, desgleichen wahrt er die Interessen der Mehl- und Brotkonsumenten. Er beaufsichtigt im Rahmen der ihm übertragenen Aufgaben den Verkehr mit Brotgetreide, Backmehl und Brot, sowie deren Preise. Der Bund trifft die nötigen Massnahmen zur Regelung der Einfuhr des Backmehls; er kann sich das ausschliessliche Recht vorbehalten, das Backmehl einzuführen. Der Bund gewährt nötigenfalls den Müllern Erleichterungen auf den Transportkosten im Innern des Landes. Er trifft zugunsten der Gebirgsgegenden Massnahmen, die geeignet sind, einen Ausgleich der Mehlpreise herbeizuführen.

Die statistische Gebühr im Warenverkehr mit dem Auslande ist zu erhöhen. Der Ertrag dieser Gebühr wird zur Deckung der aus der Getreideversorgung des Landes erwachsenden Ausgaben beitragen.

ART. 24. Der Bund hat das Recht der Oberaufsicht über die Wasserbau- und Forstpolizei.

Er wird die Korrektion und Verbauung der Wildwasser, sowie die Aufforstung ihrer Quellengebiete unterstützen und die nötigen schützenden Bestimmungen zur Erhaltung dieser Werke and der schon vorhandenen Waldungen aufstellen.

ART. 24*bis*. Die Nutzbarmachung der Wasserkräfte steht unter der Oberaufsicht des Bundes.

Die Bundesgesetzgebung stellt die zur Wahrung der öffentlichen Interessen und zur Sicherung der zweckmässigen Nutzbarmachung der Wasserkräfte erforderlichen allgemeinen Vorschriften auf. Dabei ist auch die Binnenschiffahrt nach Möglichkeit zu berücksichtigen.

Unter diesem Vorbehalt steht die Regelung der Nutzbarmachung der Wasserkräfte den Kantonen zu.

Wenn jedoch eine Gewässerstrecke, die für die Gewinnung einer Wasserkraft in Anspruch genommen wird, unter der Hoheit mehrerer Kantone steht und sich diese nicht über eine gemeinsame Konzession verständigen können, so ist die Erteilung der Konzession Sache des Bundes. Ebenso steht dem Bunde unter Beiziehung der beteiligten Kantone die Konzessionserteilung an Gewässerstrecken zu, die die Landesgrenze bilden.

Die Gebühren und Abgaben für die Benutzung der Wasserkräfte gehören den Kantonen oder den nach der kantonalen Gesetzgebung Berechtigten.

Sie werden für die vom Bunde ausgehenden Konzessionen von diesem nach Anhörung der beteiligten Kantone und in billiger Rücksichtnahme auf ihre Gesetzgebung bestimmt. Für die übrigen Konzessionen werden die Abgaben und Gebühren von den Kantonen innert den durch die Bundesgesetzgebung zu bestimmenden Schranken festgesetzt.

Die Abgabe der durch Wasserkraft erzeugten Energie ins Ausland darf nur mit Bewilligung des Bundes erfolgen.

In allen Wasserrechtskonzessionen, die nach Inkrafttreten dieses Artikels erteilt werden, ist die künftige Bundesgesetzgebung vorzubehalten.

Der Bund ist befugt, gesetzliche Bestimmungen über die Fortleitung und die Abgabe der elektrischen Energie zu erlassen.

ART. 24*ter.* Die Gesetzgebung über die Schiffahrt ist Bundessache.

ART. 25. Der Bund ist befugt, gesetzliche Bestimmungen über die Ausübung der Fischerei und Jagd, namentlich zur Erhaltung des Hochwildes, sowie zum Schutze der für die Land- und Forstwirtschaft nützlichen Vögel zu treffen.

ART. 25*bis.* Das Schlachten der Tiere ohne vorherige Betäubung vor dem Blutentzuge ist bei jeder Schlachtart und Viehgattung ausnahmslos untersagt.

ART. 26. Die Gesetzgebung über den Bau und Betrieb der Eisenbahnen ist Bundessache.

ART. 27. Der Bund ist befugt, ausser der bestehenden polytechnischen Schule, eine Universität und andere höhere Unterrichtsanstalten zu errichten oder solche Anstalten zu unterstützen.

Die Kantone sorgen für genügenden Primarunterricht, welcher ausschliesslich unter staatlicher Leitung stehen soll. Derselbe ist obligatorisch und in den öffentlichen Schulen unentgeltlich.

Die öffentlichen Schulen sollen von den Angehörigen aller Bekenntnisse ohne Beeinträchtigung ihrer Glaubens- und Gewissensfreiheit besucht werden können.

Gegen Kantone, welche diesen Verpflichtungen nicht nachkommen, wird der Bund die nötigen Verfügungen treffen.

ART. 27 *bis.* Den Kantonen werden zur Unterstützung in der Erfüllung der ihnen auf dem Gebiete des Primarunterrichtes obliegenden Pflichten Beiträge geleistet.

Das Nähere bestimmt das Gesetz.

Die Organisation, Leitung und Beaufsichtigung des Primarschulwesens bleibt Sache der Kantone, vorbehalten die Bestimmungen des Art. 27.

ART. 28. Das Zollwesen ist Sache des Bundes. Derselbe hat das Recht, Ein- und Ausfuhrzölle zu erheben.

ART. 29. Bei Erhebung der Zölle sollen folgende Grundsätze beachtet werden:
1. Eingangsgebühren:
   a. Die für die inländische Industrie und Landwirtschaft erforderlichen Stoffe sind im Zolltarife möglichst gering zu taxieren.
   b. Ebenso die zum nötigen Lebensbedarf erforderlichen Gegenstände.
   c. Die Gegenstände des Luxus unterliegen den höchsten Taxen.

Diese Grundsätze sind, wenn nicht zwingende Gründe entgegenstehen, auch bei Abschliessung von Handelsverträgen mit dem Auslande zu befolgen.
2. Die Ausgangsgebühren sind möglichst mässig festzusetzen.
3. Durch die Zollgesetzgebung sind zur Sicherung des Grenz- und Marktverkehrs geeignete Bestimmungen zu treffen.

Dem Bunde bleibt immerhin das Recht vorbehalten, unter ausserordentlichen Umständen, in Abweichung von vorstehenden Bestimmungen, vorübergehend besondere Massnahmen zu treffen.

ART. 30. Der Ertrag der Zölle fällt in die Bundeskasse.

Die den Kantonen bisher bezahlten Entschädigungen für die losgekauften Zölle, Weg- und Brückengelder, Kaufhaus- und andern Gebühren dieser Art fallen weg.

Ausnahmsweise erhalten die Kantone Uri, Graubünden, Tessin und Wallis, mit Rücksicht auf ihre internationalen Alpenstrassen, eine jährliche Entschädigung, die mit Wirkung vom 1. Januar 1925 an festgestellt wird wie folgt:

für Uri	Fr. 160,000
» Graubünden	» 400,000
» Tessin	» 400,000
» Wallis	» 100,000

ART. 31. Die Handels- und Gewerbefreiheit ist im ganzen Umfange der Eidgenossenschaft gewährleistet, soweit sie nicht durch die Bundesverfassung und die auf ihr beruhende Gesetzgebung eingeschränkt ist.

Kantonale Bestimmungen über die Ausübung von Handel und Gewerben und deren Besteuerung bleiben vorbehalten; sie dürfen jedoch, soweit die Bundesverfassung nichts anderes vorsieht, den

Grundsatz der Handels- und Gewerbefreiheit nicht beeinträchtigen. Vorbehalten bleiben auch die kantonalen Regalrechte.

ART. 31 *bis*. Der Bund trifft im Rahmen seiner verfassungsmässigen Befugnisse die zur Mehrung der Wohlfahrt des Volkes und zur wirtschaftlichen Sicherung der Bürger geeigneten Massnahmen.

Unter Wahrung der allgemeinen Interessen der schweizerischen Gesamtwirtschaft kann der Bund Vorschriften erlassen über die Ausübung von Handel und Gewerben und Massnahmen treffen zur Förderung einzelner Wirtschaftszweige oder Berufe. Er ist dabei, unter Vorbehalt von Abs. 3, an den Grundsatz der Handels- und Gewerbefreiheit gebunden.

Wenn das Gesamtinteresse es rechtfertigt, ist der Bund befugt, nötigenfalls in Abweichung von der Handels- und Gewerbefreiheit, Vorschriften zu erlassen:

a. zur Erhaltung wichtiger, in ihren Existenzgrundlagen gefährdeter Wirtschaftszweige oder Berufe sowie zur Förderung der beruflichen Leistungsfähigkeit der Selbständigerwerbenden in solchen Wirtschaftszweigen oder Berufen;

b. zur Erhaltung eines gesunden Bauernstandes und einer leistungsfähigen Landwirtschaft, sowie zur Festigung des bäuerlichen Grundbesitzes;

c. zum Schutze wirtschaftlich bedrohter Landesteile;

d. gegen volkswirtschaftlich oder sozial schädliche Auswirkungen von Kartellen und ähnlichen Organisationen;

e. über vorsorgliche Massnahmen für Kriegszeiten.

Bestimmungen gemäss lit. *a* und *b* sind nur zu erlassen, wenn die zu schützenden Wirtschaftszweige oder Berufe diejenigen Selbsthilfemassnahmen getroffen haben, die ihnen billigerweise zugemutet werden können.

Der Bund gewährleistet bei der Gesetzgebung auf Grund von Abs. 3, lit. *a* und *b*, die Entwicklung der auf gegenseitiger Hilfe beruhenden Organisationen der Wirtschaft.

ART. 31 *ter*. Die Kantone sind befugt, auf dem Wege der Gesetzgebung die Führung von Betrieben des Gastwirtschaftsgewerbes von der persönlichen Befähigung und die Zahl gleichartiger Betriebe vom Bedürfnis abhängig zu machen, sofern dieses Gewerbe durch übermässige Konkurrenz in seiner Existenz bedroht ist. Dabei ist der Bedeutung der verschiedenen Arten von Wirtschaften für das Gemeinwohl angemessen Rechnung zu tragen.

Ausserdem kann der Bund die Kantone im Rahmen seiner eigenen Gesetzgebungsbefugnisse ermächtigen, Vorschriften zu erlassen auf Gebieten, die keiner allgemeinen Regelung durch den

Bund bedürfen und für welche die Kantone nicht kraft eigenen Rechts zuständig sind.

Art. 31 *quater.* Der Bund ist befugt, über das Bankwesen Bestimmungen aufzustellen.

Diese Bestimmungen haben der besonderen Aufgabe und Stellung der Kantonalbanken Rechnung zu tragen.

Art. 31 *quinquies.* Der Bund trifft in Verbindung mit den Kantonen und der privaten Wirtschaft Massnahmen zur Verhütung von Wirtschaftskrisen und nötigenfalls zur Bekämpfung eingetretener Arbeitslosigkeit. Er erlässt Vorschriften über die Arbeitsbeschaffung.

Art. 32. Die in Art. 31*bis*, 31*ter*, Abs. 2, 31*quater* und 31*quinquies* genannten Bestimmungen dürfen nur durch Bundesgesetze oder Bundesbeschlüsse eingeführt werden, für welche die Volksabstimmung verlangt werden kann. Für Fälle dringlicher Art in Zeiten wirtschaftlicher Störungen bleibt Art. 89, Abs. 3, vorbehalten.

Die Kantone sind vor Erlass der Ausführungsgesetze anzuhören. Ihnen ist in der Regel der Vollzug der Bundesvorschriften zu übertragen.

Die zuständigen Organisationen der Wirtschaft sind vor Erlass der Ausführungsgesetze anzuhören und können beim Vollzug der Ausführungsvorschriften zur Mitwirkung herangezogen werden.

Art. 32 *bis.* Der Bund ist befugt, auf dem Wege der Gesetzgebung Vorschriften über die Herstellung, die Einfuhr, die Reinigung, den Verkauf und die fiskalische Belastung gebrannter Wasser zu erlassen.

Die Gesetzgebung ist so zu gestalten, dass sie den Verbrauch von Trinkbranntwein und dementsprechend dessen Einfuhr und Herstellung vermindert. Sie fördert den Tafelobstbau und die Verwendung der inländischen Brennereirohstoffe als Nahrungs- oder Futtermittel. Der Bund wird die Zahl der Brennapparate vermindern, indem er solche auf dem Wege der freiwilligen Übereinkunft erwirbt.

Die gewerbsmässige Herstellung gebrannter Wasser wird durch Konzession genossenschaftlichen und andern privatwirtschaftlichen Unternehmungen übertragen. Die erteilten Konzessionen sollen die Verwertung der Abfälle des Obst-, Wein- und Zuckerrübenbaues und der Überschüsse des Obst- und Kartoffelbaues ermöglichen, soweit diese Rohstoffe nicht anders zweckmässig verwendet werden können.

Das nicht gewerbsmässige Herstellen oder Herstellenlassen von Trinkbranntwein aus Obst und Obstabfällen, Obstwein, Most,

Wein, Traubentrestern, Weinhefe, Enzianwurzeln und ähnlichen Stoffen ist in den schon vorhandenen Hausbrennereien oder in fahrbaren Brennereien gestattet, wenn diese Stoffe ausschliesslich inländisches Eigen- oder Wildgewächs sind. Dieser Branntwein ist steuerfrei, soweit er im Haushalt und Landwirtschaftsbetrieb des Produzenten erforderlich ist. Die nach Ablauf einer Frist von fünfzehn Jahren, vom Zeitpunkt der Annahme dieses Artikels an, noch bestehenden Hausbrennereien bedürfen zum Weiterbetrieb einer Konzession, welche ihnen unter den im Gesetz aufzustellenden Bedingungen gebührenfrei zu erteilen ist.

Die fiskalische Belastung der Spezialitäten aus Steinobst, Wein, Traubentrestern, Weinhefe, Enzianwurzeln und ähnlichen Stoffen erfolgt in Form der Besteuerung. Dabei soll ein angemessenes Entgelt für die Rohstoffe inländischer Herkunft gewahrt bleiben.

Mit Ausnahme des steuerfreien Eigenbedarfes und der Spezialitäten ist der im Inlande hergestellte Branntwein dem Bunde abzuliefern, der ihn zu angemessenen Preisen übernimmt.

Keiner Besteuerung unterliegen die Erzeugnisse, welche ausgeführt oder durchgeführt werden oder denaturiert sind.

Die Einnahmen aus der Besteuerung des Ausschanks und des Kleinhandels innerhalb des Kantonsgebietes verbleiben den Kantonen. Die Patente für den interkantonalen und internationalen Kleinhandel werden vom Bunde ausgestellt; die Einnahmen werden auf die Kantone im Verhältnis der Wohnbevölkerung verteilt.

Von den Reineinnahmen des Bundes aus der fiskalischen Belastung gebrannter Wasser erhalten die Kantone die Hälfte, die im Verhältnis der Wohnbevölkerung unter sie zu verteilen ist; von seinem Anteil hat jeder Kanton wenigstens zehn Prozent zur Bekämpfung des Alkoholismus in seinen Ursachen und Wirkungen zu verwenden. Die andere Hälfte der Reineinnahmen verbleibt dem Bunde und ist für die Alters- und Hinterlassenenversicherung zu verwenden und bis zu deren Einführung in den bezüglichen Fonds zu legen.

ART. 32 *ter*. Fabrikation, Einfuhr, Transport, Verkauf und Aufbewahrung zum Zwecke des Verkaufs des unter dem Namen Absinth bekannten Liqueurs sind im ganzen Umfange der Eidgenossenschaft verboten. Dieses Verbot bezieht sich auch auf alle Getränke, die unter irgendwelcher Bezeichnung eine Nachahmung dieses Liqueurs darstellen. Vorbehalten bleiben der Durchgangstransport und die Verwendung zu pharmazeutischen Zwecken.

Das Verbot tritt zwei Jahre nach seiner Annahme in Kraft. Die Bundesgesetzgebung wird die infolge des Verbotes notwendig werdenden Bestimmungen treffen.

Der Bund hat das Recht, dasselbe Verbot auf dem Wege der

Gesetzgebung in bezug auf alle andern absinthhaltigen Getränke zu erlassen, welche eine öffentliche Gefahr bilden.

Art. 32 *quater.* Die Kantone können auf dem Wege der Gesetzgebung die Ausübung des Wirtschaftsgewerbes und des Kleinhandels mit geistigen Getränken den durch das öffentliche Wohl geforderten Beschränkungen unterwerfen. Als Kleinhandel mit nicht gebrannten geistigen Getränken gilt der Handel mit Mengen von weniger als zwei Litern.

Der Handel mit nicht gebrannten, geistigen Getränken in Mengen von zwei bis zehn Litern kann innerhalb der Grenzen von Art. 31, Abs. 2, von den Kantonen auf dem Wege der Gesetzgebung von einer Bewilligung und der Entrichtung einer mässigen Gebühr abhängig gemacht und der behördlichen Aufsicht unterstellt werden.

Der Verkauf nicht gebrannter, geistiger Getränke darf von den Kantonen, abgesehen von den Patentgebühren, mit keinen besondern Steuern belastet werden.

Juristische Personen dürfen von den Kantonen nicht ungünstiger behandelt werden als natürliche. Die Produzenten von Wein, Obstwein und Most können ihr Eigengewächs in Mengen von zwei und mehr Litern ohne Bewilligung und ohne Gebühr verkaufen.

Der Bund ist befugt, auf dem Wege der Gesetzgebung Vorschriften für die Ausübung des Handels mit nicht gebrannten, geistigen Getränken in Mengen von zwei und mehr Litern aufzustellen. Diese Vorschriften dürfen den Grundsatz der Handels- und Gewerbefreiheit nicht beeinträchtigen.

Das Hausieren mit geistigen Getränken, sowie ihr Verkauf im Umherziehen sind untersagt.

Art. 33. Den Kantonen bleibt es anheimgestellt, die Ausübung der wissenschaftlichen Berufsarten von einem Ausweise der Befähigung abhängig zu machen.

Auf dem Wege der Bundesgesetzgebung ist dafür zu sorgen, dass derartige Ausweise für die ganze Eidgenossenschaft gültig erworben werden können.

Art. 34. Der Bund ist befugt, einheitliche Bestimmungen über die Verwendung von Kindern in den Fabriken und über die Dauer der Arbeit erwachsener Personen in denselben aufzustellen. Ebenso ist er berechtigt, Vorschriften zum Schutze der Arbeiter gegen einen die Gesundheit und Sicherheit gefährdenden Gewerbebetrieb zu erlassen.

Der Geschäftsbetrieb von Auswanderungsagenturen und von Privatunternehmungen im Gebiete des Versicherungswesens unterliegt der Aufsicht und Gesetzgebung des Bundes.

Art. 34 bis. Der Bund wird auf dem Wege der Gesetzgebung die Kranken- und Unfallversicherung einrichten, unter Berücksichtigung der bestehenden Krankenkassen.

Er kann den Beitritt allgemein oder für einzelne Bevölkerungsklassen obligatorisch erklären.

Art. 34 ter. Der Bund ist befugt, Vorschriften aufzustellen:
a. über den Schutz der Arbeitnehmer;
b. über das Verhältnis zwischen Arbeitgebern und Arbeitnehmern, insbesondere über die gemeinsame Regelung betrieblicher und beruflicher Angelegenheiten;
c. über die Allgemeinverbindlicherklärung von Gesamtarbeitsverträgen und von andern gemeinsamen Vorkehren von Arbeitgeber- und Arbeitnehmerverbänden zur Förderung des Arbeitsfriedens;
d. über den angemessenen Ersatz des Lohn- und Verdienstausfalles infolge Militärdienstes;
e. über die Arbeitsvermittlung;
f. über die Arbeitslosenversicherung und die Arbeitslosenfürsorge;
g. über die berufliche Ausbildung in Industrie, Gewerbe, Handel, Landwirtschaft und Hausdienst.

Die Allgemeinverbindlicherklärung gemäss lit. c. ist nur für Sachgebiete, welche das Arbeitsverhältnis betreffen, und nur dann zulässig, wenn die Regelung begründeten Minderheitsinteressen und regionalen Verschiedenheiten angemessen Rechnung trägt und die Rechtsgleichheit sowie die Verbandsfreiheit nicht beeinträchtigt.

Die Durchführung der Arbeitslosenversicherung ist Sache öffentlicher und privater, sowohl paritätischer als einseitiger Kassen. Die Befugnis zur Errichtung öffentlicher Arbeitslosenversicherungskassen, sowie zur Einführung eines allgemeinen Obligatoriums der Arbeitslosenversicherung bleibt den Kantonen vorbehalten.

Die Vorschriften von Art. 32 finden entsprechende Anwendung.

Art. 34 quater. Der Bund wird auf dem Wege der Gesetzgebung die Alters- und die Hinterlassenenversicherung einrichten; er ist befugt, auf einen spätern Zeitpunkt auch die Invalidenversicherung einzuführen.

Er kann diese Versicherungszweige allgemein oder für einzelne Bevölkerungsklassen obligatorisch erklären.

Die Durchführung erfolgt unter Mitwirkung der Kantone; es können öffentliche und private Versicherungskassen beigezogen werden.

Die beiden ersten Versicherungszweige sind gleichzeitig einzuführen.

Die finanziellen Leistungen des Bundes und der Kantone dürfen sich zusammen auf nicht mehr als die Hälfte des Gesamtbedarfes der Versicherung belaufen.

Vom 1. Januar 1926 an leistet der Bund einen Beitrag in der Höhe der gesamten Einnahmen aus der fiskalischen Belastung des Tabaks an die Alters- und Hinterlassenenversicherung.

Der Anteil des Bundes an den Reineinnahmen aus einer künftigen fiskalischen Belastung gebrannter Wasser wird für die Alters- und Hinterlassenenversicherung verwendet.

ART. 34 *quinquies*. Der Bund berücksichtigt in der Ausübung der ihm zustehenden Befugnisse und im Rahmen der Verfassung die Bedürfnisse der Familie.

Der Bund ist zur Gesetzgebung auf dem Gebiete der Familienausgleichskassen befugt. Er kann den Beitritt allgemein oder für einzelne Bevölkerungsgruppen obligatorisch erklären. Er berücksichtigt die bestehenden Kassen, fördert die Bestrebungen der Kantone und der Berufsverbände zur Gründung neuer Kassen und ist befugt, eine zentrale Ausgleichskasse zu errichten. Die finanziellen Leistungen des Bundes können von angemessenen Leistungen der Kantone abhängig gemacht werden.

Der Bund ist befugt, auf dem Gebiete des Siedlungs- und Wohnungswesens Bestrebungen zugunsten der Familie zu unterstützen. Ein Bundesgesetz wird bestimmen, an welche Bedingungen die Bundesbeiträge geknüpft werden können; es wird die baupolizeilichen Bestimmungen der Kantone vorbehalten.

Der Bund wird auf dem Wege der Gesetzgebung die Mutterschaftsversicherung einrichten. Er kann den Beitritt allgemein oder für einzelne Bevölkerungsgruppen obligatorisch erklären, und es dürfen auch Personen, die nicht in den Genuss der Versicherungsleistungen kommen können, zu Beiträgen verpflichtet werden. Die finanziellen Leistungen des Bundes können von angemessenen Leistungen der Kantone abhängig gemacht werden.

Der Vollzug der auf Grund dieses Artikels ergehenden Gesetze erfolgt unter Mitwirkung der Kantone; private und öffentliche Vereinigungen können beigezogen werden.

ART. 35. Die Errichtung und der Betrieb von Spielbanken sind verboten.

Die Kantonsregierungen können unter den vom öffentlichen Wohl geforderten Beschränkungen den Betrieb der bis zum Frühjahr 1925 in den Kursälen üblich gewesenen Unterhaltungsspiele gestatten, sofern ein solcher Betrieb nach dem Ermessen der Bewilligungsbehörde zur Erhaltung oder Förderung des Fremdenverkehrs als notwendig erscheint und durch eine Kursaalunternehmung geschieht, welche diesem Zwecke dient. Die Kantone können auch Spiele dieser Art verbieten.

Über die vom öffentlichen Wohl geforderten Beschränkungen wird der Bundesrat eine Verordnung erlassen. Der Einsatz darf zwei Franken nicht übersteigen.

Jede kantonale Bewilligung unterliegt der bundesrätlichen Genehmigung.

Ein Viertel der Roheinnahmen aus dem Spielbetrieb ist dem Bunde abzuliefern, der diesen Anteil ohne Anrechnung auf seine eigenen Leistungen den Opfern von Elementarschäden sowie gemeinnützigen Fürsorgeeinrichtungen zuwenden soll.

Der Bund kann auch in Beziehung auf die Lotterien geeignete Massnahmen treffen.

Art. 36. Das Post- und Telegraphenwesen im ganzen Umfange der Eidgenossenschaft ist Bundessache.

Der Ertrag der Post- und Telegraphenverwaltung fällt in die eidgenössische Kasse.

Die Tarife werden im ganzen Gebiete der Eidgenossenschaft nach den gleichen, möglichst billigen Grundsätzen bestimmt.

Die Unverletzlichkeit des Post- und Telegraphengeheimnisses ist gewährleistet.

Art. 37. Der Bund übt die Oberaufsicht über die Strassen und Brücken, an deren Erhaltung die Eidgenossenschaft ein Interesse hat.

Die Summen, welche den im Art. 30 bezeichneten Kantonen mit Rücksicht auf ihre internationalen Alpenstrassen zukommen, werden von der Bundesbehörde zurückbehalten, wenn diese Strassen von den betreffenden Kantonen nicht in gehörigem Zustand unterhalten werden.

Art. 37 *bis*. Der Bund ist befugt, Vorschriften über Automobile und Fahrräder aufzustellen.

Den Kantonen bleibt das Recht gewahrt, den Automobil- und Fahrradverkehr zu beschränken oder zu untersagen. Der Bund kann indessen bestimmte, für den allgemeinen Durchgangsverkehr notwendige Strassen in vollem oder beschränktem Umfange offen erklären. Die Benützung der Strassen im Dienste des Bundes bleibt vorbehalten.

Art. 37 *ter*. Die Gesetzgebung über die Luftschiffahrt ist Sache des Bundes.

ART. 38. Dem Bunde steht die Ausübung aller im Münzregale begriffenen Rechte zu.

Die Münzprägung geht einzig vom Bunde aus.

Er bestimmt den Münzfuss und erlässt allfällige Vorschriften über die Tarifierung fremder Münzsorten.

ART. 39. Das Recht zur Ausgabe von Banknoten und andern gleichartigen Geldzeichen steht ausschliesslich dem Bunde zu.

Der Bund kann das ausschliessliche Recht zur Ausgabe von Banknoten durch eine unter gesonderter Verwaltung stehende Staatsbank ausüben oder, unter Vorbehalt des Rückkaufsrechts, einer zentralen Aktienbank übertragen, die unter seiner Mitwirkung und Aufsicht verwaltet wird.

Die mit dem Notenmonopol ausgestattete Bank hat die Hauptaufgabe, den Geldumlauf des Landes zu regeln, den Zahlungsverkehr zu erleichtern und im Rahmen der Bundesgesetzgebung eine den Gesamtinteressen des Landes dienende Kredit- und Währungspolitik zu führen.

Der Reingewinn der Bank über eine angemessene Verzinsung, beziehungsweise eine angemessene Dividende des Dotations- oder Aktienkapitals und die nötigen Einlagen in den Reservefonds hinaus kommt wenigstens zu zwei Dritteilen den Kantonen zu.

Die Bank und ihre Zweiganstalten dürfen in den Kantonen keiner Besteuerung unterzogen werden.

Der Bund kann die Einlösungspflicht für Banknoten und andere gleichartige Geldzeichen nicht aufheben und die Rechtsverbindlichkeit für ihre Annahme nicht aussprechen, ausgenommen in Kriegszeiten oder in Zeiten gestörter Währungsverhältnisse.

Die ausgegebenen Banknoten müssen durch Gold und kurzfristige Guthaben gedeckt sein.

Die Bundesgesetzgebung bestimmt das Nähere über die Ausführung dieses Artikels.

ART. 40. Die Festsetzung von Mass und Gewicht ist Bundessache.

Die Ausführung der bezüglichen Gesetze geschieht durch die Kantone unter Aufsicht des Bundes.

ART. 41. Fabrikation und Verkauf des Schiesspulvers stehen ausschliesslich dem Bunde zu.

Herstellung, Beschaffung und Vertrieb von Waffen, Munition, Sprengmitteln, sonstigem Kriegsmaterial und deren Bestandteilen bedürfen einer Bewilligung des Bundes. Die Bewilligung darf nur an Personen und Unternehmungen erteilt werden, die vom Standpunkte der Landesinteressen aus die nötige Gewähr bieten. Die Regiebetriebe des Bundes werden vorbehalten.

Die Einfuhr und Ausfuhr von Wehrmitteln im Sinne dieser Verfassungsbestimmung darf nur mit Bewilligung des Bundes erfolgen. Der Bund ist berechtigt, auch die Durchfuhr von einer Bewilligung abhängig zu machen.

Der Bundesrat erlässt unter Vorbehalt der Bundesgesetzgebung in einer Verordnung die zum Vollzug der Abs. 2 und 3 nötigen Vorschriften. Er stellt insbesondere die nähern Bestimmungen über Erteilung, Dauer und Widerruf der Bewilligungen und über die Überwachung der Konzessionäre auf. Er bestimmt ferner, welche Arten von Waffen, Munition, Sprengmitteln, sonstigem Material und welche Bestandteile unter diese Verfassungsbestimmung fallen.

ART. 41 *bis*. Der Bund ist befugt, Stempelabgaben auf Wertpapieren, Quittungen für Versicherungsprämien, Wechseln und wechselähnlichen Papieren, auf Frachturkunden und andern Urkunden des Handelsverkehrs zu erheben; diese Befugnis erstreckt sich nicht auf die Urkunden des Grundstückverkehrs und des Grundpfandverkehrs. Urkunden, für die der Bund die Abgabepflicht oder die Abgabefreiheit festsetzt, dürfen von den Kantonen nicht mit Stempelabgaben oder Registrierungsgebühren belastet werden.

Vom Reinertrag der Stempelabgaben fällt ein Fünftel den Kantonen zu.

Der Vollzug dieser Bestimmungen erfolgt durch die Bundesgesetzgebung.

ART. 41 *ter*. Der Bund ist befugt, den rohen und den verarbeiteten Tabak zu besteuern.

ART. 42. Die Ausgaben des Bundes werden bestritten:
a. aus dem Ertrag des Bundesvermögens;
b. aus dem Ertrag der schweizerischen Grenzzölle;
c. aus dem Ertrag der Post- und Telegraphenverwaltung;
d. aus dem Ertrag der Pulververwaltung;
e. aus der Hälfte des Bruttoertrages der von den Kantonen bezogenen Militärpflichtersatzsteuern;
f. aus den Beiträgen der Kantone, deren nähere Regulierung, vorzugsweise nach Massgabe der Steuerkraft derselben, der Bundesgesetzgebung vorbehalten ist;
g. aus dem Ertrag der Stempelabgaben.

ART. 43. Jeder Kantonsbürger ist Schweizerbürger. Als solcher kann er bei allen eidgenössischen Wahlen und Abstimmungen an seinem Wohnsitze Anteil nehmen, nachdem er sich über seine Stimmberechtigung gehörig ausgewiesen hat.

Niemand darf in mehr als einem Kanton politische Rechte ausüben.

Der niedergelassene Schweizerbürger geniesst an seinem Wohnsitze alle Rechte der Kantonsbürger und mit diesen auch alle Rechte der Gemeindsbürger. Der Mitanteil an Bürger- und Korporationsgütern, sowie das Stimmrecht in rein bürgerlichen Angelegenheiten sind jedoch hievon ausgenommen, es wäre denn, dass die Kantonalgesetzgebung etwas anderes bestimmen würde. In kantonalen und Gemeindeangelegenheiten erwirbt er das Stimmrecht nach einer Niederlassung von drei Monaten.

Die kantonalen Gesetze über die Niederlassung und das Stimmrecht der Niedergelassenen in den Gemeinden unterliegen der Genehmigung des Bundesrates.

Art. 44. Ein Schweizerbürger darf weder aus der Schweiz noch aus seinem Heimatkanton ausgewiesen werden.

Die Bedingungen für die Erteilung und den Verlust des Schweizerbürgerrechts werden durch die Bundesgesetzgebung aufgestellt.

Sie kann bestimmen, dass das Kind ausländischer Eltern von Geburt an Schweizerbürger ist, wenn seine Mutter von Abstammung Schweizerbürgerin war und die Eltern zur Zeit der Geburt in der Schweiz ihren Wohnsitz haben. Die Einbürgerung erfolgt in der früheren Heimatgemeinde der Mutter.

Die Bundesgesetzgebung stellt die Grundsätze für die Wiederaufnahme in das Bürgerrecht auf.

Die auf Grund dieser Bestimmungen eingebürgerten Personen haben die Rechte eines Gemeindebürgers, mit der Einschränkung, dass sie keinen Anteil an den Bürger- oder Korporationsgütern erhalten, soweit die kantonale Gesetzgebung es nicht anders ordnet.

Der Bund übernimmt bei den Einbürgerungen, die bei der Geburt erfolgt sind, bis zum vollendeten achtzehnten Altersjahr der Eingebürgerten wenigstens die Hälfte der den Kantonen und Gemeinden erwachsenden Unterstützungskosten. Einen gleichen Anteil übernimmt er bei Wiederaufnahmen in das Bürgerrecht während der ersten zehn Jahre nach der Aufnahme.

Die Bundesgesetzgebung bestimmt, in welchen Fällen bei Einbürgerungen Heimatloser eine Beitragsleistung an die den Kantonen und den Gemeinden erwachsenden Kosten stattfindet.

Art. 45. Jeder Schweizer hat das Recht, sich innerhalb des schweizerischen Gebietes an jedem Orte niederzulassen, wenn er einen Heimatschein oder eine andere gleichbedeutende Ausweisschrift besitzt.

Ausnahmsweise kann die Niederlassung denjenigen, welche infolge eines strafgerichtlichen Urteils nicht im Besitze der bürgerlichen Rechte und Ehren sind, verweigert oder entzogen werden.

Weiterhin kann die Niederlassung denjenigen entzogen werden, welche wegen schwerer Vergehen wiederholt gerichtlich bestraft worden sind, sowie denjenigen, welche dauernd der öffentlichen Wohltätigkeit zur Last fallen und deren Heimatgemeinde, beziehungsweise Heimatkanton, eine angemessene Unterstützung trotz amtlicher Aufforderung nicht gewährt.

In Kantonen, wo die örtliche Armenpflege besteht, darf die Gestattung der Niederlassung für Kantonsangehörige an die Bedingung geknüpft werden, dass dieselben arbeitsfähig und an ihrem bisherigen Wohnorte im Heimatkanton nicht bereits in dauernder Weise der öffentlichen Wohltätigkeit zur Last gefallen seien.

Jede Ausweisung wegen Verarmung muss von Seite der Regierung des Niederlassungskantons genehmigt und der heimatlichen Regierung zum voraus angezeigt werden.

Der niedergelassene Schweizerbürger darf von Seite des die Niederlassung gestattenden Kantons mit keiner Bürgschaft und mit keinen andern besondern Lasten behufs der Niederlassung belegt werden. Ebenso darf die Gemeinde, in welcher er seinen Wohnsitz nimmt, ihn nicht anders besteuern als den Ortsbürger.

Ein Bundesgesetz wird das Maximum der für die Niederlassungsbewilligung zu entrichtenden Kanzleigebühr bestimmen.

ART. 46. In Beziehung auf die zivilrechtlichen Verhältnisse stehen die Niedergelassenen in der Regel unter dem Rechte und der Gesetzgebung des Wohnsitzes.

Die Bundesgesetzgebung wird über die Anwendung dieses Grundsatzes, sowie gegen Doppelbesteuerung die erforderlichen Bestimmungen treffen.

ART. 47. Ein Bundesgesetz wird den Unterschied zwischen Niederlassung und Aufenthalt bestimmen und dabei gleichzeitig über die politischen und bürgerlichen Rechte der schweizerischen Aufenthalter die nähern Vorschriften aufstellen.

ART. 48. Ein Bundesgesetz wird über die Kosten der Verpflegung und Beerdigung armer Angehöriger eines Kantons, welche in einem andern Kanton krank werden oder sterben, die nötigen Bestimmungen treffen.

ART. 49. Die Glaubens- und Gewissensfreiheit ist unverletzlich.

Niemand darf zur Teilnahme an einer Religionsgenossenschaft, oder an einem religiösen Unterricht, oder zur Vornahme einer religiösen Handlung gezwungen, oder wegen Glaubensansichten mit Strafen irgendwelcher Art belegt werden.

Über die religiöse Erziehung der Kinder bis zum erfüllten 16.

Altersjahr verfügt im Sinne vorstehender Grundsätze der Inhaber der väterlichen oder vormundschaftlichen Gewalt.

Die Ausübung bürgerlicher oder politischer Rechte darf durch keinerlei Vorschriften oder Bedingungen kirchlicher oder religiöser Natur beschränkt werden.

Die Glaubensansichten entbinden nicht von der Erfüllung der bürgerlichen Pflichten.

Niemand ist gehalten, Steuern zu bezahlen, welche speziell für eigentliche Kultuszwecke einer Religionsgenossenschaft, der er nicht angehört, auferlegt werden. Die nähere Ausführung dieses Grundsatzes ist der Bundesgesetzgebung vorbehalten.

Art. 50. Die freie Ausübung gottesdienstlicher Handlungen ist innerhalb der Schranken der Sittlichkeit und der öffentlichen Ordnung gewährleistet.

Den Kantonen, sowie dem Bunde bleibt vorbehalten, zur Handhabung der Ordnung und des öffentlichen Friedens unter den Angehörigen der verschiedenen Religionsgenossenschaften, sowie gegen Eingriffe kirchlicher Behörden in die Rechte der Bürger und des Staates, die geeigneten Massnahmen zu treffen.

Anstände aus dem öffentlichen oder Privatrechte, welche über die Bildung oder Trennung von Religionsgenossenschaften entstehen, können auf dem Wege der Beschwerdeführung der Entscheidung der zuständigen Bundesbehörden unterstellt werden.

Die Errichtung von Bistümern auf schweizerischem Gebiete unterliegt der Genehmigung des Bundes.

Art. 51. Der Orden der Jesuiten und die ihm affiliierten Gesellschaften dürfen in keinem Teile der Schweiz Aufnahme finden, und es ist ihren Gliedern jede Wirksamkeit in Kirche und Schule untersagt.

Dieses Verbot kann durch Bundesbeschluss auch auf andere geistliche Orden ausgedehnt werden, deren Wirksamkeit staatsgefährlich ist oder den Frieden der Konfessionen stört.

Art. 52. Die Errichtung neuer und die Wiederherstellung aufgehobener Klöster oder religiöser Orden ist unzulässig.

Art. 53. Die Feststellung und Beurkundung des Zivilstandes ist Sache der bürgerlichen Behörden. Die Bundesgesetzgebung wird hierüber die nähern Bestimmungen treffen.

Die Verfügung über die Begräbnisplätze steht den bürgerlichen Behörden zu. Sie haben dafür zu sorgen, dass jeder Verstorbene schicklich beerdigt werden kann.

Art. 54. Das Recht zur Ehe steht unter dem Schutze des Bundes. Dieses Recht darf weder aus kirchlichen oder ökonomischen

Rücksichten, noch wegen bisherigen Verhaltens oder aus andern polizeilichen Gründen beschränkt werden.

Die in einem Kanton oder im Auslande nach der dort geltenden Gesetzgebung abgeschlossene Ehe soll im Gebiete der Eidgenossenschaft als Ehe anerkannt werden.

Durch den Abschluss der Ehe erwirbt die Frau das Heimatrecht des Mannes.

Durch die nachfolgende Ehe der Eltern werden vorehelich geborene Kinder derselben legitimiert.

Jede Erhebung von Brauteinzugsgebühren oder andern ähnlichen Abgaben ist unzulässig.

Art. 55. Die Pressfreiheit ist gewährleistet.

Über den Missbrauch derselben trifft die Kantonalgesetzgebung die erforderlichen Bestimmungen, welche jedoch der Genehmigung des Bundesrates bedürfen.

Dem Bunde steht das Recht zu, Strafbestimmungen gegen den Missbrauch der Presse zu erlassen, der gegen die Eidgenossenschaft und ihre Behörden gerichtet ist.

Art. 56. Die Bürger haben das Recht, Vereine zu bilden, sofern solche weder in ihrem Zweck, noch in den dafür bestimmten Mitteln rechtswidrig oder staatsgefährlich sind. Über den Missbrauch dieses Rechtes trifft die Kantonalgesetzgebung die erforderlichen Bestimmungen.

Art. 57. Das Petitionsrecht ist gewährleistet.

Art. 58. Niemand darf seinem verfassungsmässigen Richter entzogen, und es dürfen daher keine Ausnahmsgerichte eingeführt werden.

Die geistliche Gerichtsbarkeit ist abgeschafft.

Art. 59. Der aufrechtstehende Schuldner, welcher in der Schweiz einen festen Wohnsitz hat, muss für persönliche Ansprachen vor dem Richter seines Wohnortes gesucht und es darf daher für Forderungen auf das Vermögen eines solchen ausser dem Kanton, in welchem er wohnt, kein Arrest gelegt werden.

Vorbehalten bleiben mit Bezug auf Ausländer die Bestimmungen bezüglicher Staatsverträge.

Der Schuldverhaft ist abgeschafft.

Art. 60. Sämtliche Kantone sind verpflichtet, alle Schweizerbürger in der Gesetzgebung sowohl als im gerichtlichen Verfahren den Bürgern des eigenen Kantons gleich zu halten.

Art. 61. Die rechtskräftigen Zivilurteile, die in einem Kanton gefällt sind, sollen in der ganzen Schweiz vollzogen werden können.

ART. 62. Alle Abzugsrechte im Innern der Schweiz, sowie die Zugrechte von Bürgern des einen Kantons gegen Bürger anderer Kantone sind abgeschafft.

ART. 63. Gegen die auswärtigen Staaten besteht Freizügigkeit, unter Vorbehalt des Gegenrechtes.

ART. 64. Dem Bunde steht die Gesetzgebung zu:
über die persönliche Handlungsfähigkeit;
über alle auf den Handel und Mobiliarverkehr bezüglichen Rechtsverhältnisse (Obligationenrecht, mit Inbegriff des Handels- und Wechselrechts);
über das Urheberrecht an Werken der Literatur und Kunst;
über den Schutz gewerblich verwertbarer Erfindungen, mit Einschluss der Muster und Modelle;
über das Betreibungsverfahren und das Konkursrecht.

Der Bund ist zur Gesetzgebung auch in den übrigen Gebieten des Zivilrechts befugt.

Die Organisation der Gerichte, das gerichtliche Verfahren und die Rechtsprechung verbleiben, wie bis anhin, den Kantonen.

ART. 64 bis. Der Bund ist zur Gesetzgebung im Gebiete des Strafrechts befugt.

Die Organisation der Gerichte, das gerichtliche Verfahren und die Rechtsprechung verbleiben, wie bis anhin, den Kantonen.

Der Bund ist befugt, den Kantonen zur Errichtung von Straf-, Arbeits- und Besserungsanstalten und für Verbesserungen im Strafvollzuge Beiträge zu gewähren. Er ist auch befugt, sich an Einrichtungen zum Schutze verwahrloster Kinder zu beteiligen.

ART. 65. Wegen politischer Vergehen darf kein Todesurteil gefällt werden.

Körperliche Strafen sind untersagt.

ART. 66. Die Bundesgesetzgebung bestimmt die Schranken, innerhalb welcher ein Schweizerbürger seiner politischen Rechte verlustig erklärt werden kann.

ART. 67. Die Bundesgesetzgebung trifft die erforderlichen Bestimmungen über die Auslieferung der Angeklagten von einem Kanton an den andern; die Auslieferung kann jedoch für politische Vergehen und für Pressvergehen nicht verbindlich gemacht werden.

ART. 68. Die Ausmittlung von Bürgerrechten für Heimatlose und die Massregeln zur Verhinderung der Entstehung neuer Heimatlosen sind Gegenstand der Bundesgesetzgebung.

Art. 69. Der Bund ist befugt, zur Bekämpfung übertragbarer oder stark verbreiteter oder bösartiger Krankheiten von Menschen und Tieren gesetzliche Bestimmungen zu treffen.

Art. 69 *bis*. Der Bund ist befugt, gesetzliche Bestimmungen zu erlassen:
 a. über den Verkehr mit Nahrungs- und Genussmitteln;
 b. über den Verkehr mit andern Gebrauchs- und Verbrauchsgegenständen, soweit solche das Leben oder die Gesundheit gefährden können.

Die Ausführung der bezüglichen Bestimmungen geschieht durch die Kantone, unter Aufsicht und mit der finanziellen Unterstützung des Bundes.

Dagegen liegt die Kontrolle der Einfuhr an der Landesgrenze dem Bunde ob.

Art. 69 *ter*. Die Gesetzgebung über Ein- und Ausreise, Aufenthalt und Niederlassung der Ausländer steht dem Bunde zu.

Die Entscheidung über Aufenthalt und Niederlassung treffen nach Massgabe des Bundesrechtes die Kantone. Dem Bunde steht jedoch das endgültige Entscheidungsrecht zu gegenüber:
 a. kantonalen Bewilligungen für länger dauernden Aufenthalt, für Niederlassung und gegenüber Toleranzbewilligungen;
 b. Verletzung von Niederlassungsverträgen;
 c. kantonalen Ausweisungen aus dem Gebiete der Eidgenossenschaft;
 d. Verweigerung des Asyls.

Art. 70. Dem Bunde steht das Recht zu, Fremde, welche die innere oder äussere Sicherheit der Eidgenossenschaft gefährden, aus dem schweizerischen Gebiete wegzuweisen.

ZWEITER ABSCHNITT

BUNDESBEHÖRDEN

I. Bundesversammlung

Art. 71. Unter Vorbehalt der Rechte des Volkes und der Kantone (Art. 89 und 121) wird die oberste Gewalt des Bundes durch die Bundesversammlung ausgeübt, welche aus zwei Abteilungen besteht:
 A. aus dem Nationalrat,
 B. aus dem Ständerat.

A. NATIONALRAT

Art. 72. Der Nationalrat wird aus Abgeordneten des schweizerischen Volkes gebildet. Auf je 24,000 Seelen der Gesamtbevölkerung wird ein Mitglied gewählt. Eine Bruchzahl über 12,000 Seelen wird für 24,000 Seelen berechnet.

Jeder Kanton und bei geteilten Kantonen jeder der beiden Landesteile hat wenigstens ein Mitglied zu wählen.

Art. 73.* Die Wahlen in den Nationalrat sind direkte. Sie finden nach dem Grundsatze der Proportionalität statt, wobei jeder Kanton und jeder Halbkanton einen Wahlkreis bildet.

Die Bundesgesetzgebung trifft über die Ausführung dieses Grundsatzes die näheren Bestimmungen.

Art. 74. Stimmberechtigt bei Wahlen und Abstimmungen ist jeder Schweizer, der das 20. Altersjahr zurückgelegt hat und im übrigen nach der Gesetzgebung des Kantons, in welchem er seinen Wohnsitz hat, nicht vom Aktivbürgerrechte ausgeschlossen ist.

Es bleibt jedoch der Gesetzgebung des Bundes vorbehalten, über diese Stimmberechtigung einheitliche Vorschriften aufzustellen.

Art. 75. Wahlfähig als Mitglied des Nationalrates ist jeder stimmberechtigte Schweizerbürger weltlichen Standes.

Art. 76. Der Nationalrat wird auf die Dauer von 4 Jahren gewählt, und es findet jeweilen Gesamterneuerung statt.

Art. 77. Die Mitglieder des Ständerates, des Bundesrates und von letzterem gewählte Beamte können nicht zugleich Mitglieder des Nationalrates sein.

Art. 78. Der Nationalrat wählt aus seiner Mitte für jede ordentliche oder ausserordentliche Sitzung einen Präsidenten und Vizepräsidenten.

Dasjenige Mitglied, welches während einer ordentlichen Sitzung die Stelle eines Präsidenten bekleidete, ist für die nächstfolgende

* *Temporary provision to Article 73:*
Art. 1. Am letzten Sonntag im Oktober 1919 findet eine Gesamterneuerung des Nationalrates nach Massgabe des Bundesgesetzes betreffend die Wahl des Nationalrates nach dem Grundsatze der Proportionalität statt.

Der neugewählte Nationalrat tritt am ersten Montag des Monats Dezember 1919 zur konstituierenden Sitzung in der Bundesstadt zusammen. An dem diesem Tage vorhergehenden Sonntag endigt die Amtsdauer des gegenwärtigen Nationalrates.

Die Amtsdauer des neuen Nationalrates endigt an dem dem ersten Montag des Monats Dezember 1922 vorangehenden Sonntag.

Art. 2. In der Dezembersession 1919 findet eine Gesamterneuerung des Bundesrates statt. Die Amtsdauer des neugewählten Bundesrates endigt im Dezember 1922.

ordentliche Sitzung weder als Präsident noch als Vizepräsident wählbar. Das gleiche Mitglied kann nicht während zwei unmittelbar aufeinanderfolgenden ordentlichen Sitzungen Vizepräsident sein.

Der Präsident hat bei gleich geteilten Stimmen zu entscheiden; bei Wahlen übt er das Stimmrecht aus wie jedes Mitglied.

ART. 79. Die Mitglieder des Nationalrates werden aus der Bundeskasse entschädigt.

B. STÄNDERAT

ART. 80. Der Ständerat besteht aus 44 Abgeordneten der Kantone. Jeder Kanton wählt zwei Abgeordnete, in den geteilten Kantonen jeder Landesteil einen Abgeordneten.

ART. 81. Die Mitglieder des Nationalrates und des Bundesrates können nicht zugleich Mitglieder des Ständerates sein.

ART. 82. Der Ständerat wählt für jede ordentliche oder ausserordentliche Sitzung aus seiner Mitte einen Präsidenten und Vizepräsidenten.

Aus den Abgeordneten desjenigen Kantons, aus welchem für eine ordentliche Sitzung der Präsident gewählt worden ist, kann für die nächstfolgende ordentliche Sitzung weder der Präsident noch der Vizepräsident gewählt werden.

Abgeordnete des gleichen Kantons können nicht während zwei unmittelbar aufeinanderfolgenden ordentlichen Sitzungen die Stelle eines Vizepräsidenten bekleiden.

Der Präsident hat bei gleich geteilten Stimmen zu entscheiden; bei Wahlen übt er das Stimmrecht aus wie jedes Mitglied.

ART. 83. Die Mitglieder des Ständerates werden von den Kantonen entschädigt.

C. BEFUGNISSE DER BUNDESVERSAMMLUNG

ART. 84. Der Nationalrat und der Ständerat haben alle Gegenstände zu behandeln, welche nach Inhalt der gegenwärtigen Verfassung in die Kompetenz des Bundes gehören und nicht einer andern Bundesbehörde zugeschieden sind.

ART. 85. Die Gegenstände, welche in den Geschäftskreis beider Räte fallen, sind insbesondere folgende:

1. Gesetze über die Organisation und die Wahlart der Bundesbehörden.
2. Gesetze und Beschlüsse über diejenigen Gegenstände, zu deren Regelung der Bund nach Massgabe der Bundesverfassung befugt ist.

3. Besoldung und Entschädigung der Mitglieder der Bundesbehörden und der Bundeskanzlei; Errichtung bleibender Beamtungen und Bestimmung ihrer Gehalte.

4. Wahl des Bundesrates, des Bundesgerichtes, des Kanzlers, sowie des Generals der eidgenössischen Armee.

Der Bundesgesetzgebung bleibt vorbehalten, auch die Vornahme oder Bestätigung weiterer Wahlen der Bundesversammlung zu übertragen.

5. Bündnisse und Verträge mit dem Auslande, sowie die Gutheissung von Verträgen der Kantone unter sich oder mit dem Auslande. Solche Verträge der Kantone gelangen jedoch nur dann an die Bundesversammlung, wenn vom Bundesrat oder einem andern Kanton Einsprache erhoben wird.

6. Massregeln für die äussere Sicherheit, für Behauptung der Unabhängigkeit und Neutralität der Schweiz, Kriegserklärungen und Friedensschlüsse.

7. Garantie der Verfassungen und des Gebietes der Kantone; Intervention infolge der Garantie; Massregeln für die innere Sicherheit, für Handhabung von Ruhe und Ordnung; Amnestie und Begnadigung.

8. Massregeln, welche die Handhabung der Bundesverfassung, die Garantie der Kantonalverfassungen, die Erfüllung der bundesmässigen Verpflichtungen zum Zwecke haben.

9. Verfügungen über das Bundesheer.

10. Aufstellung des jährlichen Voranschlages und Abnahme der Staatsrechnung, sowie Beschlüsse über Aufnahme von Anlehen.

11. Die Oberaufsicht über die eidgenössische Verwaltung und Rechtspflege.

12. Beschwerden gegen Entscheidungen des Bundesrates über Administrativstreitigkeiten (Art. 113).

13. Kompetenzstreitigkeiten zwischen Bundesbehörden.

14. Revision der Bundesverfassung.

ART. 86. Die beiden Räte versammeln sich jährlich einmal zur ordentlichen Sitzung an einem durch das Reglement festzusetzenden Tage.

Sie werden ausserordentlich einberufen durch Beschluss des Bundesrates, oder wenn ein Viertel der Mitglieder des Nationalrates oder fünf Kantone es verlangen.

ART. 87. Um gültig verhandeln zu können, ist die Anwesenheit der absoluten Mehrheit der Mitglieder des betreffenden Rates erforderlich.

Art. 88. Im Nationalrat und Ständerat entscheidet die absolute Mehrheit der Stimmenden.

Art. 89. Für Bundesgesetze und Bundesbeschlüsse ist die Zustimmung beider Räte erforderlich.

Bundesgesetze, sowie allgemeinverbindliche Bundesbeschlüsse, sind dem Volke zur Annahme oder Verwerfung vorzulegen, wenn es von 30,000 stimmberechtigten Schweizerbürgern oder von 8 Kantonen verlangt wird.

Staatsverträge mit dem Auslande, welche unbefristet oder für eine Dauer von mehr als 15 Jahren abgeschlossen sind, sind ebenfalls dem Volke zur Annahme oder Verwerfung vorzulegen, wenn es von 30,000 stimmberechtigten Schweizerbürgern oder von 8 Kantonen verlangt wird.

Art. 89 *bis*. Allgemeinverbindliche Bundesbeschlüsse, deren Inkrafttreten keinen Aufschub erträgt, können durch die Mehrheit aller Mitglieder in jedem der beiden Räte sofort in Kraft gesetzt werden; ihre Gültigkeitsdauer ist zu befristen.

Wird von 30,000 stimmberechtigten Schweizerbürgern oder von acht Kantonen eine Volksabstimmung verlangt, treten die sofort in Kraft gesetzten Beschlüsse ein Jahr nach ihrer Annahme durch die Bundesversammlung ausser Kraft, soweit sie nicht innerhalb dieser Frist vom Volke gutgeheissen wurden; in diesem Falle können sie nicht erneuert werden.

Die sofort in Kraft gesetzten Bundesbeschlüsse, welche sich nicht auf die Verfassung stützen, müssen innert Jahresfrist nach ihrer Annahme durch die Bundesversammlung von Volk und Ständen genehmigt werden; andernfalls treten sie nach Ablauf dieses Jahres ausser Kraft und können nicht erneuert werden.

Art. 90. Die Bundesgesetzgebung wird bezüglich der Formen und Fristen der Volksabstimmung das Erforderliche feststellen.

Art. 91. Die Mitglieder beider Räte stimmen ohne Instruktionen.

Art. 92. Jeder Rat verhandelt abgesondert. Bei Wahlen (Art. 85, Ziffer 4,), bei Ausübung des Begnadigungsrechtes und für Entscheidung von Kompetenzstreitigkeiten (Art. 85, Ziffer 13) vereinigen sich jedoch beide Räte unter der Leitung des Präsidenten des Nationalrates zu einer gemeinschaftlichen Verhandlung, so dass die absolute Mehrheit der stimmenden Mitglieder beider Räte entscheidet.

Art. 93. Jedem der beiden Räte und jedem Mitgliede derselben steht das Vorschlagsrecht (die Initiative) zu.

Das gleiche Recht können die Kantone durch Korrespondenz ausüben.

Art. 94. Die Sitzungen der beiden Räte sind in der Regel öffentlich.

II. Bundesrat

Art. 95. Die oberste vollziehende und leitende Behörde der Eidgenossenschaft ist ein Bundesrat, welcher aus 7 Mitgliedern besteht.

Art. 96. Die Mitglieder des Bundesrates werden von der Bundesversammlung aus allen Schweizerbürgern, welche als Mitglieder des Nationalrates wählbar sind, auf die Dauer von 4 Jahren ernannt. Es darf jedoch nicht mehr als ein Mitglied aus dem nämlichen Kanton gewählt werden.

Nach jeder Gesamterneuerung des Nationalrates findet auch eine Gesamterneuerung des Bundesrates statt.

Die in der Zwischenzeit ledig gewordenen Stellen werden bei der nächstfolgenden Sitzung der Bundesversammlung für den Rest der Amtsdauer wieder besetzt.

Art. 97. Die Mitglieder des Bundesrates dürfen keine andere Beamtung, sei es im Dienste der Eidgenossenschaft, sei es in einem Kantone, bekleiden, noch irgendeinen andern Beruf oder Gewerbe treiben.

Art. 98. Den Vorsitz im Bundesrat führt der Bundespräsident, welcher, sowie auch der Vizepräsident, von den vereinigten Räten aus den Mitgliedern desselben für die Dauer eines Jahres gewählt wird.

Der abtretende Präsident ist für das nächstfolgende Jahr weder als Präsident noch als Vizepräsident wählbar. Das gleiche Mitglied kann nicht während zwei unmittelbar aufeinanderfolgenden Jahren die Stelle eines Vizepräsidenten bekleiden.

Art. 99. Der Bundespräsident und die übrigen Mitglieder des Bundesrates beziehen einen jährlichen Gehalt aus der Bundeskasse.

Art. 100. Um gültig verhandeln zu können, müssen wenigstens vier Mitglieder des Bundesrates anwesend sein.

Art. 101. Die Mitglieder des Bundesrates haben bei den Verhandlungen der beiden Abteilungen der Bundesversammlung beratende Stimme und auch das Recht, über einen in Beratung liegenden Gegenstand Anträge zu stellen.

Art. 102. Der Bundesrat hat innert den Schranken der gegenwärtigen Verfassung vorzüglich folgende Befugnisse und Obliegenheiten:

1. Er leitet die eidgenössischen Angelegenheiten, gemäss den Bundesgesetzen und Bundesbeschlüssen.

2. Er hat für Beobachtung der Verfassung, der Gesetze und Beschlüsse des Bundes, sowie der Vorschriften eidgenössischer Konkordate zu wachen; er trifft zur Handhabung derselben von sich aus oder auf eingegangene Beschwerde, soweit die Beurteilung solcher Rekurse nicht nach Art. 113 dem Bundesgerichte übertragen ist, die erforderlichen Verfügungen.

3. Er wacht für die Garantie der Kantonalverfassungen.

4. Er schlägt der Bundesversammlung Gesetze und Beschlüsse vor und begutachtet die Anträge, welche von den Räten des Bundes oder von den Kantonen an ihn gelangen.

5. Er vollzieht die Bundesgesetze und Bundesbeschlüsse, die Urteile des Bundesgerichts, sowie die Vergleiche oder schiedsrichterlichen Sprüche über Streitigkeiten zwischen Kantonen.

6. Er hat diejenigen Wahlen zu treffen, welche nicht der Bundesversammlung und dem Bundesgerichte oder einer andern Behörde übertragen werden.

7. Er prüft die Verträge der Kantone unter sich oder mit dem Auslande und genehmigt dieselben, sofern sie zulässig sind (Art. 85, Ziffer 5).

8. Er wahrt die Interessen der Eidgenossenschaft nach aussen, wie namentlich ihre völkerrechtlichen Beziehungen, und besorgt die auswärtigen Angelegenheiten überhaupt.

9. Er wacht für die äussere Sicherheit, für die Behauptung der Unabhängigkeit und Neutralität der Schweiz.

10. Er sorgt für die innere Sicherheit der Eidgenossenschaft, für Handhabung von Ruhe und Ordnung.

11. In Fällen von Dringlichkeit ist der Bundesrat befugt, sofern die Räte nicht versammelt sind, die erforderliche Truppenzahl aufzubieten und über solche zu verfügen, unter Vorbehalt unverzüglicher Einberufung der Bundesversammlung, sofern die aufgebotenen Truppen zweitausend Mann übersteigen oder das Aufgebot länger als drei Wochen dauert.

12. Er besorgt das eidgenössische Militärwesen und alle Zweige der Verwaltung, welche dem Bunde angehören.

13. Er prüft die Gesetze und Verordnungen der Kantone, welche seiner Genehmigung bedürfen; er überwacht diejenigen Zweige der Kantonalverwaltung, welche seiner Aufsicht unterstellt sind.

14. Er sorgt für die Verwaltung der Finanzen des Bundes, für die

Entwerfung des Voranschlages und die Stellung der Rechnungen über die Einnahmen und Ausgaben des Bundes.

15. Er hat die Aufsicht über die Geschäftsführung aller Beamten und Angestellten der eidgenössischen Verwaltung.

16. Er erstattet der Bundesversammlung jeweilen bei ihrer ordentlichen Sitzung Rechenschaft über seine Verrichtungen, sowie Bericht über den Zustand der Eidgenossenschaft im Innern sowohl als nach aussen, und wird ihrer Aufmerksamkeit diejenigen Massregeln empfehlen, welche er zur Beförderung gemeinsamer Wohlfahrt für dienlich erachtet.

Er hat auch besondere Berichte zu erstatten, wenn die Bundesversammlung oder eine Abteilung derselben es verlangt.

ART. 103. Die Geschäfte des Bundesrates werden nach Departementen unter die einzelnen Mitglieder verteilt. Der Entscheid über die Geschäfte geht vom Bundesrat als Behörde aus.

Durch die Bundesgesetzgebung können bestimmte Geschäfte den Departementen oder ihnen untergeordneten Amtsstellen unter Vorbehalt des Beschwerderechtes zur Erledigung überwiesen werden.

Die Bundesgesetzgebung bezeichnet die Fälle, in denen ein eidgenössisches Verwaltungsgericht für die Behandlung der Beschwerde zuständig ist.

ART. 104. Der Bundesrat und seine Departemente sind befugt, für besondere Geschäfte Sachkundige beizuziehen.

III. Bundeskanzlei

ART. 105. Eine Bundeskanzlei, welcher ein Kanzler vorsteht, besorgt die Kanzleigeschäfte bei der Bundesversammlung und beim Bundesrat.

Der Kanzler wird von der Bundesversammlung auf die Dauer von 4 Jahren jeweilen gleichzeitig mit dem Bundesrat gewählt.

Die Bundeskanzlei steht unter der besondern Aufsicht des Bundesrates.

Die nähere Organisation der Bundeskanzlei bleibt der Bundesgesetzgebung vorbehalten.

IV. Organisation und Befugnisse des Bundesgerichts

ART. 106. Zur Ausübung der Rechtspflege, soweit dieselbe in den Bereich des Bundes fällt, wird ein Bundesgericht aufgestellt.

Für Beurteilung von Straffällen (Art. 112) werden Schwurgerichte (Jury) gebildet.

Art. 107. Die Mitglieder des Bundesgerichts und die Ersatzmänner werden von der Bundesversammlung gewählt. Bei der Wahl derselben soll darauf Bedacht genommen werden, dass alle drei Amtssprachen des Bundes vertreten seien.

Das Gesetz bestimmt die Organisation des Bundesgerichtes und seiner Abteilungen, die Zahl der Mitglieder und Ersatzmänner, deren Amtsdauer und Besoldung.

Art. 108. In das Bundesgericht kann jeder Schweizerbürger ernannt werden, der in den Nationalrat wählbar ist.

Die Mitglieder der Bundesversammlung und des Bundesrates und die von diesen Behörden gewählten Beamten können nicht gleichzeitig Mitglieder des Bundesgerichtes sein.

Die Mitglieder des Bundesgerichtes dürfen keine andere Beamtung, sei es im Dienste der Eidgenossenschaft, sei es in einem Kantone, bekleiden, noch irgendeinen andern Beruf oder Gewerbe treiben.

Art. 109. Das Bundesgericht bestellt seine Kanzlei.

Art. 110. Das Bundesgericht beurteilt zivilrechtliche Streitigkeiten:
1. zwischen dem Bunde und den Kantonen;
2. zwischen dem Bunde einerseits und Korporationen oder Privaten andererseits, wenn der Streitgegenstand eine durch die Bundesgesetzgebung zu bestimmende Bedeutung hat und wenn diese Korporationen oder Privaten Kläger sind;
3. zwischen den Kantonen unter sich;
4. zwischen den Kantonen einerseits und Korporationen oder Privaten andererseits, wenn der Streitgegenstand von einer durch die Bundesgesetzgebung zu bestimmenden Bedeutung ist und eine Partei es verlangt.

Das Bundesgericht urteilt ferner über Anstände betreffend Heimatlosigkeit, sowie über Bürgerrechtsstreitigkeiten zwischen Gemeinden verschiedener Kantone.

Art. 111. Das Bundesgericht ist verpflichtet, die Beurteilung auch anderer Fälle zu übernehmen, wenn dasselbe von beiden Parteien angerufen wird und der Streitgegenstand von einer durch die Bundesgesetzgebung zu bestimmenden Bedeutung ist.

Art. 112. Das Bundesgericht urteilt mit Zuziehung von Geschwornen, welche über die Tatfrage absprechen, in Straffällen:
1. über Hochverrat gegen die Eidgenossenschaft, Aufruhr und Gewalttat gegen die Bundesbehörden;
2. über Verbrechen und Vergehen gegen das Völkerrecht;

3. über politische Verbrechen und Vergehen, die Ursache oder Folge derjenigen Unruhen sind, durch welche eine bewaffnete eidgenössische Intervention veranlasst wird, und ...
4. in Fällen, wo von einer Bundesbehörde die von ihr ernannten Beamten ihm zur strafrechtlichen Beurteilung überwiesen werden.

ART. 113. Das Bundesgericht urteilt ferner:
1. über Kompetenzkonflikte zwischen Bundesbehörden einerseits und Kantonalbehörden andererseits;
2. über Streitigkeiten staatsrechtlicher Natur zwischen Kantonen;
3. über Beschwerden betreffend Verletzung verfassungsmässiger Rechte der Bürger, sowie über solche von Privaten wegen Verletzung von Konkordaten und Staatsverträgen.

Vorbehalten sind die durch die Bundesgesetzgebung näher festzustellenden Administrativstreitigkeiten.

In allen diesen Fällen sind jedoch die von der Bundesversammlung erlassenen Gesetze und allgemein verbindlichen Beschlüsse, sowie die von ihr genehmigten Staatsverträge für das Bundesgericht massgebend.

ART. 114. Es bleibt der Bundesgesetzgebung überlassen, ausser den in den Artikeln 110, 112 und 113 bezeichneten Gegenständen auch noch andere Fälle in die Kompetenz des Bundesgerichtes zu legen, insbesondere die Befugnisse festzustellen, welche ihm nach Erlassung der im Artikel 64 vorgesehenen eidgenössischen Gesetze behufs einheitlicher Anwendung derselben zu übertragen sind.

IV bis. EIDGENÖSSISCHE VERWALTUNGS- UND DISZIPLINARGERICHTSBARKEIT

ART. 114 bis. Das eidgenössische Verwaltungsgericht beurteilt die in den Bereich des Bundes fallenden Administrativstreitigkeiten, die die Bundesgesetzgebung ihm zuweist.

Dem Verwaltungsgericht steht auch die Beurteilung von Disziplinarfällen der Bundesverwaltung zu, die ihm durch die Bundesgesetzgebung zugewiesen werden, soweit dafür nicht eine besondere Gerichtsbarkeit geschaffen wird.

Die Bundesgesetzgebung und die von der Bundesversammlung genehmigten Staatsverträge sind für das eidgenössische Verwaltungsgericht massgebend.

Die Kantone sind mit Genehmigung der Bundesversammlung befugt, Administrativstreitigkeiten, die in ihren Bereich fallen, dem eidgenössischen Verwaltungsgericht zur Beurteilung zuzuweisen.

Die Organisation der eidgenössischen Verwaltungs- und Diszi-
plinargerichtsbarkeit, sowie das Verfahren wird durch das Gesetz
bestimmt.

V. Verschiedene Bestimmungen

Art. 115. Alles, was sich auf den Sitz der Bundesbehörden
bezieht, ist Gegenstand der Bundesgesetzgebung.

Art. 116. Das Deutsche, Französische, Italienische und Räto-
romanische sind die Nationalsprachen der Schweiz.

Als Amtssprachen des Bundes werden das Deutsche, Französische
und Italienische erklärt.

Art. 117. Die Beamten der Eidgenossenschaft sind für ihre
Geschäftsführung verantwortlich. Ein Bundesgesetz wird diese
Verantwortlichkeit näher bestimmen.

DRITTER ABSCHNITT

REVISION DER BUNDESVERFASSUNG

Art. 118. Die Bundesverfassung kann jederzeit ganz oder teil-
weise revidiert werden.

Art. 119. Die Totalrevision geschieht auf dem Wege der
Bundesgesetzgebung.

Art. 120. Wenn eine Abteilung der Bundesversammlung die
Totalrevision beschliesst und die andere nicht zustimmt, oder wenn
fünfzigtausend stimmberechtigte Schweizerbürger die Totalrevision
der Bundesverfassung verlangen, so muss im einen wie im andern
Falle die Frage, ob eine solche stattfinden soll oder nicht, dem
schweizerischen Volke zur Abstimmung vorgelegt werden.

Sofern in einem dieser Fälle die Mehrheit der stimmenden
Schweizerbürger über die Frage sich bejahend ausspricht, so sind
beide Räte neu zu wählen, um die Totalrevision an die Hand zu
nehmen.

Art. 121. Die Partialrevision kann sowohl auf dem Wege der
Volksanregung (Initiative) als der Bundesgesetzgebung vorgenom-
men werden.

Die Volksanregung umfasst das von fünfzigtausend stimmberechtigten Schweizerbürgern gestellte Begehren auf Erlass, Aufhebung
oder Abänderung bestimmter Artikel der Bundesverfassung.

Wenn auf dem Wege der Volksanregung mehrere verschiedene

Materien zur Revision oder zur Aufnahme in die Bundesverfassung vorgeschlagen werden, so hat jede derselben den Gegenstand eines besonderen Initiativbegehrens zu bilden.

Die Initiativbegehren können in der Form der allgemeinen Anregung oder des ausgearbeiteten Entwurfs gestellt werden.

Wenn ein solches Begehren in Form der allgemeinen Anregung gestellt wird und die eidgenössischen Räte mit demselben einverstanden sind, so haben sie die Partialrevision im Sinne der Initianten auszuarbeiten und dieselbe dem Volke und den Ständen zur Annahme oder Verwerfung vorzulegen. Stimmen die eidgenössischen Räte dem Begehren nicht zu, so ist die Frage der Partialrevision dem Volke zur Abstimmung zu unterbreiten und, sofern die Mehrheit der stimmenden Schweizerbürger sich bejahend ausspricht, die Revision von der Bundesversammlung im Sinne des Volksbeschlusses an die Hand zu nehmen.

Wird das Begehren in Form eines ausgearbeiteten Entwurfs gestellt und stimmt die Bundesversammlung demselben zu, so ist der Entwurf dem Volke und den Ständen zur Annahme oder Verwerfung vorzulegen. Im Falle der Nichtzustimmung kann die Bundesversammlung einen eigenen Entwurf ausarbeiten oder die Verwerfung des Vorschlages beantragen und ihren Entwurf oder Verwerfungsantrag gleichzeitig mit dem Initiativbegehren der Abstimmung des Volkes und der Stände unterbreiten.

Art. 122. Über das Verfahren bei den Volksbegehren und den Abstimmungen betreffend Revision der Bundesverfassung wird ein Bundesgesetz das Nähere bestimmen.

Art. 123. Die revidierte Bundesverfassung, beziehungsweise der revidierte Teil derselben, treten in Kraft, wenn sie von der Mehrheit der an der Abstimmung teilnehmenden Bürger und von der Mehrheit der Kantone angenommen sind.

Bei Ausmittlung der Mehrheit der Kantone wird die Stimme eines Halbkantons als halbe Stimme gezählt.

Das Ergebnis der Volksabstimmung in jedem Kantone gilt als Standesstimme desselben.

ÜBERGANGSBESTIMMUNGEN

Art. 1. In betreff der Verwendung der Zoll- und Posteinnahmen bleiben die bisherigen Verhältnisse unverändert, bis der Übergang der bis jetzt von den Kantonen getragenen Militärlasten auf den Bund sich vollzieht.

Ausserdem ist auf dem Wege der Bundesgesetzgebung zu bewirken, dass denjenigen Kantonen, für welche die durch die Artikel 20, 30, 36, zweites Alinea, und 42e herbeigeführten Veränderungen im Gesamtergebnisse eine fiskalische Einbusse zur Folge haben, diese Einbusse nicht auf einmal in ihrem vollen Umfange, sondern nur allmählich während einer Übergangsperiode von einigen Jahren erwachse.

Diejenigen Kantone, welche sich bis zum Zeitpunkte, in welchem der Artikel 20 in Kraft tritt, mit den ihnen durch die bisherige Bundesverfassung und die Bundesgesetze obliegenden militärischen Leistungen im Rückstande befinden, sind verpflichtet, diese Leistungen auf eigene Kosten nachzuholen.

Art. 2. Diejenigen Bestimmungen der eidgenössischen Gesetzgebung, der Konkordate, der kantonalen Verfassungen und Gesetze, welche mit der neuen Bundesverfassung im Widerspruch stehen, treten mit Annahme derselben, beziehungsweise der Erlassung der darin in Aussicht genommenen Bundesgesetze, ausser Kraft.

Art. 3. Die neuen Bestimmungen betreffend die Organisation und die Befugnisse des Bundesgerichts treten erst nach Erlassung der bezüglichen Bundesgesetze in Kraft.

Art. 4. Den Kantonen wird zur Einführung der Unentgeltlichkeit des öffentlichen Primarunterrichts (Art. 27) eine Frist von fünf Jahren eingeräumt.

Art. 5. Personen, welche den wissenschaftlichen Berufsarten angehören und welche bis zum Erlasse der im Artikel 33 vorgesehenen Bundesgesetzgebung von einem Kanton oder von einer, mehrere Kantone repräsentierenden Konkordatsbehörde den Ausweis der Befähigung erlangt haben, sind befugt, ihren Beruf in der ganzen Eidgenossenschaft auszuüben.

Also dem Volke und den Ständen vorzulegen beschlossen vom Nationalrate.

Bern, den 31. Jänner 1874.

Der Präsident: Ziegler.
Der Protokollführer: Schiess.

Also dem Volke und den Ständen vorzulegen beschlossen vom Ständerate.

Bern, den 31. Jänner 1874.

Der Präsident: A. Kopp.
Der Protokollführer: J. L. Lütscher.

ART. 7. Der Bund richtet den Kantonen für die Jahre 1951 bis 1954 die Hälfte des Reinertrages des Zolles auf Treibstoffen für motorische Zwecke aus. Die Ausrichtung erfolgt in Form von
  a. Beiträgen an die allgemeinen Kosten der dem Motorfahrzeug geöffneten Strassen;
  b. Beiträgen an die Kosten des Neu- oder Ausbaues der Hauptstrassen, die zu einem vom Bundesrat zu bezeichnenden Netz gehören und deren Ausführung bestimmten technischen Anforderungen genügt;
  c. zusätzlichen Beiträgen an die Strassenbaulasten der Kantone mit geringer Finanzkraft.

Die auf Grund von Artikel 30, Absatz 3, der Bundesverfassung den Kantonen Uri, Graubünden, Tessin und Wallis, mit Rücksicht auf ihre internationalen Alpenstrassen, jährlich auszurichtenden Entschädigungen werden für die Jahre 1951 bis 1954 erhöht auf:
  240 000 Franken für Uri,
  600 000 Franken für Graubünden,
  600 000 Franken für Tessin,
  150 000 Franken für Wallis.

ART. 8. Beschlüsse, durch die einmalige Ausgaben von mehr als fünf Millionen Franken oder wiederkehrende Ausgaben von mehr als 250 000 Franken bewilligt oder beschlossene Ausgaben um den gleichen Betrag erhöht werden sollen, bedürfen in jedem der beiden Räte der Zustimmung der absoluten Mehrheit aller Mitglieder, wenn über sie die Volksabstimmung nicht verlangt werden kann.

ART. 9. Zur Bekämpfung von Wirtschaftskrisen, welche während der Geltungsdauer dieses Bundesbeschlusses allenfalls auftreten, sind in erster Linie vorhandene Kredite und Mittel aus früheren Arbeitsbeschaffungsaktionen, der Kriegsgewinnsteuer-Rückstellung und der Verrechnungssteuer-Rückstellung bis zum Gesamtbetrag von 400 Millionen Franken zu verwenden.

BEFRISTETE WEITERFÜHRUNG EINER BESCHRÄNKTEN PREISKONTROLLE

(*26. Sept. 1952*)

I

Die Bundesverfassung vom 29. Mai 1874 erhält folgenden Zusatz:

ART. 1. Der Bund kann Vorschriften erlassen über Miet- und Pachtzinse sowie zum Schutze der Mieter. Er kann seine Befugnisse den Kantonen übertragen.

Er kann ferner für Waren, die für das Inland bestimmt sind und deren Preisbildung durch Schutzmassnahmen, wie insbesondere durch Einfuhrbeschränkungen oder damit verbundene Zollzuschläge, sowie durch Hilfsmassnahmen des Bundes beeinflusst wird, Höchstpreisvorschriften erlassen und Preisausgleichsmassnahmen treffen.

Art. 2. Beantragt der Bundesrat der Bundesversammlung Höchstpreisvorschriften für lebenswichtige, für das Inland bestimmte Waren zu erlassen, so ist er befugt, diese Vorschriften mit sofortiger Wirkung selbst in Kraft zu setzen.

Diese Vorschriften fallen dahin, wenn sie nicht in der auf ihr Inkrafttreten folgenden Session von der Bundesversammlung durch einen dem Referendum unterstellten Bundesbeschluss genehmigt werden.

Art. 3. Der Bundesratsbeschluss vom 15. Oktober 1941/ 8. Februar 1946 betreffend Massnahmen gegen die Wohnungsnot sowie die am 31. Dezember 1952 noch geltenden, auf den erwähnten Bundesratsbeschluss oder auf den Bundesratsbeschluss vom 1. September 1939 betreffend die Kosten der Lebenshaltung und den Schutz der regulären Marktversorgung gestützten Vorschriften bleiben längstens bis zum 31. Dezember 1953 in Kraft.

Die Strafbestimmungen des Bundesratsbeschlusses vom 1. September 1939 betreffend die Kosten der Lebenshaltung und den Schutz der regulären Marktversorgung bleiben längstens bis zum 31. Dezember 1953 in Kraft.

Die Strafverfolgung und Beurteilung von Widerhandlungen, die nach dem 31. Dezember 1952 begangen werden, ist Sache der Kantone.

II

Dieser Beschluss gilt vom 1. Januar 1953 bis 31. Dezember 1956. Er ist der Abstimmung des Volkes und der Stände zu unterbreiten.

BROTGETREIDEVERSORGUNG DES LANDES
(26. Sept. 1952)

I

Die Bundesverfassung erhält folgenden Zusatz:

Art. 1. Der Bund kann Vorschriften über eine befristete Ergänzung der auf Artikel 23*bis* der Bundesverfassung beruhenden Getreideordnung erlassen. Diese Vorschriften betreffen:
 a) Einfuhr, Lagerung, Verteilung, Verwendung und Vermahlung des Brotgetreides (einschliesslich Hartweizen);

b) Herstellung, Abgabe, Bezug, Preise, Verwendung und Ausfuhr von Mahlerzeugnissen aus Brotgetreide (einschliesslich Hartweizen) und von Brot;
c) Sicherheitsleistung der Handelsmüller.

Art. 2. Die am 31. Dezember 1952 noch geltenden und auf die nachstehend aufgeführten Bundesratsbeschlüsse gestützten Vorschriften bleiben noch bis zum 31. Dezember 1953 in Kraft.

a) Bundesratsbeschluss vom 1. September 1939 betreffend die Kosten der Lebenshaltung und den Schutz der regulären Marktversorgung und Bundesratsbeschluss vom 17. Oktober 1939 über die Sicherstellung der Landesversorgung mit Lebens- und Futtermitteln, soweit die in Frage stehenden Vorschriften die Brotgetreideversorgung des Landes betreffen;
b) Bundesratsbeschluss vom 15. November 1940/29. April 1949 über die Getreide- und Futtermittelversorgung;
c) Bundesratsbeschluss vom 29. Dezember 1947 betreffend die Sicherstellung der Landesversorgung mit Lebens- und Futtermitteln (Kontingentierung der Handelsmühlen);
d) Bundesratsbeschluss vom 30. Mai 1950 betreffend die Überwachung der Ausfuhr von Mehl und Brot.

Der Bundesrat kann die erforderlichen Straf- und Strafverfahrensbestimmungen erlassen.

II

Dieser Beschluss gilt bis zum 31. Dezember 1957.
Er ist der Abstimmung des Volkes und der Stände zu unterbreiten.

SELECT BIBLIOGRAPHY

A. GENERAL CHARACTERISTICS OF BOOKS ON SWISS GOVERNMENT

1. ENGLISH BOOKS

The treatment of Swiss institutions in English books is disappointing. The only general work in English on Swiss government which is indubitably of permanent value is Adams and Cunningham's *The Swiss Confederation*. Of those books which still retain a topical value, Brooks's *Government and Politics of Switzerland*, supplemented by Professor Rappard's study and Dr. Tripp's useful dissertation, will take the reader as far as he can proceed in English. The other general books merely cover the same ground again. Lord Bryce's examination of Switzerland in *Modern Democracies*, however, deserves to be read on account of the celebrity and experience of its author. There are useful examinations of particular topics in books not dealing mainly with Switzerland, and of these Professor Wheare's *Federal Government* is especially valuable.

It is not easy to account for the small number of masterpieces on this subject, for English people know Switzerland better than any other foreign country, and the Swiss Constitution dates substantially from 1848, and is of intrinsic interest. Two factors to some extent account for this poverty. In the first place the Swiss presentation in the English language of their own institutions has been such that it deters readers from taking any further interest. An assumption of complete ignorance, a note of sustained panegyric, and comparisons betraying a complete lack of knowledge of British institutions—these are refreshing traits on the first occasion, but become unbearable upon constant repetition. And secondly, there is the German language. It is an unpalatable fact that, with rare exceptions, the general books on Swiss institutions in French are no better than those in English, whereas there are numerous excellent books in German on the subject. Even the weaknesses of French style have a charm for English people, whereas German writers cultivate as virtues what in England are regarded as the deadliest vices, and the style, the language, and the cast of mind are alike strange to us. Behind this barrier lies a territory of legal literature and scholarship well worth exploring, abounding in riches. No thorough study of Switzerland can be made without reading German.

2. FOREIGN BOOKS

There are three types of book likely to be immediately of use to a student of Swiss institutions—documents, commentaries, and dissertations.

(i) *Documents*. None of these quite corresponds to its English counterpart. The reports of the Federal Council, for example, will be quoted in the

Courts to interpret a law, and so may, on occasion, the Stenographic Bulletin, whereas the precedent of the Federal Tribunal will occasionally be rather lightly brushed aside. It is always necessary to relate the document being studied to the whole Constitution of Switzerland.

(ii) *Commentaries, &c.* Foremost among these are the great works of Giacometti and Burckhardt. In general the commentaries, regarding the Constitution as a 'pure ought', will freely give an interpretation of the law in terms which do not describe what actually happens but what should happen—an occasional footnote 'The practice of the authorities is otherwise, wrongly' gives the clue. But the opinion of the commentary cannot be disregarded, for it will very likely alter the practice. It is in its way also a document, also a source of law, for the hard line which with us separates the professions and pronouncements of the judge and the university lecturer is not drawn in Switzerland. The same consideration applies in diminishing degree to the whole learned hierarchy of commentary, manual, outline, and *Beitrag*, and to articles in learned periodicals.

(iii) *Dissertations*. These are the proletariat of legal literature, and are much relied upon by the commentators. The present writer is deeply indebted to them.

Dissertations come into being because law-students try to become Doktors, and this requires a thesis or dissertation—there is no B.A. or M.A. in German-Swiss universities. The value of them varies; at their worst they are (with great humility) pretty bad, but often they are of permanent worth. The pattern on which German theses are constructed varies little. They start with the 'Begriff', the concept of what is under discussion. These Begriffs display marvellous subtlety, distinguishing the most unitary concepts into broader and narrower, material and formal, ideal and functional senses (the thesis is perhaps upon the hunting laws or absinthe). Once the reader has accustomed himself to the mode, he can skip the Begriffs, for on their particular plane they can be trusted to be orthodox. What remains after the Begriffs have been purged is often of great value—accurate, conscientious, subtle, and accessible. French language theses are on the whole less scholastic, more elegant, and shorter, and because of a difference in the university system they are usually written by riper scholars. At their worst, to say nothing at length in French is pleasanter for English ears than saying it in German.

(i) DOCUMENTS

(Where the French and German texts are of equal authority, the French text is listed rather than the German. The titles given in SMALL CAPITALS are the customary abbreviations.)

RECUEIL OFFICIEL *des Lois et Ordonnances de la Confédération suisse* (Amtliche Sammlung). Since 1848 (1874), continued to the present day. Contains Laws and Federal Arrêtés and Arrêtés, *Ordonnances*, &c., of the Federal Council, and to some extent also of departments. Appears weekly, and is collected into two (or more) annual volumes.

RECUEIL SYSTÉMATIQUE *des Lois et Ordonnances 1848–1947* (Bereinigte Sammlung). Ten volumes, plus 2 volumes of Treaties. Contains the law in force on 1 Jan. 1948, i.e. all laws since 1848 in force on that date, collected under headings (e.g. all the Federal rules concerning Public Health are to be found in vol. iv). In some ways this is the student's most convenient source for statutes, &c., but the text given is that as revised to 1948, and it is often of greater interest to see the text as it originally was than as it is today. For these purposes the *Recueil officiel* must be used, the current volume of which includes a *table systématique* of amendments since 1948.

The contents of the *Recueil systématique* are:

Vol. i. The Constitution, the Laws on the organization of the Confederation and on citizenship. The Standing Orders of the Councils. This volume contains most of what the student of politics requires.

Vol. ii. Civil Law.

Vol. iii. Bankruptcy, Penal Law, Civil and Penal Procedure.[1]

Vol. iv. Education, Public Health and Works.

Vol. v. Army.

Vol. vi. Finance, Alcohol.

Vol. vii. Transport.

Vol. viii. Social Legislation.

Vol. ix. Agriculture, Game Laws.

Vol. x. Trade, Cost of Living.

Volumes xi and xii. Treaties.

FEUILLE FÉDÉRALE (Bundesblatt). Also since 1848 (1874). Three or four volumes a year, numbered by year and volume. Chief contents: messages and reports of the Federal Council, the texts of Laws, &c., subject to referendum, the results of Federal votations and elections, projects of Laws, reports on projected Laws and treaties, and the projected guarantee of Cantonal Constitutions, &c. When the text of a Law is consulted, the message which originally accompanied it should also be read.

SAMMLUNG DER BUNDES- UND KANTONSVERFASSUNGEN. A single fat volume, published by the Federal Chancellery from time to time. The last edition was in 1948. The Cantonal Constitutions are given in their original texts, accompanied by brief introductions, and indexes. The Federal Constitution is in its three languages.

RAPPORTS DE GESTION *du Conseil fédéral* (Geschaeftsbericht). The Annual Reports to the Assembly of the Chancellor, the departments, the Federal Tribunal, &c. The reports before 1934 were much fuller, and are still of interest. They give a good picture of the year's business. The Federal Assembly's debates upon the report of 1945 were printed in the *Bulletin sténographique* of that year: otherwise such debates can usually only be consulted in newspaper reports or in unpublished records.

[1] The Civil Code, the Penal Code, and the Law on Judicial Organization (and ancillary documents) are each printed and obtainable separately. There exist commentaries upon each. The three separate documents are more convenient for the student than vols. ii and iii of the *Recueil systématique*, and contain all he will normally want.

BULLETIN STÉNOGRAPHIQUE. National Council and Council of States, separately. The Swiss Hansard; since 1890. Appears at the end of every session, the French speeches in French, the German in German. Only the debates on Laws and on *arrêtés de portée générale* are regularly reported in it, though other debates are occasionally included. Makes dull reading.

RÉSUMÉ DES DÉLIBÉRATIONS DE L'ASSEMBLÉE FÉDÉRALE. Contains the texts of motions and postulates, summaries of written questions and petitions, and the lists of members of *commissions*. Cf. Commons' and Lords' Journals.

ARRÊTS DU TRIBUNAL FÉDÉRAL (Entscheidungen des Bundesgerichts). The official Federal Law Reports, since 1875. Contains only a selection of cases, in the language in which the decision was given. Annual and decennial indices. Two or three volumes a year, of which vol. i contains the cases on Public Law.

PRAXIS DES BUNDESGERICHTS. A brief non-official résumé of cases before the Federal Tribunal.

ANNUAIRE STATISTIQUE *de la Suisse* (Statistisches Jahrbuch). Annual since 1891. Bilingual. Contains much of political interest.

In addition to the above sources, there are certain very useful collections of precedents and decisions. In particular:

'ULLMER', i.e. Die staatsrechtliche Praxis der schweizerischen Bundesbehoerden, by R. E. Ullmer (also in a French translation, *Droit public suisse*). Vol. i, 1848–60; vol. ii contains additional reports for the earlier period, and continues the work down to 1863. A semi-official collection of precedents, decisions of the Federal Council, Assembly, Tribunal, &c., taken chiefly from the *Feuille fédérale*.

'SALIS', i.e. Schweizerisches Bundesrecht, by L. R. von Salis. Performs the same functions as 'Ullmer' (omitting reports of the Federal Tribunal) for the years 1875–1902. Five volumes, of which the last contains the index. There is a French translation.

'BURCKHARDT', i.e. Schweizerisches Bundesrecht, by W. Burckhardt. Performs the same functions as 'Salis' for the years 1903–27. Five very substantial volumes, and a separate index volume. There is a French translation.

VERWALTUNGSENTSCHEIDE der Bundesbehörden (*Jurisprudence des autorités administratives de la Confédération*). Annual, from 1927. An official publication which to some extent continues the work of 'Burckhardt'. It contains decisions not published elsewhere. It is now about 10 years in arrears.

'CURTI', i.e. Saemtliche Entscheidungen des schw. Bundesgerichts. Abridged reports of the decisions of the Federal Tribunal for the first 30 years.

There is nothing to fill the gap between 'Ullmer' and 'Salis'.

(ii) COMMENTARIES

There are many Commentaries, Handbooks, &c., in German which display an impeccably high standard of scholarship. The most useful today are:

Z. GIACOMETTI, *Schweizerisches Bundesstaatsrecht*. Zürich, 1949 (971 pages).

WALTHER BURCKHARDT, *Kommentar der schw. Bundesverfassung*. 3rd edn., Bern, 1931 (2nd edn., 1914, 848 pages).

F. FLEINER. *Schweizerisches Bundesstaatsrecht*, deals more fully than Giacometti with certain matters, e.g. the Swiss army, and is in some ways a more attractively written book, but it is now rather out of date (1921, Tübingen).

These three books give full references to other commentaries on the subject.

B. SELECTED LITERATURE

The best introduction to Swiss history is:
Historischer Atlas der Schweiz: Atlas historique de la Suisse, edited by Hektor Ammann and Karl Schib. Aarau, 1951.

A book presenting an unfamiliar, but now influential and important, viewpoint—and extremely interesting—is:
GONZAGUE DE REYNOLD, *La Démocratie et la Suisse*. Berne, 1929.

For modern history:
WILLIAM RAPPARD, *L'Individu et l'État dans l'évolution constitutionnelle de la Suisse*. Zurich, 1936,
provides a guiding line. A thoroughly satisfactory modern history is extremely difficult to find, and perhaps has not yet been written. There has recently been a revival of interest in the Old Confederation (before 1798) and this has led to some excellent historical writing. The reader should be on his guard against histories of the 'Swiss Confederation', especially those written as the success-story of the three Forest Cantons, for these seldom avoid the dangers of historical 'backsight'. It is after all possible that if Switzerland had disappeared in 1798 or 1848, or even in the 1870s, its history would now be written as a part of the success-story of Brandenburg-Prussia. And the emphasis on the Confederation is also a distortion in another direction, for the real history of Swiss soil before 1798 is the history of each of the ancient Cantons, of their allies and of their subjects, and of the republics of the Grisons and Valais. Furthermore, Berne, and even Zurich, have claims to be considered the nodal points of the ancient Union. It is only in very recent times that a critical attitude has been adopted to the Old Confederation—an attitude which has political implications, for it rehabilitates aristocracy as a form of government, and ceases to regard the French Revolution as the nativity of the Swiss State.

There is an elementary source-book on Swiss history which is sometimes obtainable in England, and which is useful:
Quellenbuch zur Schweizergeschichte, ed. W. Oechsli. Zürich, 1886.

The following can be used as an introduction to the 1874 Constitution:
F. O. ADAMS and C. D. CUNNINGHAM, *The Swiss Confederation*. London, 1889.
R. C. BROOKS, *Government and Politics of Switzerland*. London, 1920.
W. E. RAPPARD, *The Government of Switzerland*. New York, 1936.

To bridge the gulf between these introductory works and Giacometti's great commentary, the following are useful:

M. L. TRIPP, *The Swiss and United States Federal Constitutional Systems* (Zurich thesis). Paris, 1940. There is also a German translation edited by H. Huber which, being the work of perhaps the most experienced and acute student of public law now in Switzerland, must be considered as the superior text;

K. C. WHEARE, *Federal Government*. Oxford (3rd edition).

Beyond these there are few general works which the present writer knows and is able to recommend as easy to read, containing new information, and perceptive—except the great commentaries listed above. Before tackling the commentaries, the English reader might care to familiarize himself with the general background of jurisprudence in *General Theory of Law and State*, by Hans Kelsen (Cambridge, Mass., 1949), after which he is referred to Giacometti's *Bundesstaatsrecht* cited above.

C. BIBLIOGRAPHIES

Giacometti's book contains a full apparatus of footnotes which serves as a bibliography. The *Schweizerische Buchhändlerverein* issues a catalogue of lawbooks still in print, from time to time, and this catalogue can be obtained from a Swiss bookseller. The *Zeitschrift für schweizerisches Recht* (the leading law journal; a serious student should be familiar with its back numbers) notices current publications on public law, and so do other legal periodicals.

INDEX

The figures refer to *pages*. There is an alphabetical analysis of the text of the Constitution on page 143, and of the Law on the Relations between the Councils on page 166: these are in some respects more complete than the present Index.

Aargau, Canton, 26, 66, 82, 85.
'Absolute majority', 99, 107, 210.
Administrative law, 93, 95, 97, 112, 117, 124, 126 seq., 130–1.
Alcohol, 24, 36, 85, 141.
Amnesty, 95.
Annual Report, 115, 151, 161, 215.
Appenzell, Inner Rhodes, 4, 24, 29, 36, 61, 64, 74, 82, 85, 88, 89, 132, 141.
— Outer Rhodes, 4, 42, 64, 82–83, 88.
Arbitrariness: prohibited, *see* Equality before the Law.
Aristocracy, *8*, 53, 107, 217.
Army, Federal, 13–20, 28, 63, 70, 77, 96, 114, 127, 139, 170, 217. *See also* General, Federal.
Arrêtés, Federal; meaning of word, 92, 100; cited, *see* Laws.
Assizes, Federal, *see* Jury.
Association, freedom of, 70.
Augsburg, Peace of, 61.
Authorities, Federal; meaning of term, 92–93; seat of, 128, responsibility of, 130.

Banishment, 54.
Bankrupts, 72, 74, 77, 85, 125.
Banks, 20, 34, 43, 46.
Barcelona, Declaration of, 25.
Basle, town, Canton, bishopric, 4, 12, 27, 61, 82, 138–9.
Berne, town, Canton, 4, 27, 53, 61, 65, 78, 82–3, 88, 108, 128–9, 217.
Bicameralism, 91, 100, 104. See also *Divergences*.
Biel (Bienne), 128.
Births, deaths, and marriages, registration of, 67, 117.
Books: Documents and authors, cited:
Adams & Cunningham, 213, 217.
Ammann & Schib, 217.
Annuaire statistique, 53, 55, 86, 120, 216.
Brooks, 213, 217.
Bryce, Lord, 213.
Bulletin sténographique, 106, 159, 215–16.

Burckhardt, W., (Kommentar) 135, 214, 216; (Bundesrecht) 21, 86, 216.
Carr, Sir C., 169.
Cron, 152.
Curti, 10, 216.
Eichenberger, 152.
Eidgenössische Abschiede, 57.
Élections au Conseil national, 84.
Feuille fédérale (Bundesblatt) 12, 33, 40, 43, 51, 59, 69, 96–97, 101, 104, 115, 119, 134, 136–7, 151, 163, 215.
Fleiner, 217. *See also* Giacometti.
Giacometti, (Bundesstaatsrecht) 135, 214, 216, 218; (Vollmachten) 169.
Huber, H., 218.
Kapani, 169.
Kelsen, 218.
Lachenal, 89, 104.
Manuel des chambres fédérales, 97.
Marti, Hans, 169.
Oechsli, 217.
Orelli, von, 72.
Parliamentary Affairs, 169.
Rappard, 213, 217.
Raton, 3.
Recueil officiel, 49, 69, 119, 151, 163–4, 214.
Recueil systématique, 38, 45, 56, 60, 97, 104, 136, 138, 159, 214 seq.
Reynold, G. de, 217.
Répertoire général, Arrêts du Tribunal fédéral, 7, 216.
Salis, L. R. von, 216.
Sammlung der Bundes- & Kantonsverfassungen, 215.
Tripp, 213, 218.
Ullmer, 59, 71, 216.
Verwaltungsentscheide der Bundesbehörden, 31, 216.
Wheare, K. C., 213, 218.
White, L., 115.
Williams, I., 74.
Zeitschrift für schw. Recht, 218.
Bosco-Gurin, 128.

INDEX

Broadcasting, 43, 114–15.
Budget, Federal (Estimates), 96, 161. See also Finance, Federal.
Burckhardt, family, 8; see also Books.
Bureaucracy, 67, 71, 84, 100–1, 107, 115, 171. For Officials, Federal see those words.
Bureaux, 87, 154.
Burials, 60, 67, 117.

Cantonal execution of Federal Laws, 5–6, 19, *23*, 26, 34, 43, 75–76, 80, *91*, 113, 140.
Cantons, see Citizenship, Concordats, Constitutions, Cantonal; Half-cantons; Sovereignty, Cantonal; *and the names of individual cantons*.
Capitulations, military, 13, 14.
Cases, cited:
 Basles, reunion of, 138.
 Commune of Willihof, 59.
 Hauri *v.* Aargau, 10.
 Fribourg tribunals, 71.
 Knellwolf, Pastor, 86.
 Mariahilfskirche. 65.
 Nicole (senior) 122, (junior) 69.
 Public works, military, 21.
 Thurgau *v.* St. Gall (double tax) 58–59.
 — reports of decided cases, 7, 216.
Cereals, 22, 211–12.
Challenge, the legislative, see Referendum.
Chancellery, Federal, 92, 109–10, 116, *118–19*, 152, 159, 215.
Church and State, see Religion.
Circular letters, 95.
Citizenship, 52–55, 70, 73, 77–79, 82, 117.
Civil code, *74–75*, 215; *cited*, 8, 11, 21, 56, 58, 68, 70, 72–73, 125, 133.
Code Napoléon, 73.
Coinage, 45, 125.
Collective contracts, 40.
Commissioner, Federal, 16–17.
Commissions, parliamentary, 71, 87–88, 90, 95, 106, 113, *151*, *160–2*, 171, 216.
'Communal autonomy', 90, 123, 164.
Communes, 21, 27, 52–59, 61, 71, 78–79, 164.
Communist party, 69, 84.
Concordats, 6, *11–13*, 45–46, 57, 73, 114, 123.

Conscience, Freedom of, 61–64. See also Religion.
Constitution, Federal, nature of, 3–4, 31, 92, 106, 169; text of, 1, 2, 37, 57, 73, 100, 103.
Constitutional judge, 71.
Constitutions, Cantonal, 4, 8–11, 32, 94, 113, 117, 123, 137–9, 215.
Contingents, Cantonal, 19, 49.
Corporal punishment, 76–77.
Corporations, 52, 55, 68, 78.
Council of States, 88 seq., 153 seq.
Criminal Code, *see* Penal Code.
Customs duties, 24, *29–31*, 51, 58, 139.

Death Penalty, 76, 105.
Decorations, prohibited foreign, 14, 89, 133.
Delegated legislation, 39, 43, 80, 93, 113, 124.
Denial of Justice, remedied, *see* Equality before the Law.
Department of Justice and Police, 69, 117.
Departments of Federal Council, 109–10, 116–17.
Deprivation of political rights, 57, 77, 85–86.
Dicey, A. V., 127, 130.
Disorder, internal, 16, 64–65, 95, 114, 122.
Divergences, 105, 134, 151, *155–6*.
'Domicile', meaning of word, 53, 56, 72.
Double Taxation, 12, 56, *58–59*, 124.
Droit de retrait, 73.
Droz, Numa, 110.
Dufour, General, 17.

'Economic Articles', the, 33 seq., 133.
Economic theories, influence of, 34.
Education, *27–29*, 79, 85, 93, 126–7, 150, 214; religious, 27–28, 62, 66.
Emergency Powers, *169* seq., 18, 43, 49–51, 69, 81, 94, 124.
— procedure, *see* Urgency procedure.
Emigration agencies, 39.
Epidemics, 79.
Equality before the Law, *6–8*, 43, 53, 63, 71–72, 88, 123–4, 139–40.
Escher, family, 8.
Execution, Federal, 9, 15–16, 95.
'Exclusively Federal matters', 1, 26.

INDEX

Factory Laws, 38.
Federal Assembly, 81 seq., &c.; competences of, 91 seq.
— Council, 106 seq., &c.; collegiality of, 116; competences, 112 seq. *See also* Emergency Powers.
— Insurance Tribunal, 39, 93, 97, 124.
'Federal Law breaks Cantonal Law', *139-40*, 123-6, 5, 9, 11, 23, 32, 43, 76, 81, 95, 114.
— Tribunal, 93, 97, 119 seq. &c. *See also* Incompatibility.
Federalism, 88, 90, 104, *140*. *See also* Sovereignty, Cantonal; Constitution, Federal, nature of.
Finance, Federal, 29-30, *48-51*, 101, 139, 142, 208 seq.; control of, 96-97, 161-2.
Foreigners, 24, 54-55, 70, 80, 82, 117.
Franchise, 53, 85, 88.
Freedom-rights, 71, 123, &c.
Fribourg, town, Canton, 4, 27, 66, 71, 82, 88, 128, 132, 141.
Full Powers, *see* Emergency Powers.
Foreign relations, 12, 74, 109-10, 117. *See also* Treaties.

General, 16-18, 93, 95-96, 130.
Geneva, town, Canton, bishopric, 16, 27, 65, 78, 82, 88, 102, 122.
Gipsies, 78-79.
Glarus, 61, 82, 88.
Great Britain, comparisons with, 5, 71, 76, 80, 87, 88, 90, 96, 98-99, 102, *107*, 115-16, 127, 130-1, 149 seq., 155, 160.
Grisons, 30, 61, 82, 128-9, 217.
Guarantee, Federal. *See* Sovereignty, Cantonal.
Gunpowder, 47-48.
Gotthard, pass, tunnel, 18, 30, 102.

Half-cantons, 3-4, 82, 88-89, 101, 105, 138. *See also* Appenzell; Basle; Unterwalden.
Heimatlos, 54, 68, *77-79*, 121.
Heimatschein, 52, 56.
High treason, 77, 122.
Hunting, 25.

Incapacity and incompatibility, 85-89, 109, 120.

Initiative; constitutional, *132 seq.*, 69, 76, 82-83, 108, 115; parliamentary, 105. *See also* Referendum.
Insurances; private, 39, 117; social, 39, 41.
Interpellations, 150, 160.
Intervention, Federal, 9, *15-16*, 92, 95, 113-14.

Jesuits, 62, 66, 117, 127.
Jews, 25-26.
Joint session, 93, 95, 97, 105, 107, 119, 120, 130, 158.
Joos, National Councillor, 132.
Judges, Cantonal, 7, 76, 164.
Jury, Federal, 95, 119, 122, 125-6.

Landsgemeinde, 88, 100, 105, 152.
Languages, 1, 20, 29, 44, *88-9*, 108, 119-20, *128-9*, 158.
Lausanne, 27, 128.
Laws, cited:
 Federal Law of—
 1849, Chancellery fee, 57.
  Federal Administration, 109.
  Relations of Councils, 164.
 1850, Expropriation, 21.
  Heimatlosat, 78.
  Responsibility, 106, 130.
 1851, Guarantees, *see* Law of 1934.
 1852, Extradition for crimes, 77.
 1872, Elections, 82, 104, 138.
 1874, *État civil*, 67.
  Referendum, 101-3, 163, 165.
 1875, Paupers' Burials, 60.
  Weights and Measures, 47.
 1877, Factories, 38.
 1881, Banks, 46.
 1886, Vaccination, 79.
 1889, Bankruptcy, 72-73, 125.
  Military Penal Procedure, 130.
 1891, *Séjour* and Settlement, 58, 60.
 1892, Initiatives, 104, 136, 138.
 1893, Judicial Organization, 70. *See also* Law of 1943.
 1897, Railways, 26.
 1900, Voting, 82.
 1902, Relations of Councils, *153-87*, 96, 98, 104, 113, 134, 149-51.
 1903, Education, 29, 151.
  Naturalization, 55.
 1907, Military Organization, 18.
 1911, Insurance, 39.

LAWS, cited (*contd.*):
Federal Law of (contd.)—
1912, Judicial Organization, 70.
1914, Factories, 38.
    Federal Administration, 109–10, 117–18.
1916, Water Power, 24.
1919, Chancellery, 118.
    Proportional Representation, 83, 104.
1922, Factories, Young People, 38.
1923, Payment of Councillors, 90.
1924, Narcotics, 79.
1927, Officials, 93, 115.
1928, Administrative Jurisdiction, 126.
    Relations of Councils (Amendment), 165.
1930, Expropriation, 21.
1931, Foreigners, 80.
1932, Alcohol Monopoly, 36.
    Road Traffic, 45.
1934, Guarantees, 20, 26, 53, 105, 108, 128, 130.
    Penal Procedure, 125–6.
1939, Relations of Councils (Amendment), 156, 165.
1943, Judicial Organization, 57, 72, 97, 113, 120–1, 125–6, 215.
1947, Civil Procedure, 125.
    Old Age Insurance, 41.
1948, Aerial Navigation, 45.
1950, Initiatives (Amendment), 104, 136.
1953, Education, 150.
    Nationality, 55.
Federal Arrêtés cited, (Finance) 49–50, (Full Powers) 169–71, (others), 68–9, 110, 118.
Arrêtés of Federal Council, 49–50, 56, 65, 69, 117–8.
See also Civil Code, Concordats, Penal Code, *Règlements*.
[The Constitution of the Helvetic Republic, the Federal Treaty, and the Constitutions of 1848 and 1874, and Laws which were frustrated by referendums, are not indexed.]
League of Nations, 94, 100.
Learned professions, 37–8, 141.
Legislative procedure, 86, 105, *151*.
Lichtenstein, 3.
Locke, John, 93.

Lotteries, 42, 44.
Lucerne, town, Canton, lake, 39, 59, 65–66, 74, 82, 88, 128, 141.

Madison, 93.
Marriage, 67–68, 72.
Messages, of Federal Council, 33, 41, 75, 113, 115–16, 149–51. *See also* Reports; Annual Report.
Monasteries, 66.
Monopolies, Federal, 22, 24, 25, 36, 43, 46–47; Cantonal, 25, 31, 44.
Montesquieu, 93.
Motions, of Assembly, 105, 149, 160.

National Council, 82 seq., 149 seq., &c.
Nationalism, 2, 24.
Navigation, 25.
Neufchatel, town, Canton, 10, 27, 78–79, 82, 88.
Neutrality, 43, 55, *94*, 169–71.
Nicole, (senior) 122; (junior) 69.

Officials, Federal, 17, 26, 70, 87, 89, 92, 97, 114, *115*, 119, 130, 151.
Orders; religious, 66. *See also* Jesuits; Decorations, foreign.
Ordonnances, of Federal Council, 42–43, 93, *124*. *See also* LAWS, Arrêtés of Federal Council.

Pardon, 95, 105.
Parties, political, 7, 41–42, 61, 67–69, 74–76, *82–84*, 88–89, 91, 96, 99, 102, *104*, *108*, 160, 164, 171.
Patents, 74, 117.
Patriotism, 24, 80.
Penal Code, 56, 68–69, *74–77*, 95, 122, 125–7, 133, 215.
Petition, right of, 71.
'Political', use of the word, 77.
Polytechnic, 27, 115.
Poor law, 52–53, *56–58*, 85.
Posts, 20–21, 23, *43–45*.
Postulates, 150, 156, 160.
Préfet (Statthalter), 13, 164.
President of Confederation, 109–10, 119, 152.
— of Council, 87, 89, 100, 158.
Press, freedom of the, 63, *68–69*, 77, 137.
Procedure, parliamentary, 149 seq., &c.

Professional politicians, 88. *See also* Learned professions.
Project of 1872, 141.
Property, right to, 123.
Proportional representation, *82–84*, 86–88.
'Public law', 93, 115, 123, 127, 131.
— works, 21, 26, 44.
— worship, 64. *See also* Religion.

Question, parliamentary, 150, 160.
Quorum, of Assembly, 98–99, 154; of Federal Council, 110.

Railways, 20–21, 23–24, 43, 114–15, 163.
Referendum: constitutional amendment, *132–8*, 10, 76, 81–83, 103, 106, 119; legislative challenge, *100–3*, 22, 26, 32, 39–41, 66, 74, 79, 92–94, 154, 171; of 1866, 46–47, 59, 74, 76, 83, 132; in Cantons, 10.
Règlements, of legislative Councils, 95, 97–99, 105–6, 110, 113, 127, 155, 158–9, 215.
Religion, *61–68*, 2, 17, 25, *27–28*, 38, 70, 72, 85, 115, 119, 126–9.
Reports of Federal Council, 97, 105, 111, 113, *115*, 134, *136–7*, 149–52, 213, 215. *See also* Annual Report; Messages.
Responsibility, of officials, 130; in Swiss government, 101.
Revision of Constitution, 132–8, 157. *See also* Unconstitutionality.
Rousseau, J.-J., 78.

St. Gall, 58–59, 82, 85, 88.
Salis, family, 8. *See also* Books.
Salvation army, 62, 65, 70.
Schaffhausen, 82, 85.
Schwyz, 4, 42, 66, 82, 85, 88, 141.
Secession, forbidden, 3.
Secret session, Assembly, 106; Federal Council, 117.
Séjour, 60.
Separation of powers, doctrine of, 81, 90–92, 106, 121, *123*, *140*.
Session, annual, 76, 87, 98.
Settlement; freedom of, 54, *56–60*, 63, 117, 124; treaty of, 70, 80.
Sierre, 128.

Sonderbund, 11, 61, *66*, 71, *88*, 141.
Sovereignty, Cantonal, *3*, *5–6*, 8–9, 12–13, 21, 25–27, 34, 44, 48, 58, 63–64, 73, 78, 81, 90, 92, 122, *139–40*, 164.
Statthalter, *see Préfet.*
Subsidies, 21–23, 27–31, 44, 50, 75–76, 80, 101.
Supervision, Federal, 19, *23*, 25, 44, 97.
Supreme power, the, 81, 93, 106, 169.

Taxation, Cantonal, 7, *20*, 34, 48–51, *58–59*, 63.
Ticino, 4, 16, 30, 52, 58, 82, 85, 128–9.
Thurgau, 58, 82, 85.
Tobacco, taxation of, 48, 51.
Trade and Industry, freedom of, *31* seq., 36–37, 63–64, 123–4, 126, 133. *See also* Customs duties; Monopolies; Subsidies; Economic Articles.
Traite foraine, 73.
Treaties, 11–12, *93–94*, *102*, 114; Cantonal, *see* Concordats. *See also* Treaties of Settlement.

Unconstitutional initiatives, 137.
Unconstitutionality, 24, 33, 39, 50, 103, 124, 137, 169; *examples of,* 22, 105, 169.
United Nations Organization, 94.
United States of America, comparison with, 64, 140, 218.
Unity of material, principle of, 137.
'Universally binding', 100.
Universities, 27, 129, 214.
Unterwalden (Nid- and Obwald), 4, 66, 82, 88, 132, 141.
Urgency procedure, 22, 24, 34, 49–50, 100–3, 114, 142, 156.
Uri, 30, 42, 66, 82, 88, 141.

Valais, 30, 66, 82, 88, 132, 141, 217.
Vaud, 61, 78, 82.
Vorarlberg, 3.

Weights and measures, 46–47.
Wireless, 43, 114–15.
Women, *8*, 43, 56, 75, 85, 134.

Zug, Canton, 42, 66, 74, 82, 85, 88, 141.
Zurich, town, Canton, 16, 27, 61, 82–83, 108, 217.

PRINTED IN
GREAT BRITAIN
AT THE
UNIVERSITY PRESS
OXFORD
BY
CHARLES BATEY
PRINTER
TO THE
UNIVERSITY